Grade K

Your Turn

Practice Book

Education

Bothell, WA • Chicago, IL • Columbus, OH • New York, NY

Contents

Start Smart • Let's Get Started!

Week 1

Week 2

My Family and Me

Week 3

I Can!

Unit 1 • Take a New Step

Week 1

Make New Friends

Week 2

Get Up and Go!

Week 3

Use Your Senses

Unit 2 • Let's Explore

Week 1

Tools We Use

Contents

Contents

Contents

Unit 7 • The Animal Kingdom

Week 1

Baby Animals

Week 2

Pet Pals

Week 3

Animal Habitats

Unit 8 • From Here to There

Week 1

On the Move

Week 2

My U.S.A.

Week 3

Look to the Sky

Contents

Unit 9 • How Things Change

Week 1

Growing Up

Week 2

Good Citizens

Week 3

Our Natural Resources

Unit 10 • Thinking Outside the Box

Week 1

Problem Solvers

Week 2

Sort It Out

Week 3

Protect Our Earth

Name ______________________________

Aa Bb Cc Dd Ee Ff Gg Hh Ii Jj Kk Ll Mm
Nn Oo Pp Qq Rr Ss Tt Uu Vv Ww Xx Yy Zz

A B A B

a b a b

Letter Recognition: ***Aa, Bb***
Name each letter. Draw a line to connect the capital and lowercase forms of the same letter.

Name ______________________________

I  .

I  .

I  .

I  .

High-Frequency Word: *I*
Read the sentences: *I paint. I read. I run. I eat.*

Name ________________________________

Illustrated by Teri Weidner

Illustrated by Teri Weidner

Respond to the Interactive Read-Aloud: ***The Ugly Duckling***
Tell what is happening in each box. Then draw a picture of something else that happened in the story.

Name ______________________________

Category Words: Names
Look at the pictures. Put a marker on each picture where you see a name.

Name ______________________________

Aa Bb Cc Dd Ee Ff Gg Hh Ii Jj Kk Ll Mm
Nn Oo Pp Qq Rr Ss Tt Uu Vv Ww Xx Yy Zz

C D E F

c d e f

Letter Recognition: *Cc, Dd, Ee, Ff*
Name each letter. Draw a line to connect the capital and lowercase forms of the same letter.

Name ______________________________

Aa Bb Cc Dd Ee Ff Gg Hh Ii Jj Kk Ll Mm
Nn Oo Pp Qq Rr Ss Tt Uu Vv Ww Xx Yy Zz

G H G H

g h g h

Letter Recognition: ***Gg, Hh***
Name each letter. Draw a line to connect the capital and lowercase forms of the same letter.

Name ______________________

I nap!

High Frequency Word: ***I***
Read the book aloud to a partner. Reread for fluency.

I hop

I hop.

Copyright © The McGraw-Hill Companies, Inc.

I  throw .

I dig .

Name ______________________________

Aa Bb Cc Dd Ee Ff Gg Hh Ii Jj Kk Ll Mm
Nn Oo Pp Qq Rr Ss Tt Uu Vv Ww Xx Yy Zz

I J K L

i j k l

Letter Recognition: ***Ii, Jj, Kk, Ll***
Name each letter. Draw a line to connect the capital and lowercase forms of the same letter.

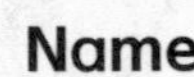

Name ______________________________

I can  .

I can  .

I can  .

I can  .

High-Frequency Word: *can*
Read the sentences: *I can clap. I can sing. I can jump. I can kick.*
Then circle the picture that shows what you like to do best.

Draw

Name ______________________________

Illustrated by Marcin Piwowarski

Illustrated by Marcin Piwowarski

Respond to the Interactive Read-Aloud: *Tikki Tikki Tembo*
Name the characters in the boxes. Then draw another character from the story. Circle your favorite character.

Name ______________________________

5 D 10

2 4 a

L 3 7

Category Words: Numbers
Put a marker on each number on the page. Say each number.

Name ____

Aa Bb Cc Dd Ee Ff Gg Hh Ii Jj Kk Ll Mm
Nn Oo Pp Qq Rr Ss Tt Uu Vv Ww Xx Yy Zz

M N O P

m n o p

Letter Recognition: ***Mm, Nn, Oo, Pp***
Name each letter. Draw a line to connect the capital and lowercase forms of the same letter.

Name ______________________________

Aa Bb Cc Dd Ee Ff Gg Hh Ii Jj Kk Ll Mm
Nn Oo Pp Qq Rr Ss Tt Uu Vv Ww Xx Yy Zz

Q R Q R

q r q r

Letter Recognition: *Qq, Rr*
Name each letter. Draw a line to connect the capital and lowercase forms of the same letter.

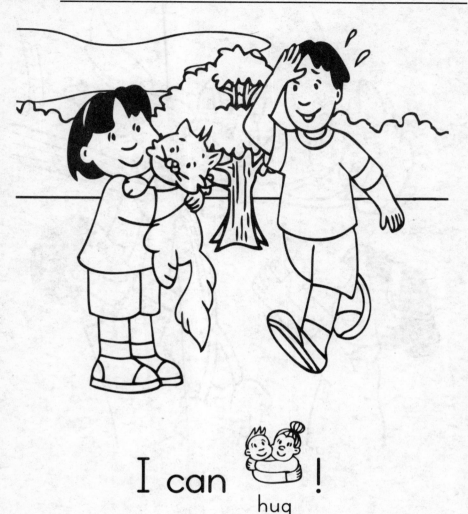

Name ______________________

I can hug !

High Frequency Word: *can*
Read the book aloud to a partner. Reread for fluency.

I Can hug !

I can see !

I can  yell .

I can  catch .

Name ____

Respond to the Big Book: ***Animals in the Park:*** *An ABC Book*
Name the animals. Then draw another animal from the story.

Name ________________________________

Aa Bb Cc Dd Ee Ff Gg Hh Ii Jj Kk Ll Mm
Nn Oo Pp Qq Rr Ss Tt Uu Vv Ww Xx Yy Zz

S T U V

s t u v

Letter Recognition: ***Ss, Tt, Uu, Vv***
Name each letter. Draw a line to connect the capital and lowercase forms of the same letter.

Name ______________________________

I can  .

I can  .

I can  .

I can  .

High-Frequency Words: *I, can*
Read the sentences: *I can dance. I can mix. I can ride. I can play.*
Then circle the picture that shows something that you can do.

Draw

Name ____________________

Mary Kate Denny/PhotoEdit

Alyson Aliano/Taxi/Getty Images

Respond to the Interactive Read-Aloud: *Kindergarteners Can!*
Tell what the children in each box are doing. Then draw a picture that shows something else a kindergartener can do.

Name ____

abcdef
ghijklm
nopqrs
tuvwxyz

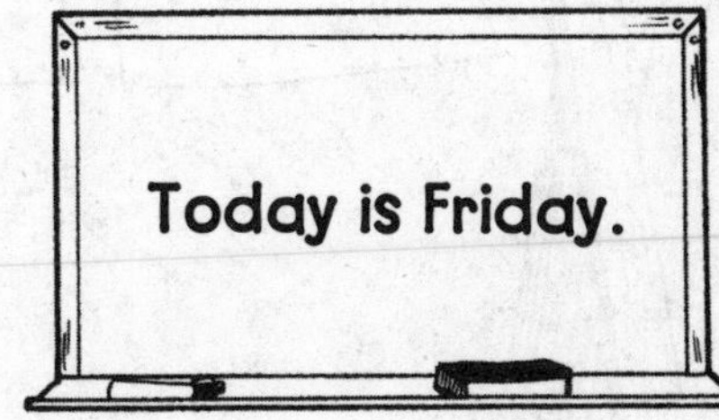

can

Category Words: Days of the Week
Look at the pictures. Put a marker on each picture where you might see a day of the week.

Draw

Name ____________________

Aa Bb Cc Dd Ee Ff Gg Hh Ii Jj Kk Ll Mm
Nn Oo Pp Qq Rr Ss Tt Uu Vv Ww Xx Yy Zz

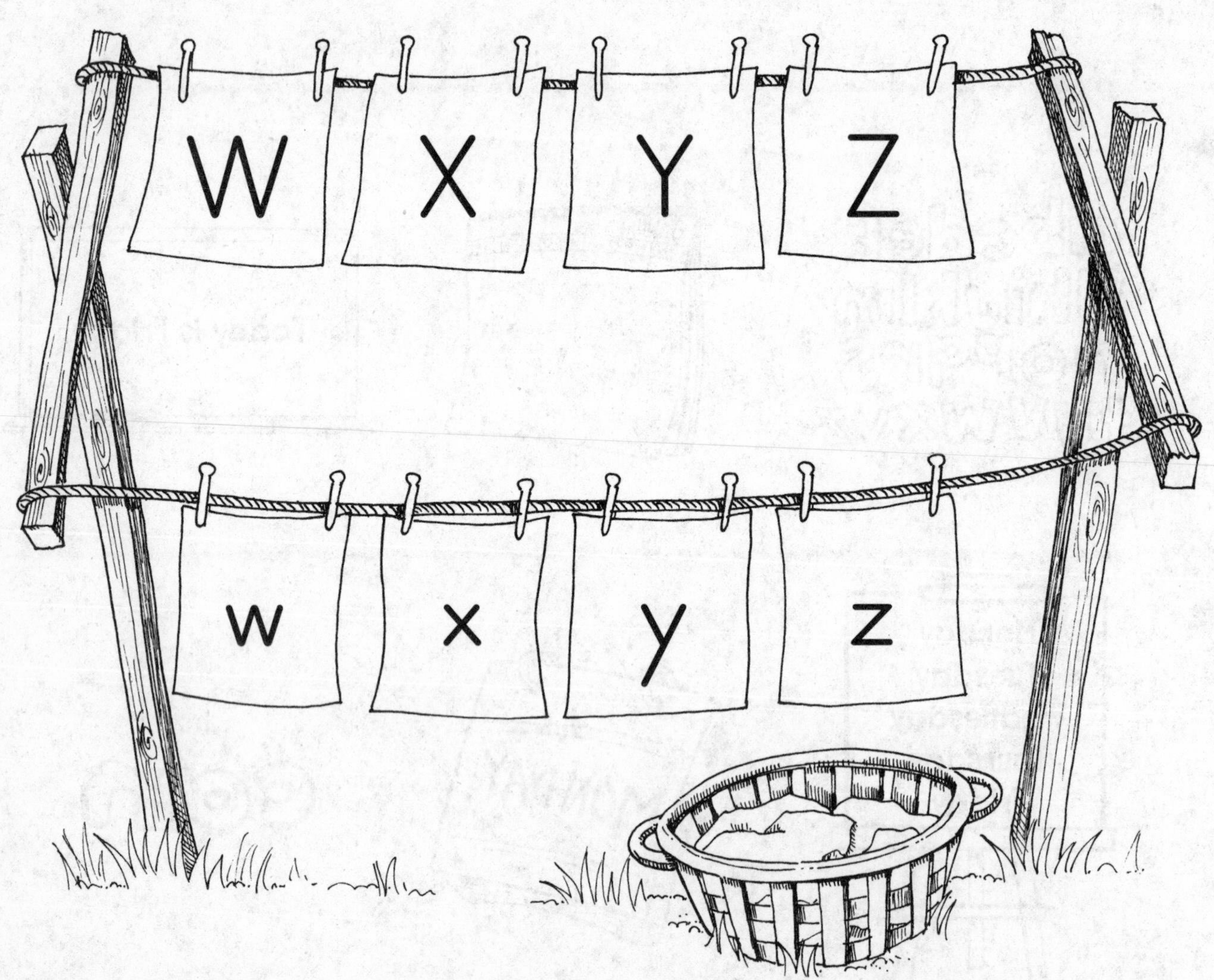

Letter Recognition: *Ww, Xx, Yy, Zz*
Name each letter. Draw a line to connect the capital and lowercase forms of the same letter.

Name ______________________________

I can give !

High Frequency Word: *I, can*
Read the book aloud to a partner. Reread for fluency.

I Can give !

I can  cut .

I can tie.

I can hide.

Name ______________________________

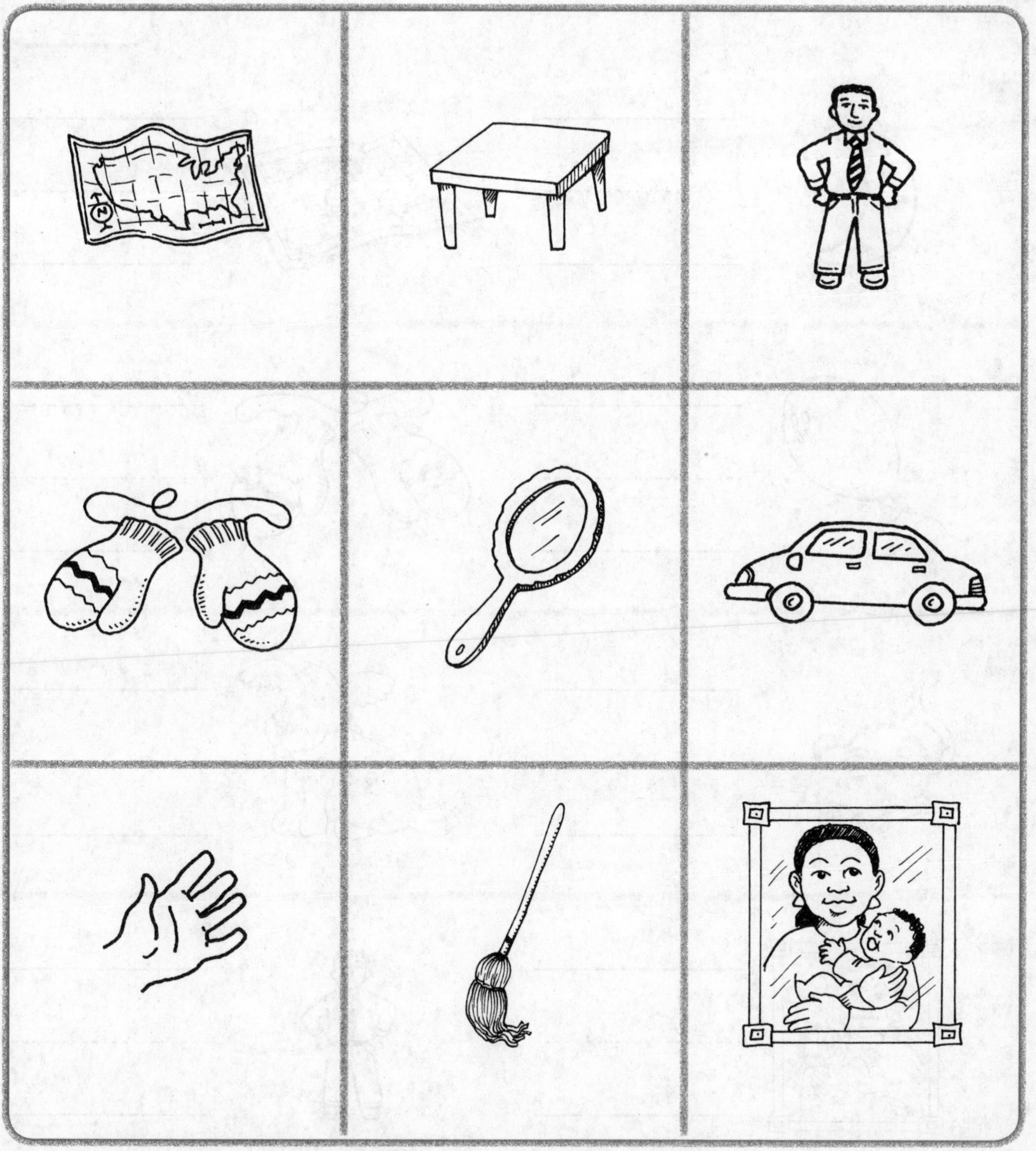

Phonemic Awareness: /m/

Say the name of each picture. Put a marker on each picture if its name begins with the /m/ sound.

Name

m

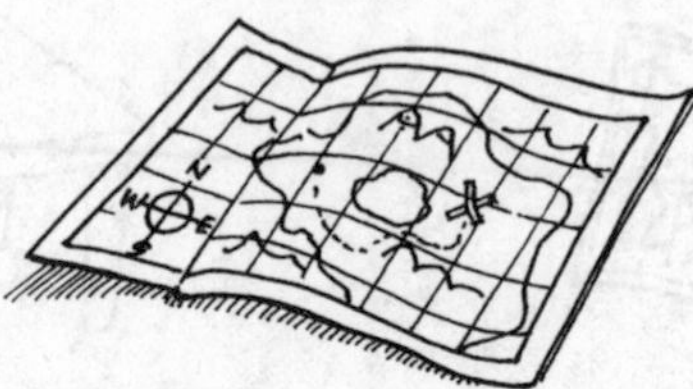

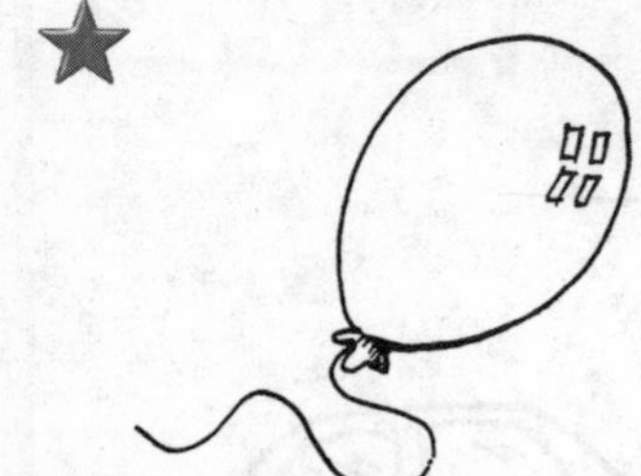

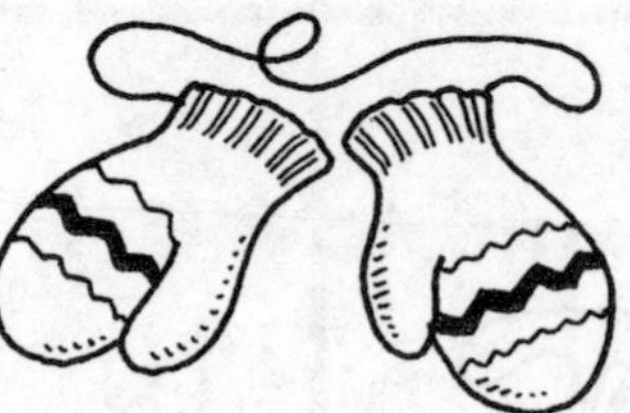

Phonics: /m/*m*

Say the name of each picture. Write the letter *m* next to each picture whose name begins with the /m/ sound.

Name ____________________

Comprehension: Key Details

Circle the picture that shows Bear feeling mad.
★Circle the picture that shows Goose feeling happy.
Circle the picture that shows Fox feeling sad.

Write

Name ___

m

Phonics: /m/*m*
Look at the picture. Say the name of each item. Circle each item whose name begins with the same sound as *map*. Write the letter.

Name ________________

the  friends

High Frequency Word: ***the***
Read the book aloud to a partner. Reread for fluency.

The  friends

the girl

the boy

the  dog

Name ______________________________

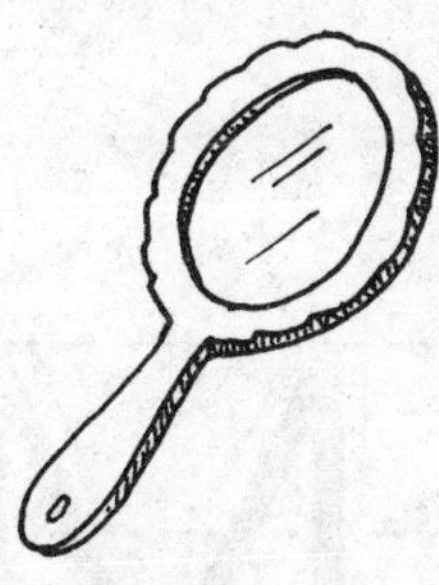

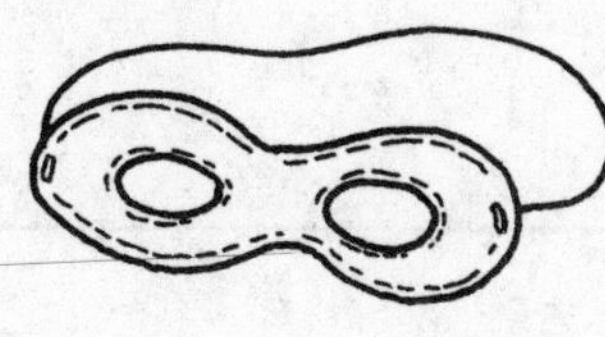

Category Words: Feeling Words
Tell about each picture. Put a marker on each picture if it shows a feeling.

Name ______________________________

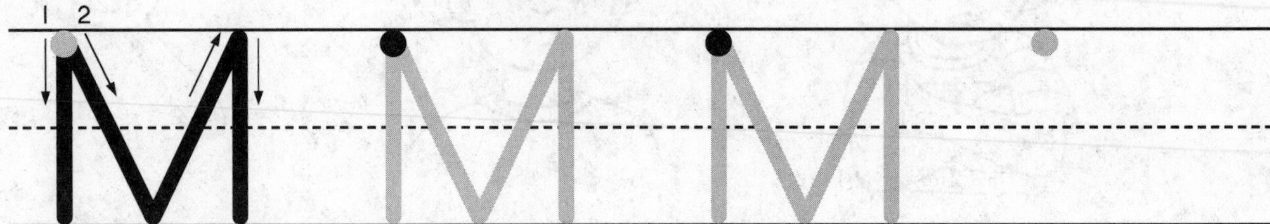

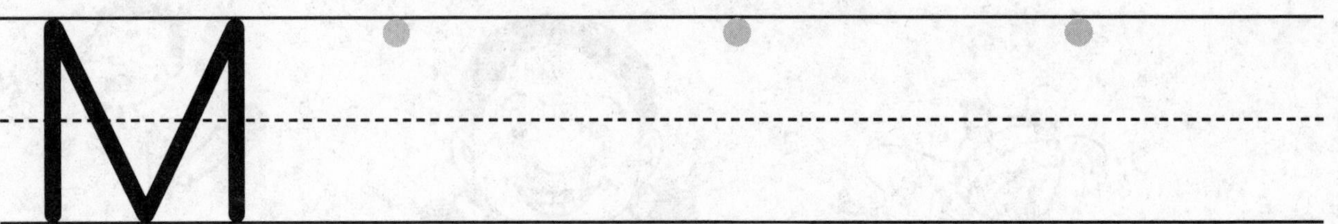

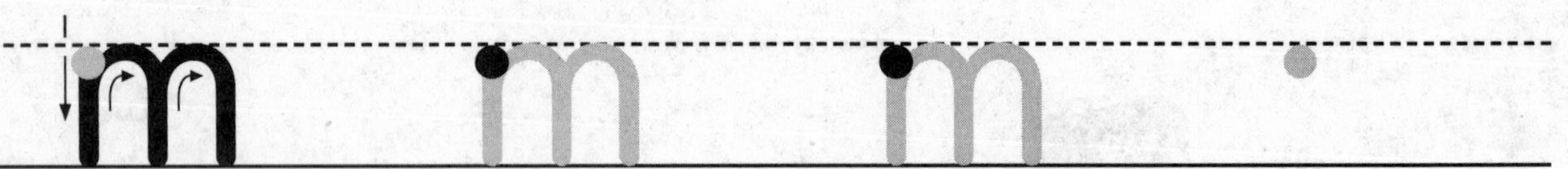

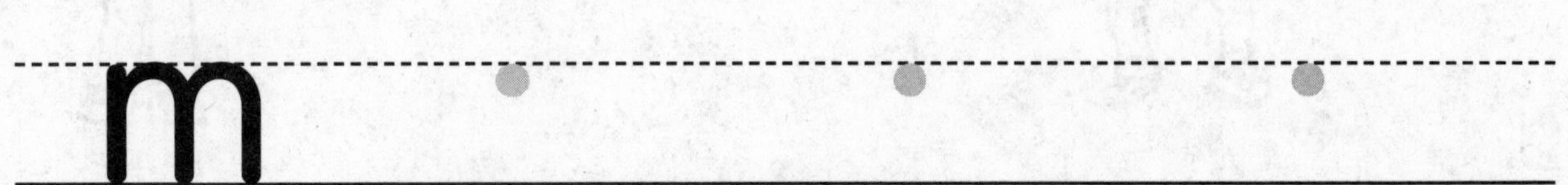

Handwriting: *Mm*
Trace and write each capital letter *M.* Then trace and write each lowercase letter *m.*

Name ________________________________

Phonemic Awareness: /a/

Say the name of each picture. Put a marker on each picture if its name begins with the /a/ sound.

Name ________________________________

a

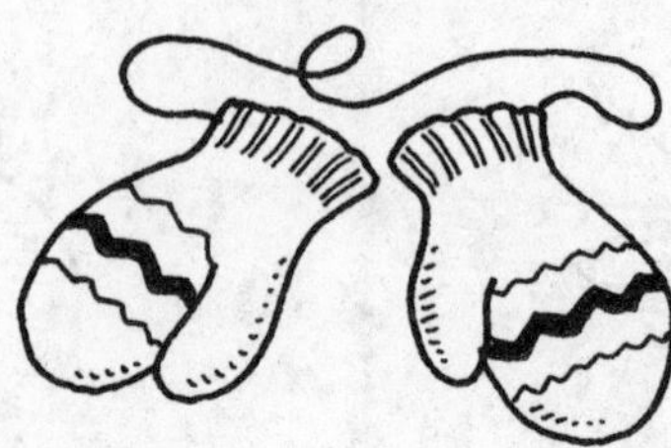

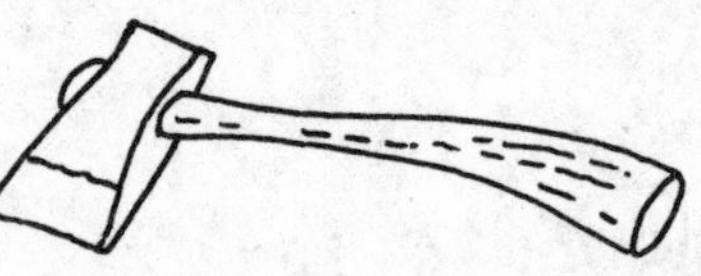

ABCDEFG
HIJKLMN
OPQRSTU
VWXYZ

Phonics: /a/*a*
Say the name of each picture. Write the letter *a* next to each picture whose name begins with the /a/ sound.

Name ___________________________________

Comprehension: Key Details
🍎Which animals hop? Circle the pictures.
★Which animals fly? Circle the pictures.
Tell a partner why you circled each picture.

Write

Name ____________________

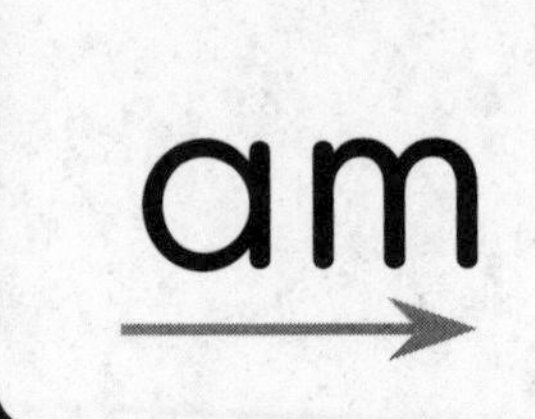

I am

I

I

Phonics: Blending *am*
Blend the sounds and say the word. Write the word. Read the sentence.

Name ________________________________

We can  dig .

High Frequency Word: ***we***
Read the book aloud to a partner. Reread for fluency.

We Can!

We can  hop .

We can  run .

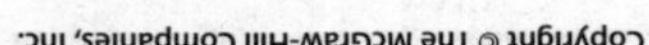

We can 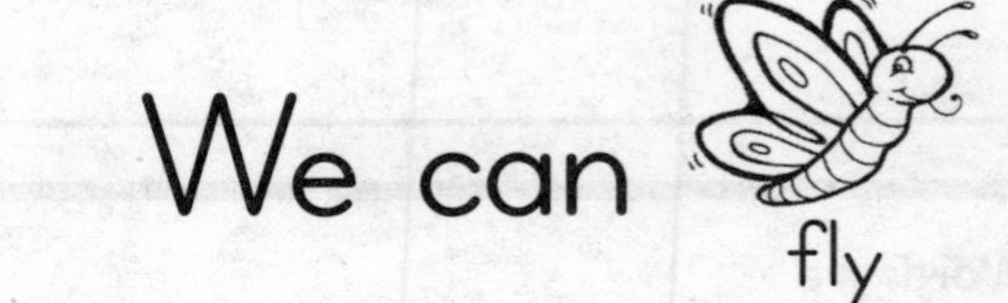 fly !

Name ______________________________

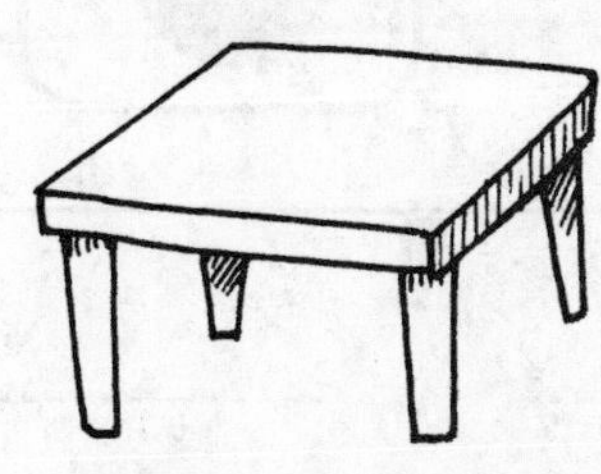

Category Words: Family Words
Tell about each picture. Put a marker on each picture if it shows a family word.

Name ____

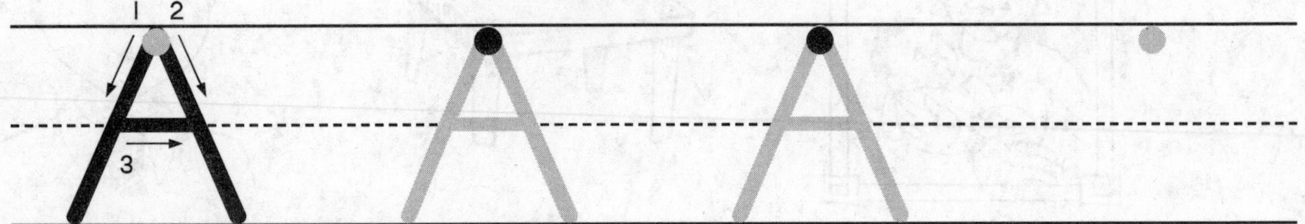

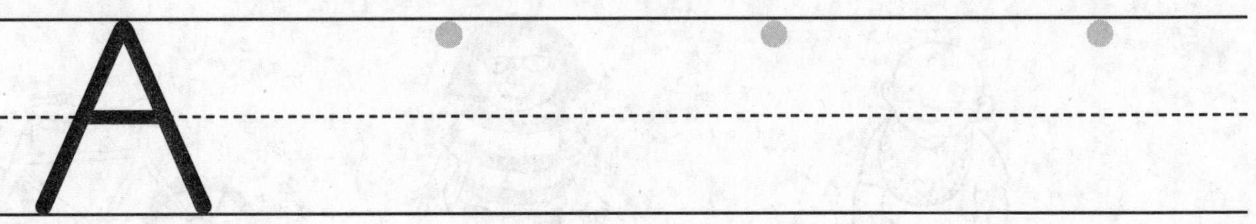

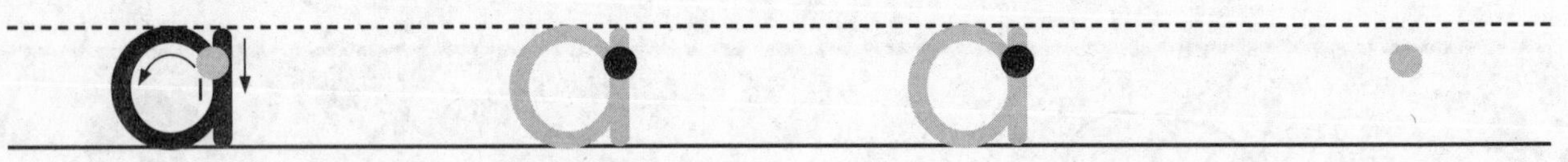

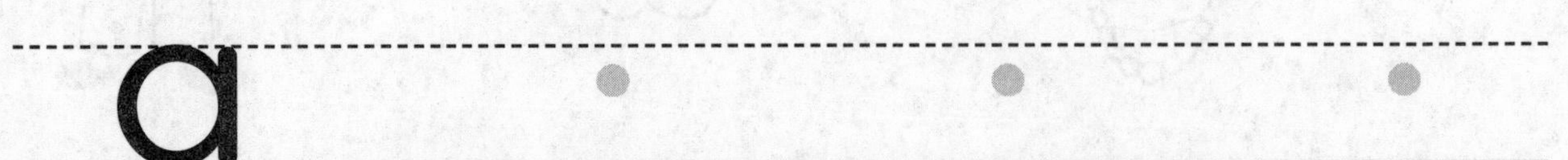

Handwriting: *Aa*
Trace and write each capital letter *A*. Then trace and write each lowercase letter *a*.

Name ______________________________

6

Phonemic Awareness: /s/
Say the name of each picture around the sun. Put a marker on each picture if its name begins with the /s/ sound.

Name ______________________

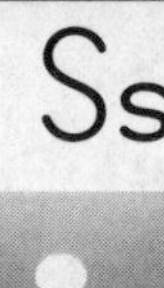

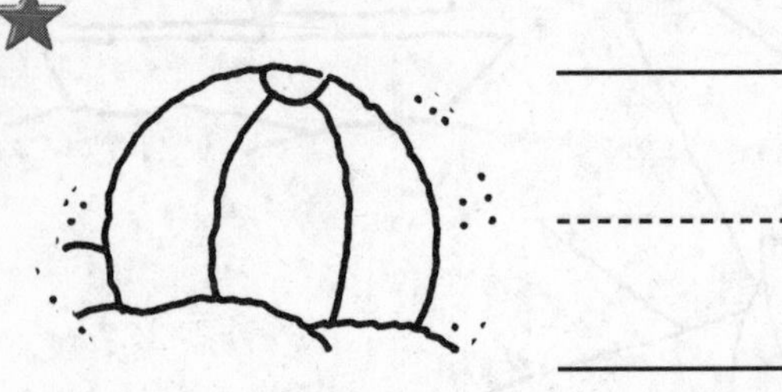

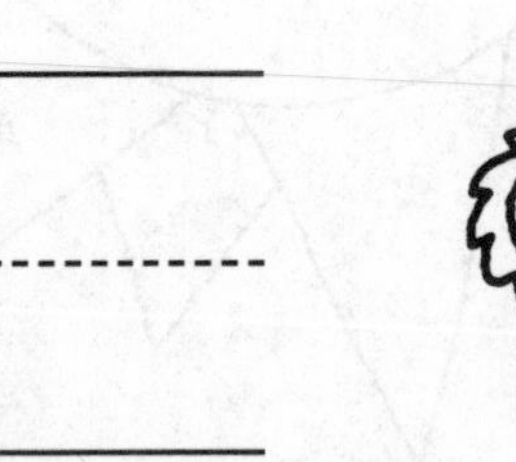

Phonics: /s/*s*

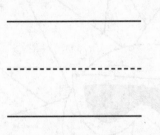

Say the name of each picture. Write the letter *s* next to each picture whose name begins with the /s/ sound.

Name ______________________________

Comprehension: Key Details

Circle the child who is looking at a sailboat.
★Circle the child who is tasting a sandwich.
Circle the child who is feeling the water.

Name ______________________

Sam

Am I Sam ?

I am ________ .

I like ________ .

Phonics: Blending /s/s
Blend the sounds and say the word. Read the sentence. Write the word *Sam*. Read the sentence again.

Name ____________________

We see the garden.

High Frequency Words: ***see***
Read the book aloud to a partner. Reread for fluency.

I See

I see the worm.

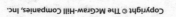

I see the  pumpkin .

I see the corn .

Name ____

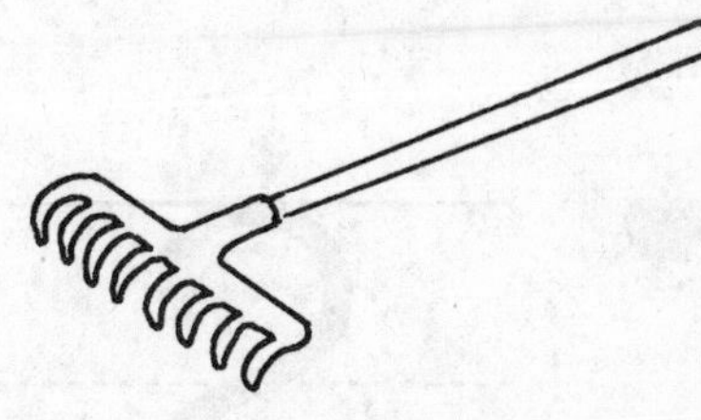

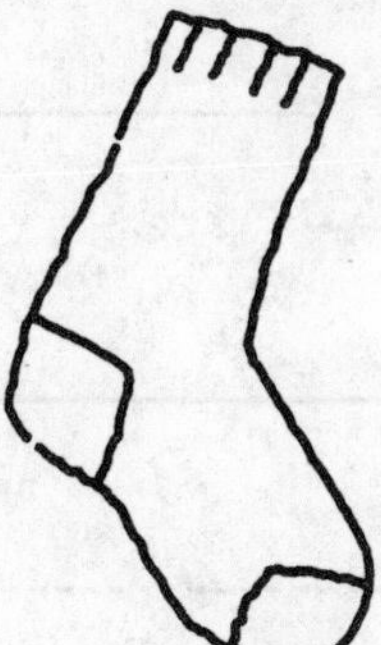

Category Words: Sensory Words
Tell about each picture. Put a marker on each picture if it shows someone using her or his senses.

Name ____________________

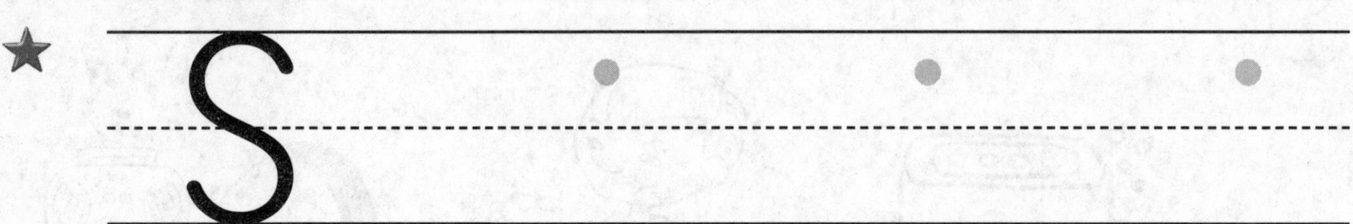

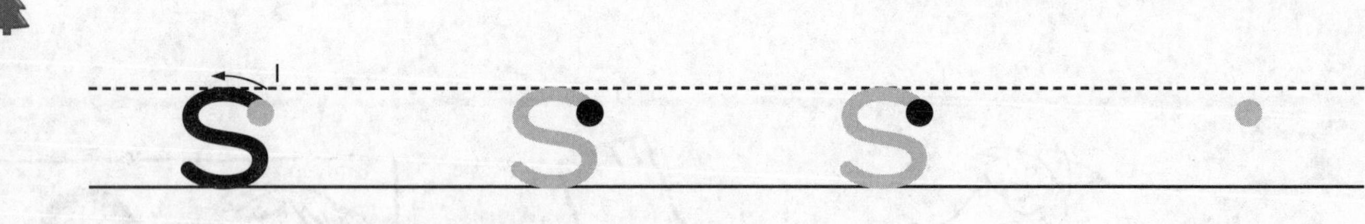

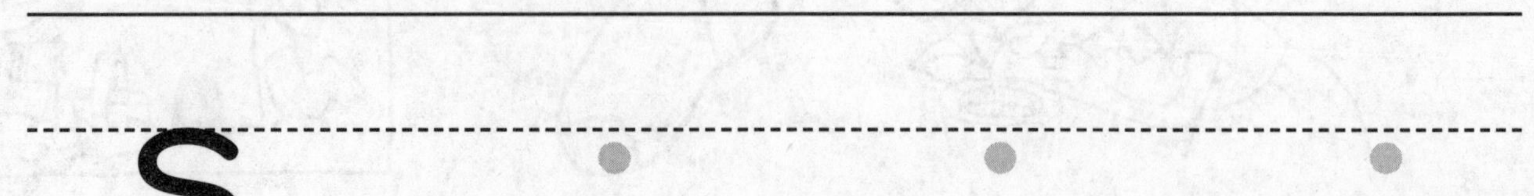

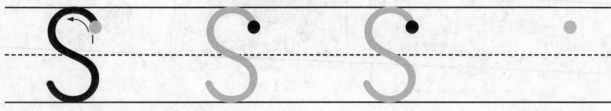

Handwriting: *Ss*
Trace and write each capital letter *S*. Then trace and write each lowercase letter *s*.

Name ______________________________

Phonemic Awareness: /p/
Say the name of each picture. Put a marker on each picture if its name begins with the /p/ sound.

Name

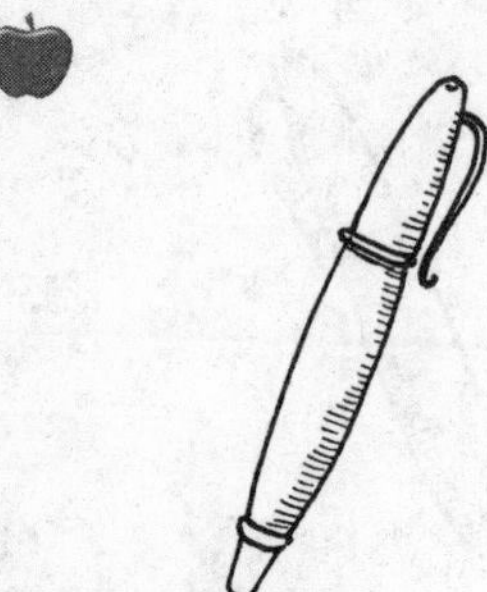

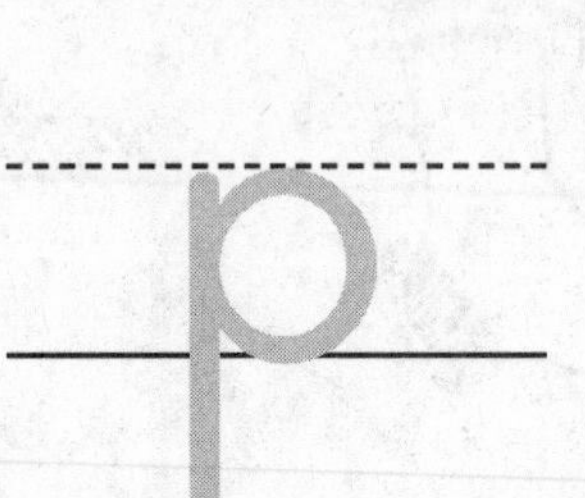

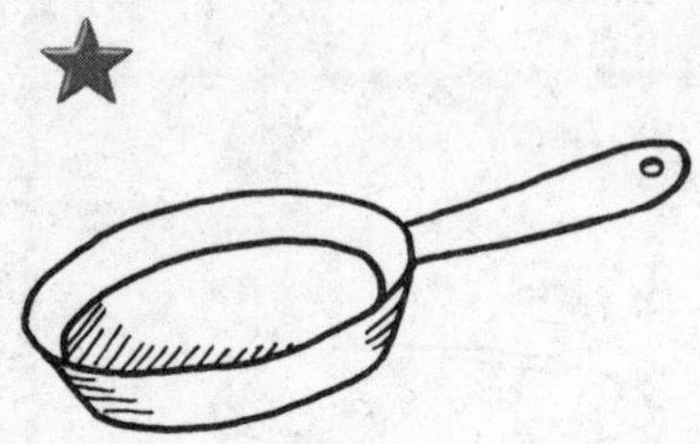

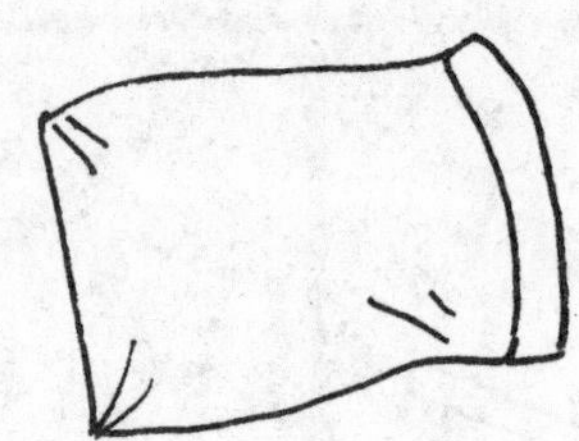

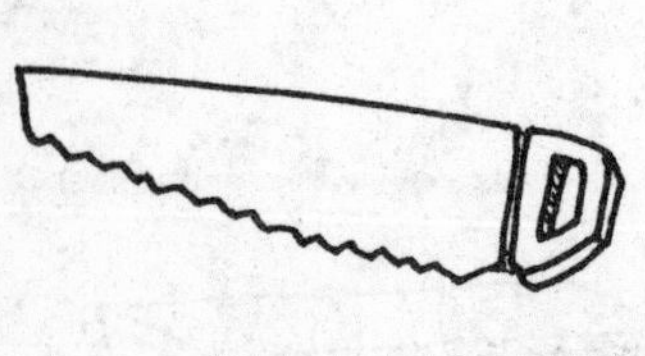

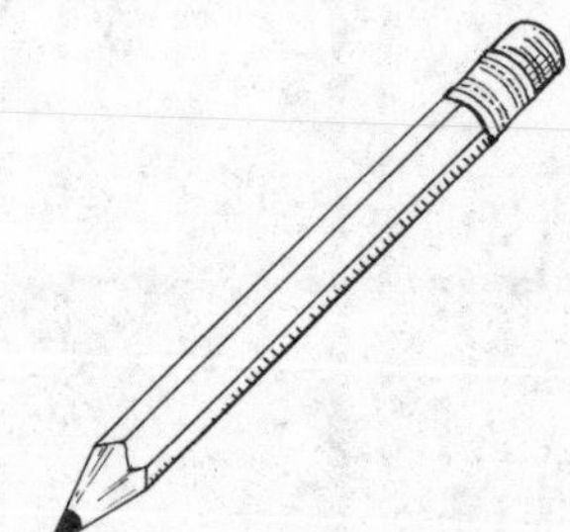

Phonics: /p/*p*
Say the name of each picture. Write the letter *p* next to each picture whose name begins with the /p/ sound.

Name ____

Comprehension: Key Details
Look at the pictures in each row. Circle the child that is using a tool. Tell a partner why you circled each picture.

Name ______________________

map sap Pam

map

sap

Pam

Phonics: Blending /p/*p*
Blend the sounds and say the word. Write the word. Repeat the word.

Name ______________________

I see a bird!

High Frequency Words: ***a***
Read the book aloud to a partner. Reread for fluency.

A  Walk

I see a bird.

I see a 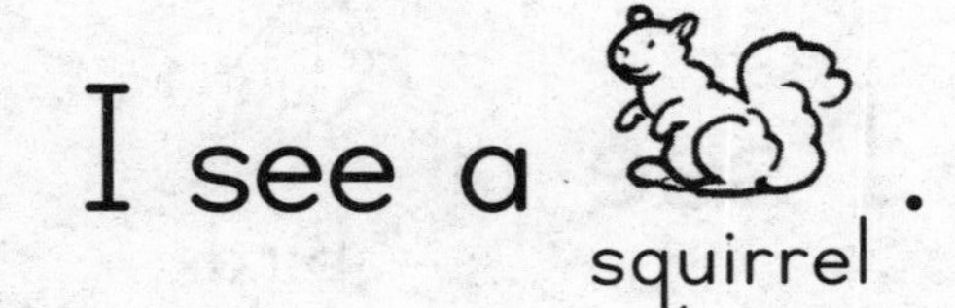 squirrel .

I see a 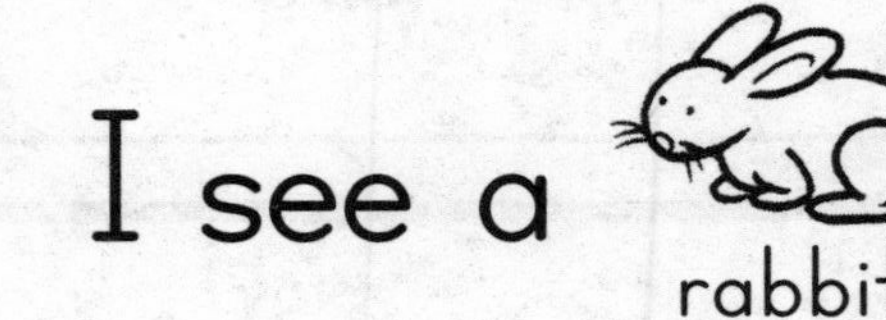 rabbit .

Name ______________________________

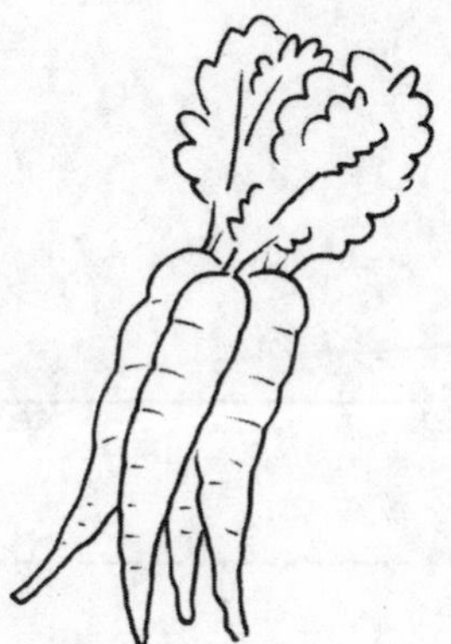

Category Words: Colors

Color the pictures in this row that are orange.

★Color the pictures in this row that are green.

Color the pictures in this row that are yellow.

Tell why you colored the pictures.

Name ____________________

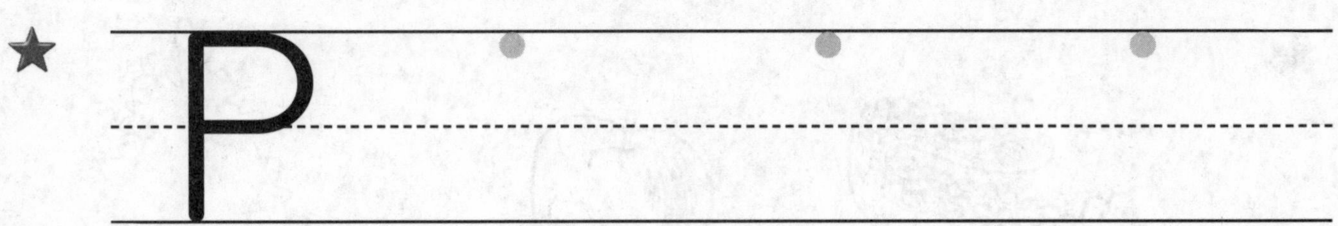

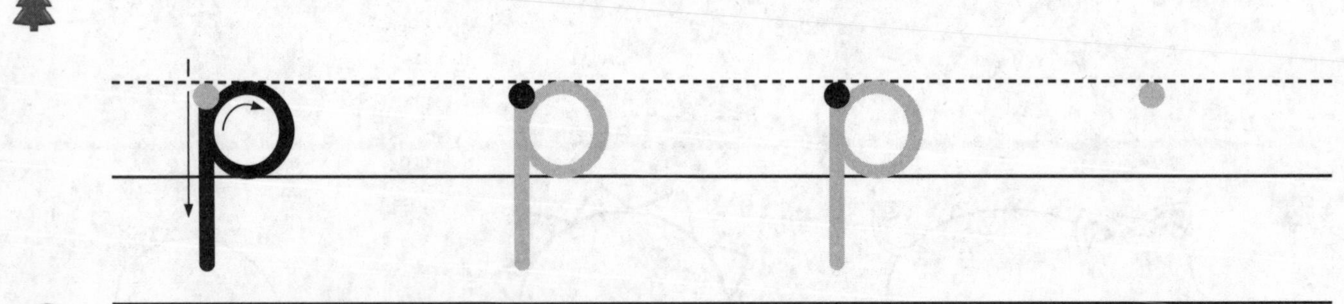

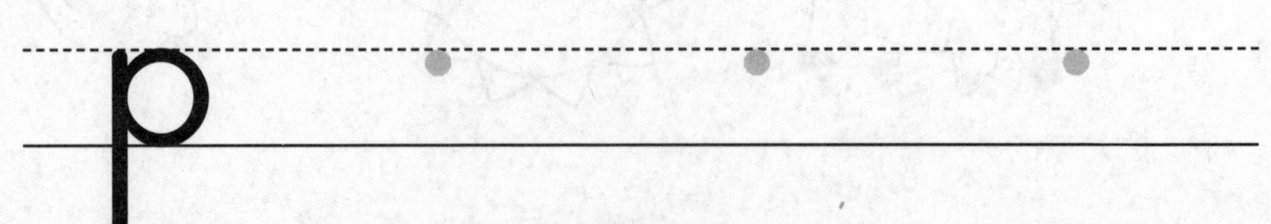

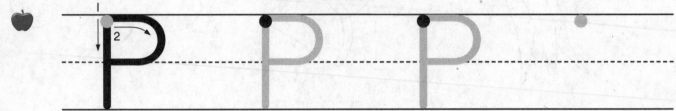

Handwriting: *Pp*
Trace and write each capital letter *P*. Then trace and write each lowercase letter *p*.

Name ____

Phonemic Awareness: /t/
Say the name of each picture. Circle each picture if its name begins with the /t/ sound.

Name ______________________________

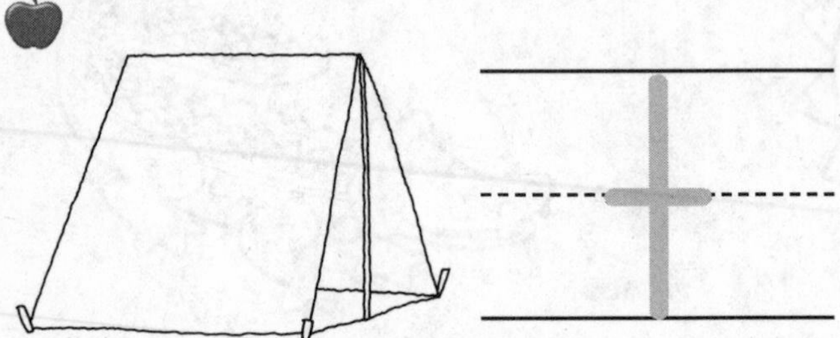

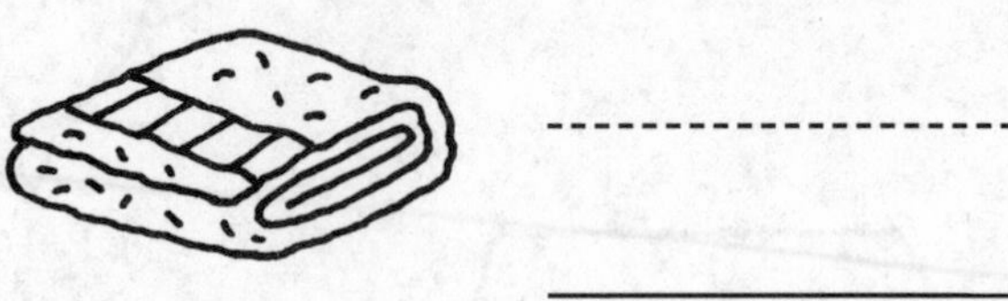

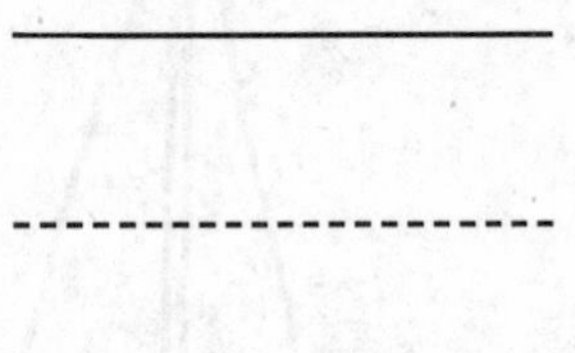

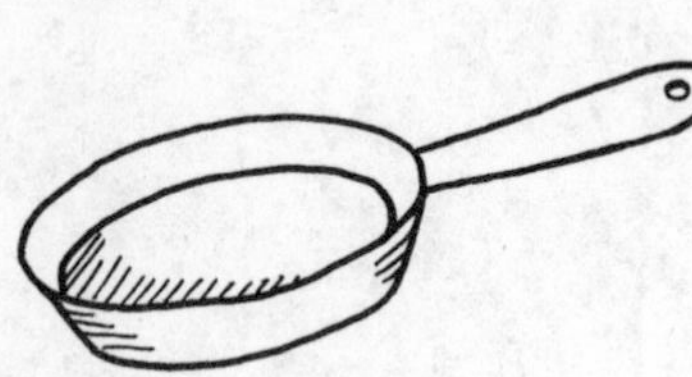

Phonics: /t/*t*
Say the name of each picture. Write the letter *t* next to each picture whose name begins with the /t/ sound.

Name ________________________________

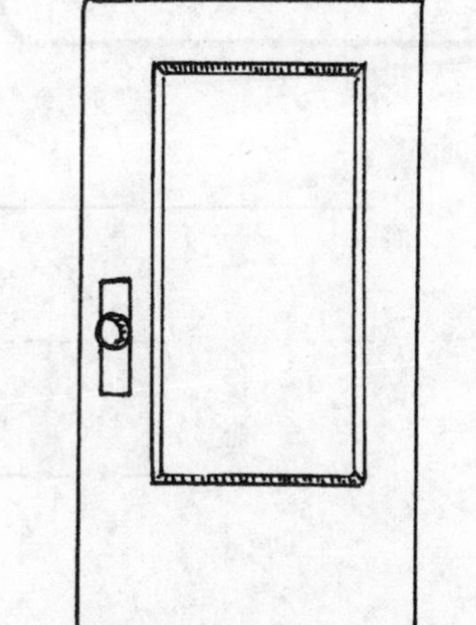

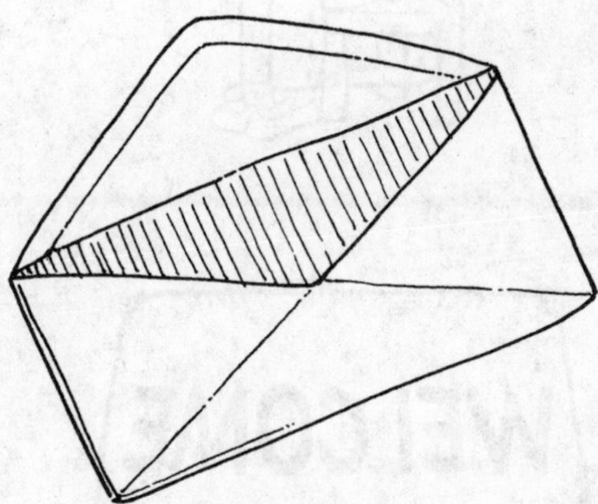

Comprehension: Key Details
Look at the pictures. Find circles, rectangles, triangles, and squares in the pictures. Trace each shape in a different color. Tell a partner about each shape you traced.

Name ______________________

tap sat mat

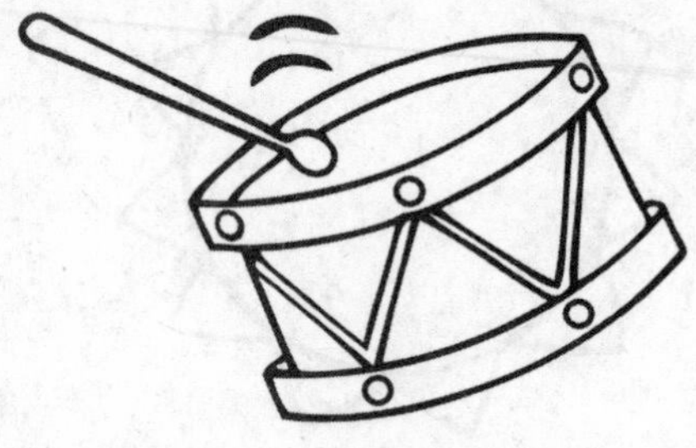

tap tap

sat

mat

Phonics: Blending /t/t
Blend the sounds and say the word. Write the word. Repeat the word.

Name ____________________

We like the shapes !

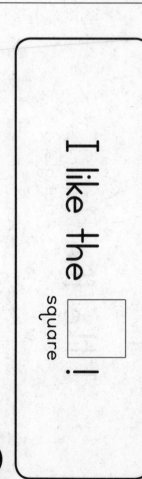

High Frequency Words: *like*
Read the book aloud to a partner. Reread for fluency.

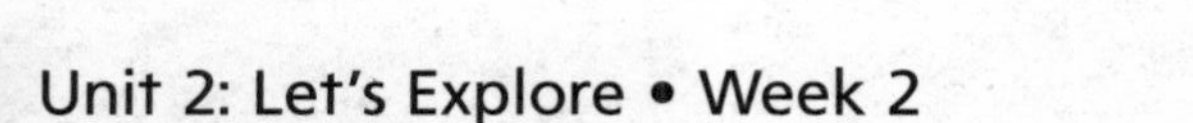

We Like!

I like the square !

I like the △ triangle.

I like the ▭ rectangle.

Name ______________________________

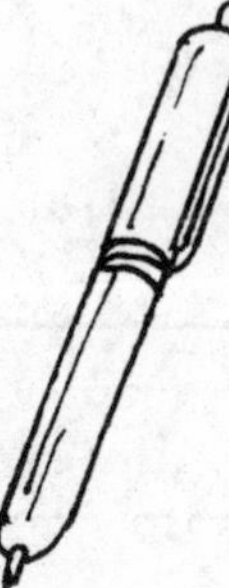
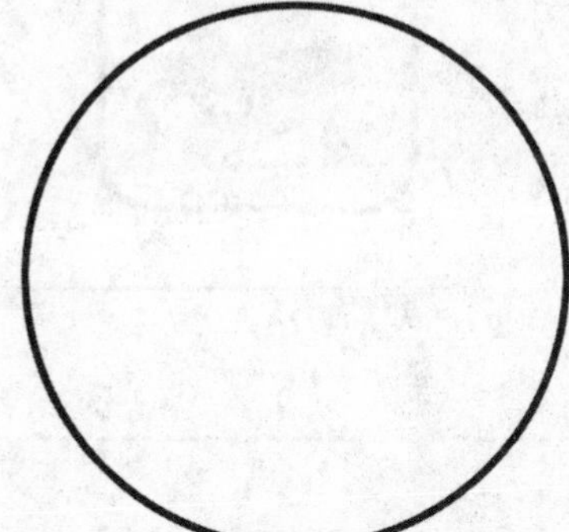

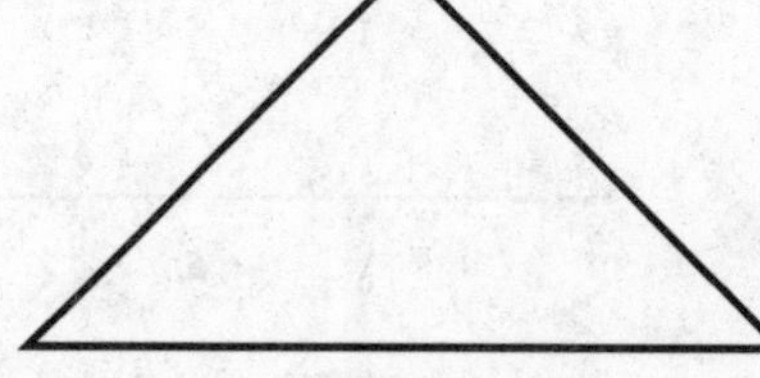

Category Words: Shapes
Tell about each picture. Circle each picture if it shows a shape.
Say the name of each shape you circled.

Name ______________________________

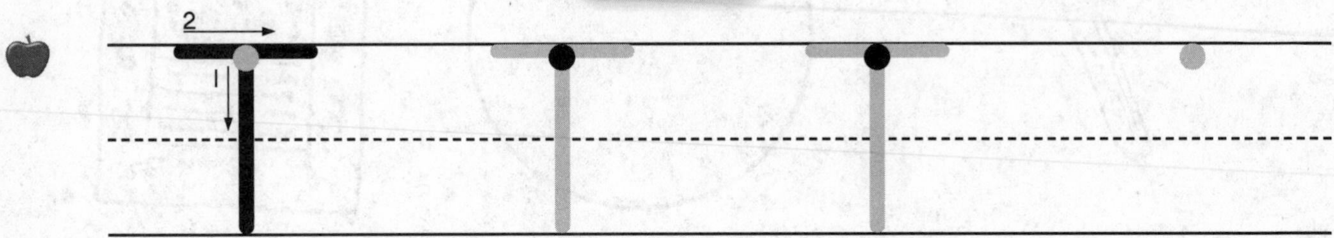

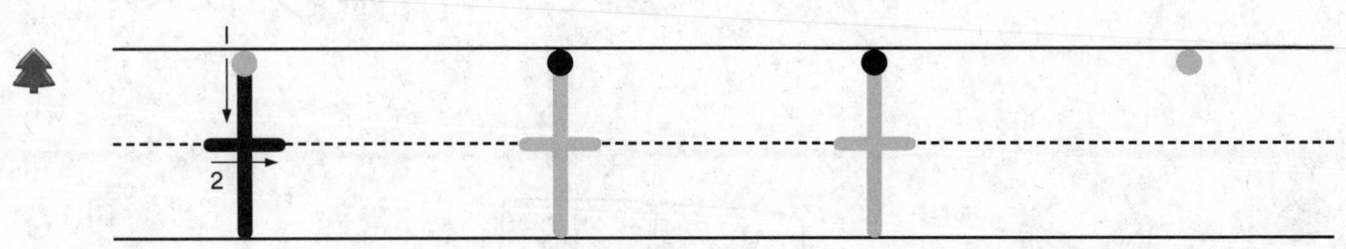

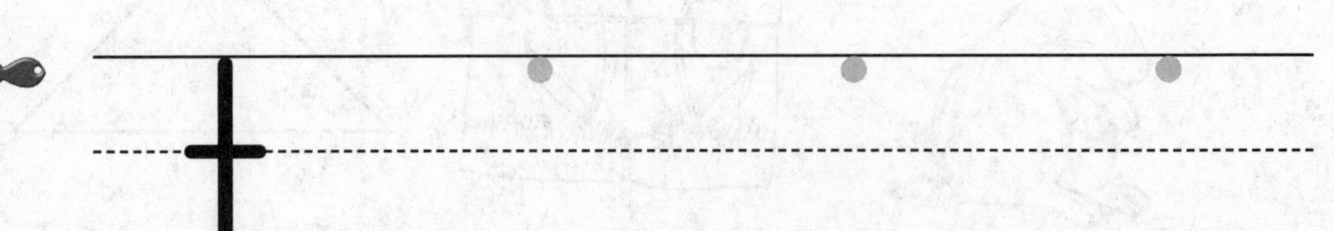

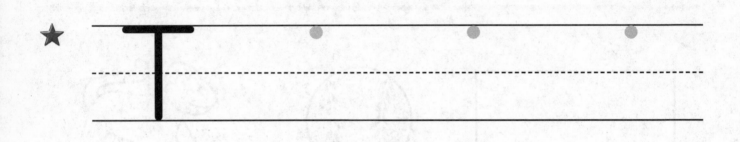

Handwriting: *Tt*
Trace and write each capital letter *T*. Then trace and write each lowercase letter *t*.

Name

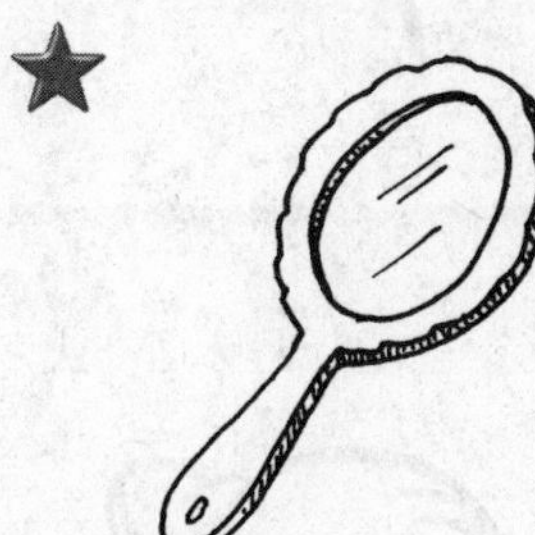

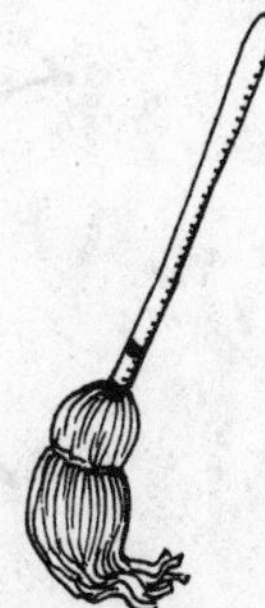

Review Phonics: /m/m, /a/a, /p/p
Say the name of each picture. Write the letter that begins each picture name: *m, a,* or *p.*

Circle

Name ______________________________

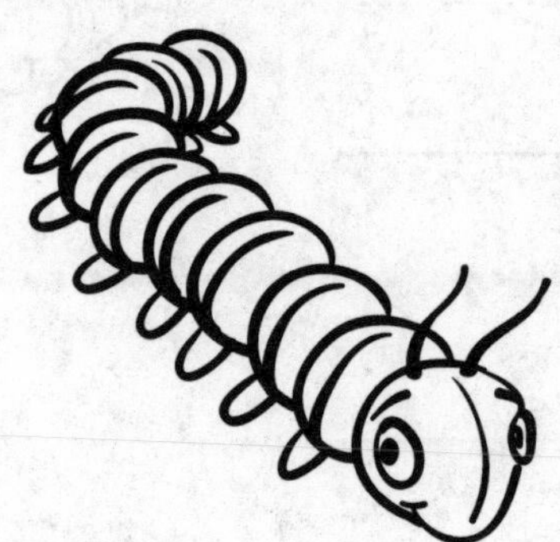

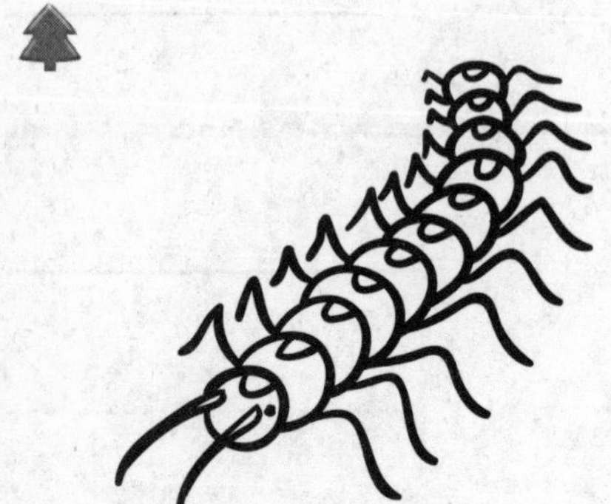

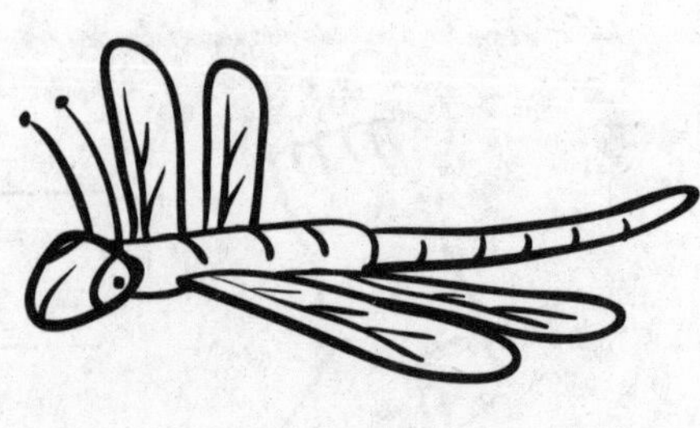

Comprehension: Key Details

🍎 Which bugs fly? Circle the pictures.

★ Which bugs crawl? Circle the pictures.

🌲 Which bugs hop? Circle the picture.

Name ______________________________

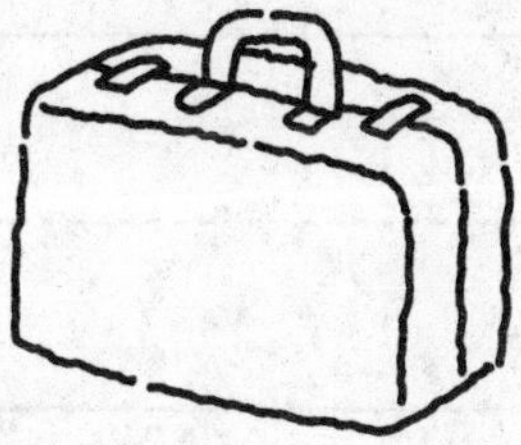

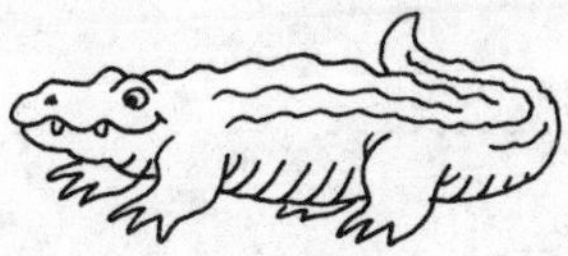

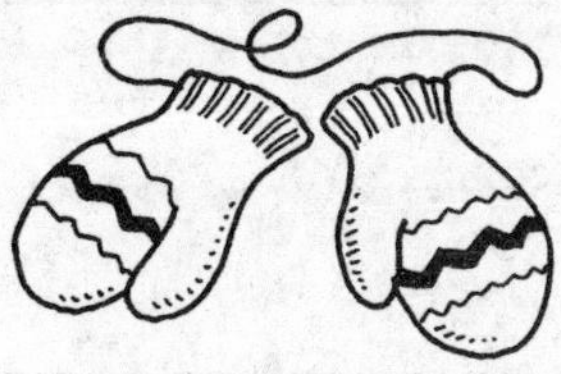

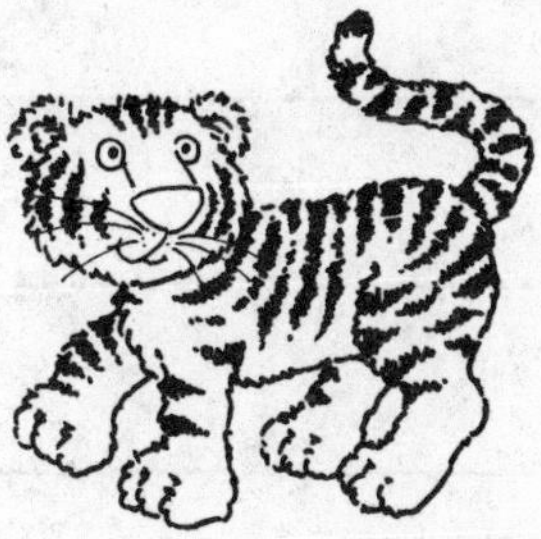

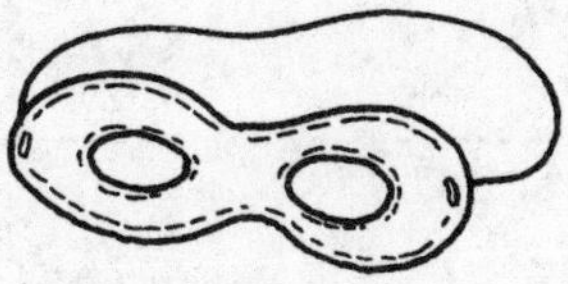

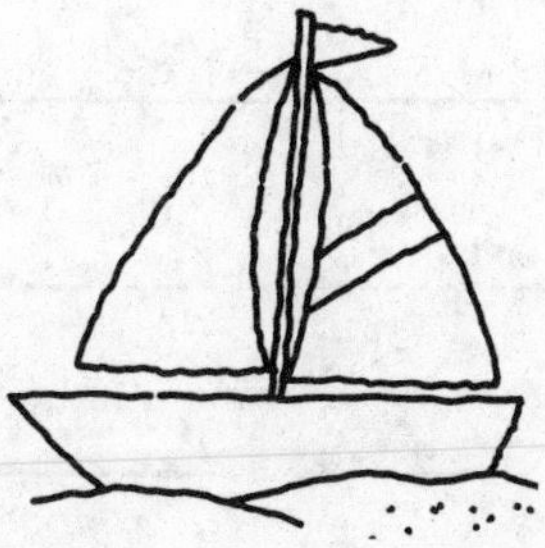

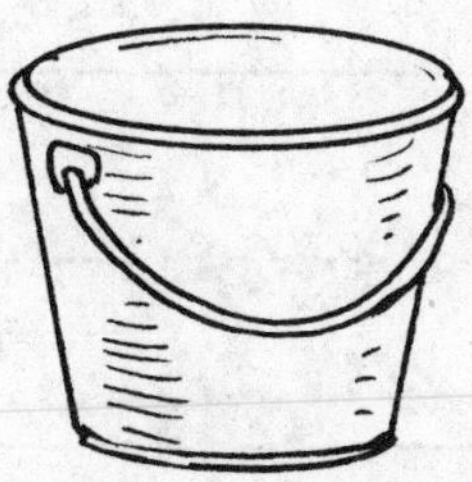

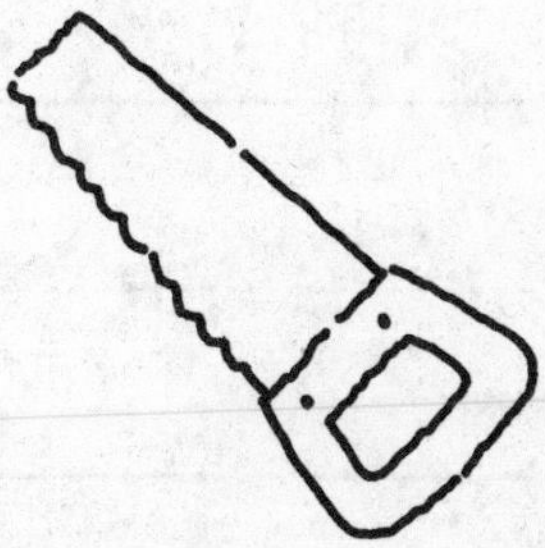

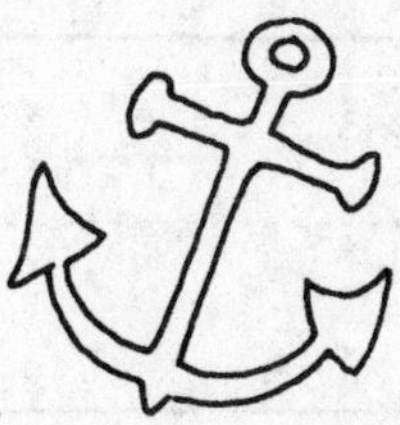

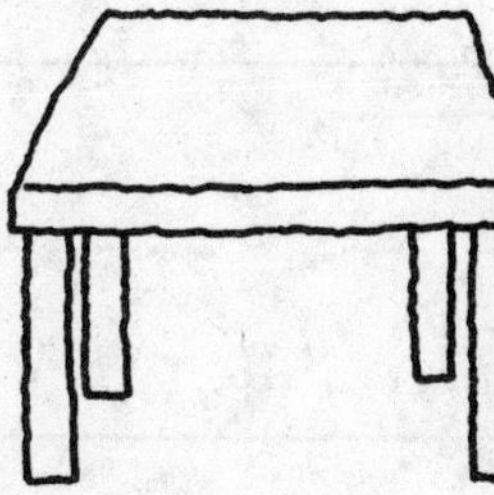

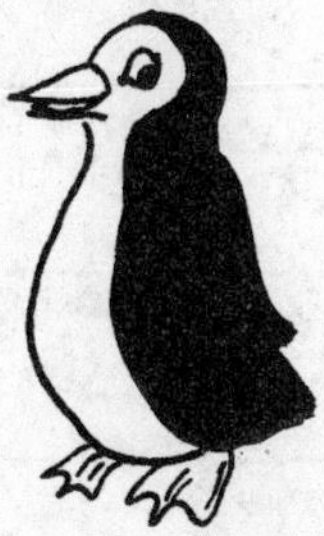

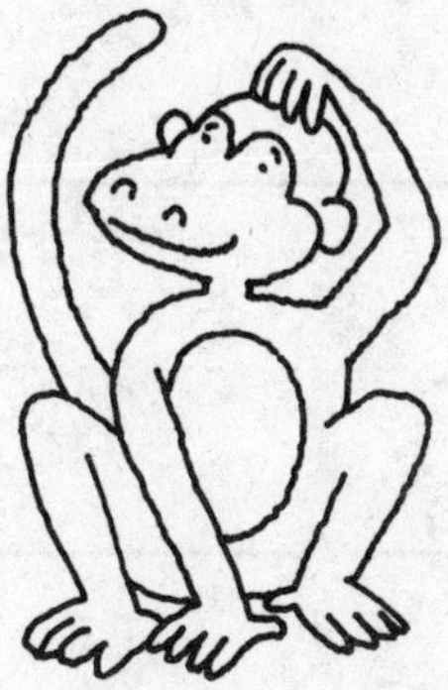

Phonics Review Game: /m/*m*, /a/*a*, /s/*s*, /p/*p*, /t/*t*
Say the name of each item and the letter it begins with. Turn the picture over and trace the letters. With a partner, think of other things whose names begin with each sound and letter.

Write

Name ______________________

t	m	a	s
s	p	s	m
m	p	t	a

Phonics Review Game: /m/*m*, /a/*a*, /s/*s*, /p/*p*, /t/*t*
Trace the letters. Say each letter and its sound. Then name a word that begins with the letter.

Name ____________________

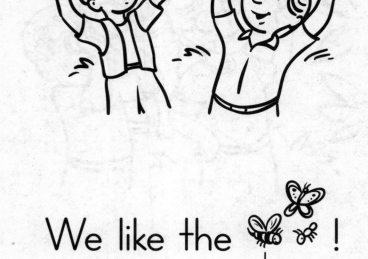

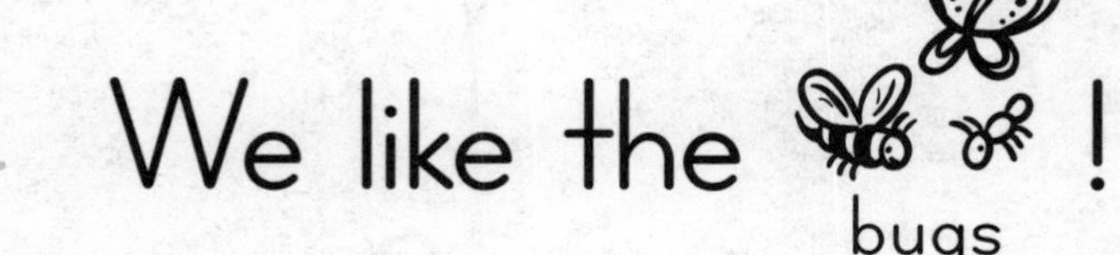
We like the bugs!

Review High Frequency Words: ***the, a, see, we, like***
Read the book aloud to a partner. Reread for fluency.

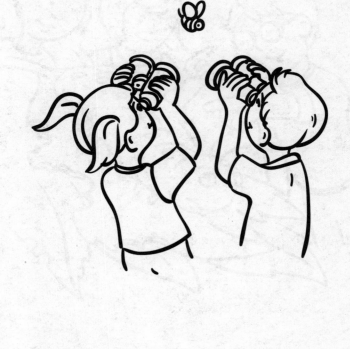

See the bugs!

We see a bee.

We see a caterpillar.

We see a butterfly.

Name ________________________________

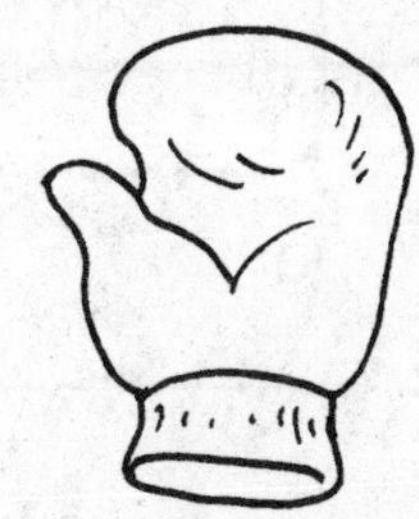

Category Words: Movement Words
Tell about each picture. Put a marker on each picture if it shows movement.

Name ____________________

mat map sap

mat mat

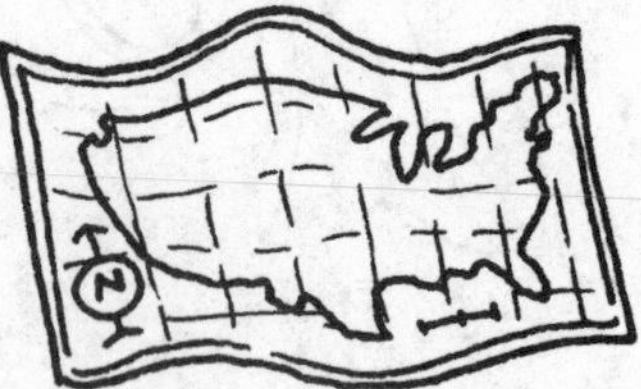

map

sap

Review Phonics: Blending
Blend the sounds and say the word. Write the word.
Repeat the word.

Name ______________________________

tap pat Sam

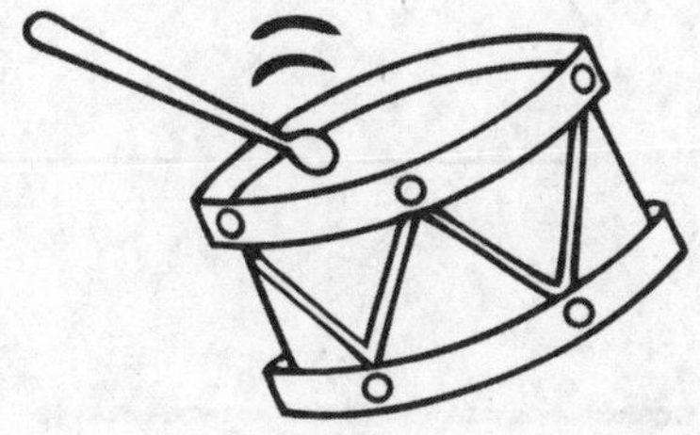

tap tap

pat

Sam

Review Phonics: Blending
Blend the sounds and say the word. Write the word.
Repeat the word.

Write

Name

sat

pat

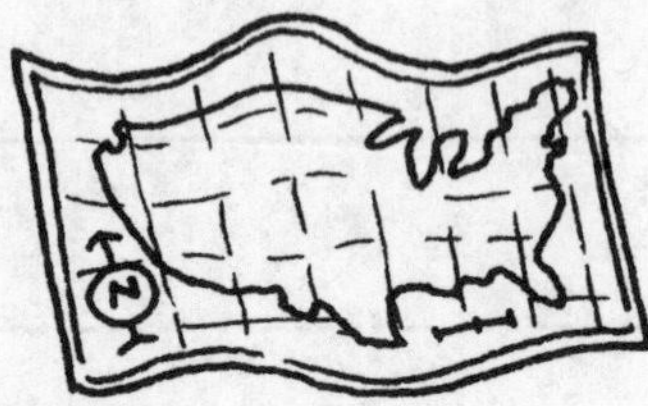

map

Handwriting Review
Say each word as you trace it and write it. Then read each word to a partner.

Play

Name ___

You're invited to a PARTY

1

Phonemic Awareness: /i/

Say the name of each picture. Put a marker on each picture if its name begins with the /i/ sound.

Name ______________________

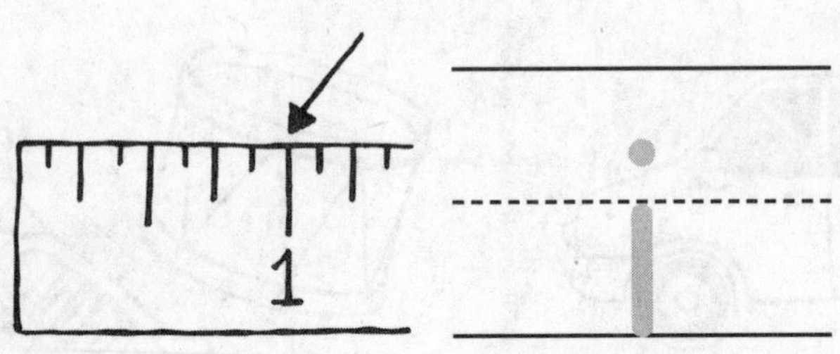

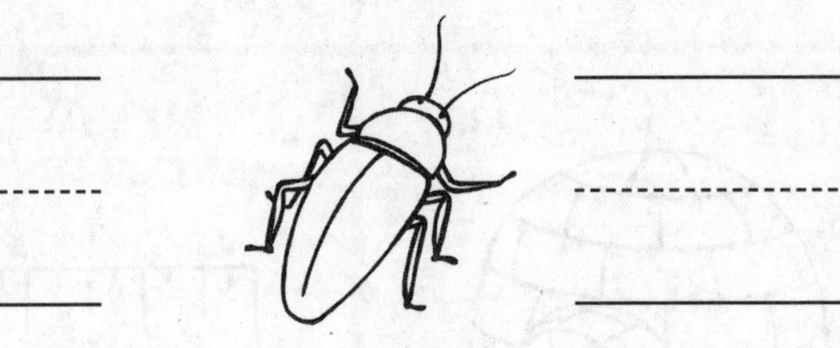

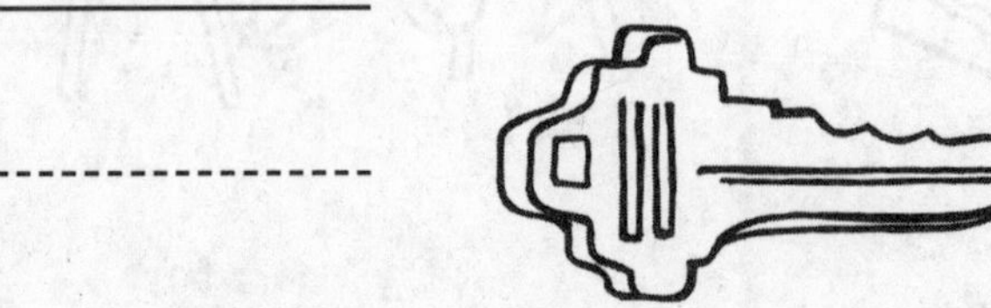

Phonics: /i/i
Say the name of each picture. Write the letter i next to each picture whose name begins with the /i/ sound.

Name ______________________________

Comprehension: Key Details

Look at the pictures about the story *How Do Dinosaurs Go to School?*

🍎Circle the dinosaur with spots.

★Circle the dinosaur with a bell.

🌲Circle the dinosaur with a helmet.

Name ______________________

tip pin pit

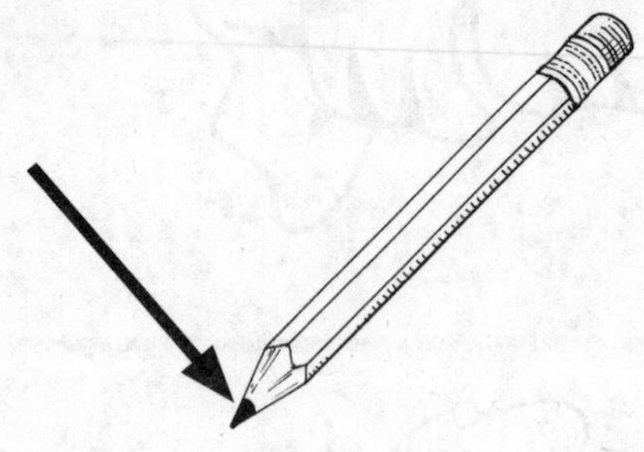

tip

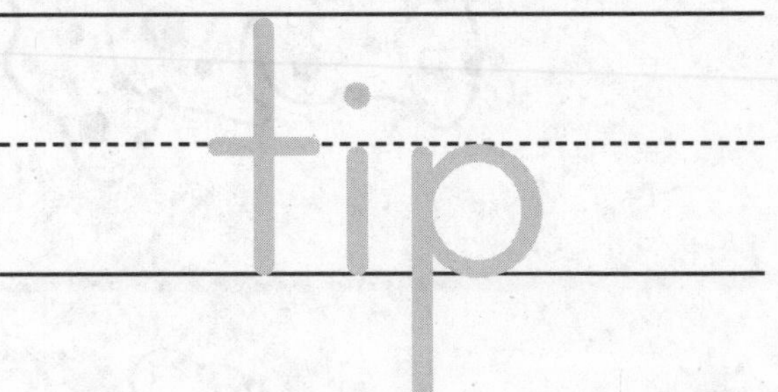

pin

pit

Phonics: Blending *-ip, -in, -it*
Blend the sounds and say the word. Write the word.
Repeat the word.

Name ____________________

I like to tap to the ♫ (music)!

High Frequency Words: *to*
Read the book aloud to a partner. Reread for fluency.

We Like to Tap

I like to tap the (piano).

I like to tap the drum.

I like to tap the .

Name ____

Category Words: Action Words
Tell about each picture. Put a marker on each picture if it shows an action.

Name ______________________________

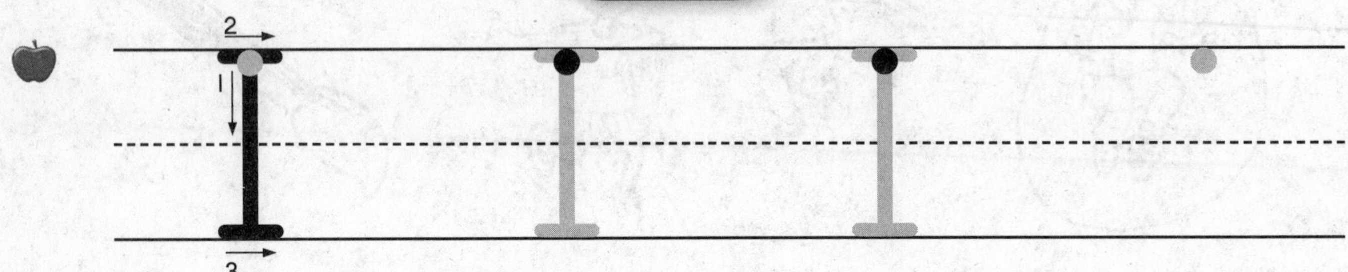

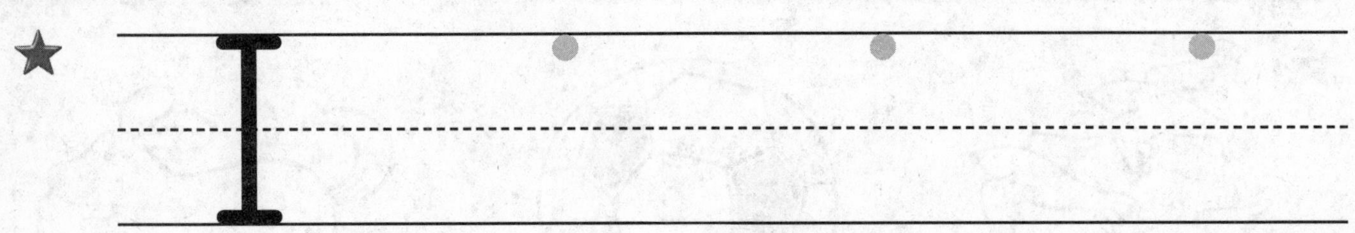

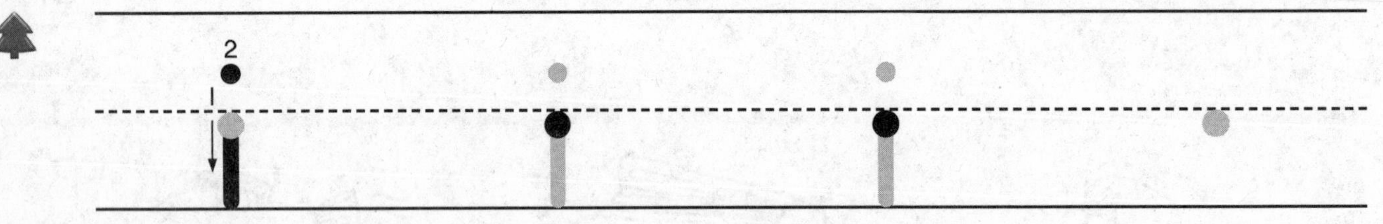

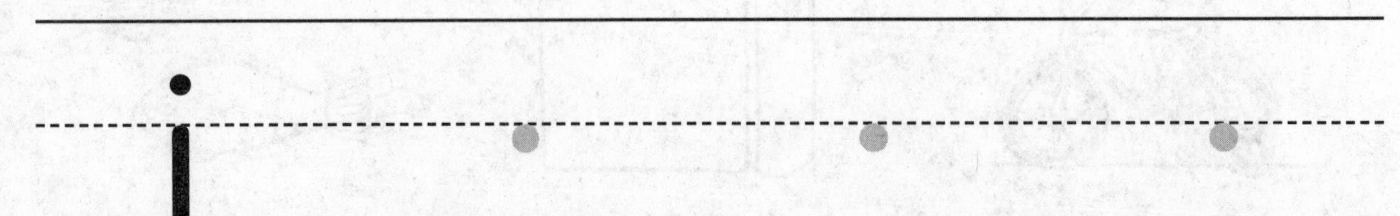

Handwriting: *Ii*
Trace and write each capital letter *I*. Then trace and write each lowercase letter *i*.

Name ______________________________

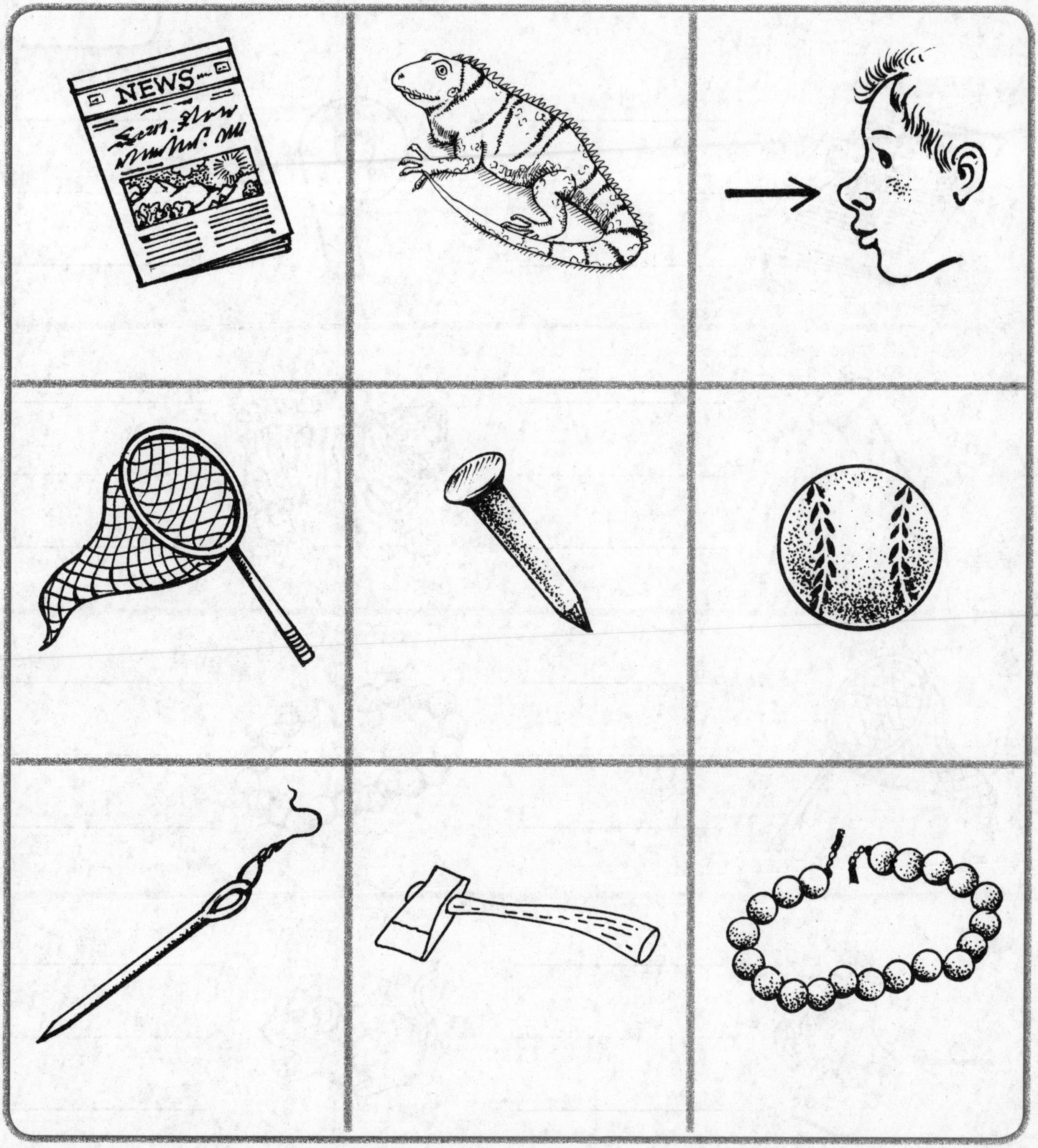

Phonemic Awareness: /n/

Say the name of each picture. Put a marker on each picture if its name begins with the /n/ sound.

Write

Name ____________________

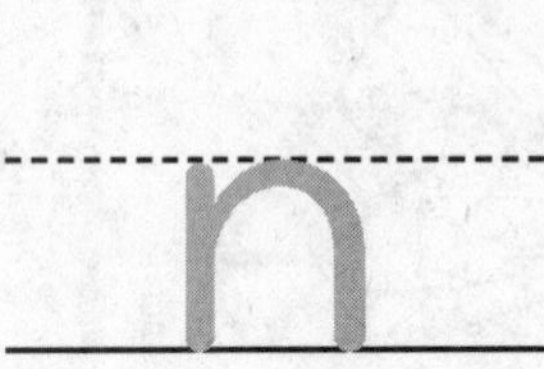

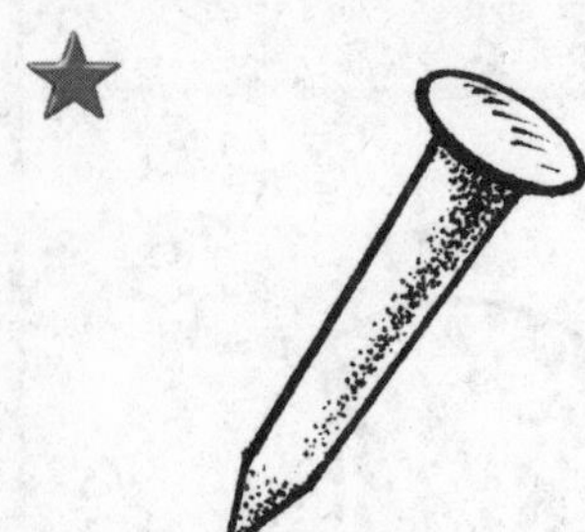

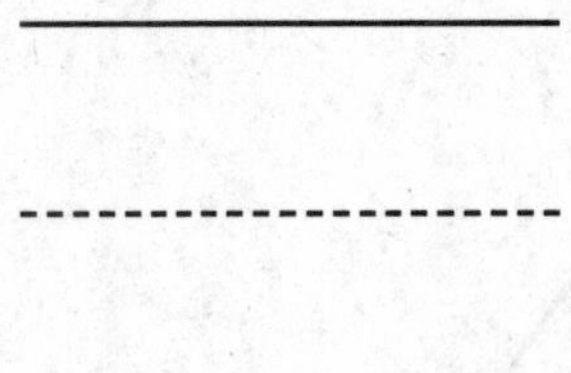

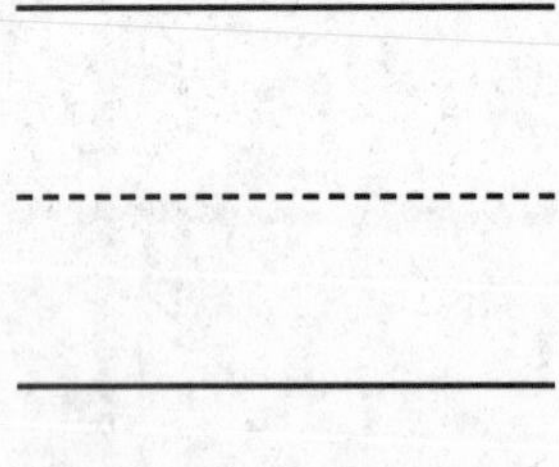

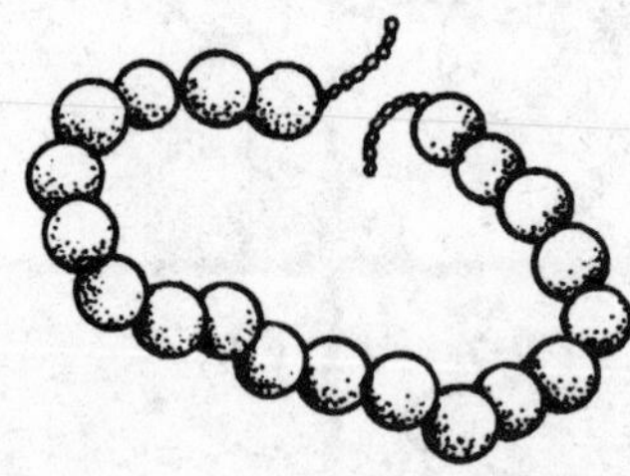

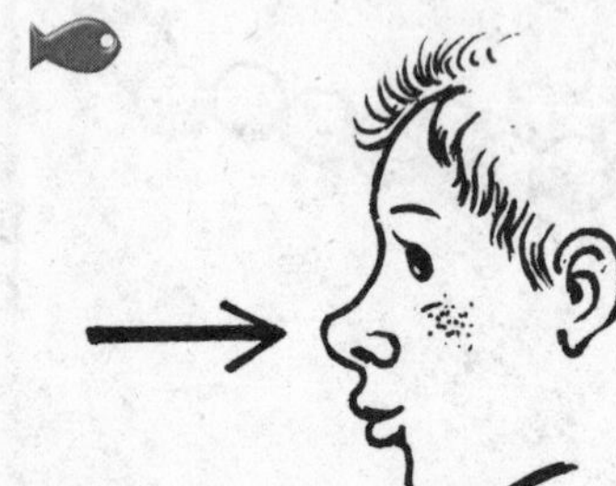

Phonics: /n/*n*
Say the name of each picture. Write the letter *n* next to each picture whose name begins with the /n/ sound.

Name ____

Comprehension: Key Details
Look at each picture. Tell what you see. Tell what sounds you would hear. Circle one part of each picture that would make noise. Tell a partner why you circled each picture.

Name ______________________

Nan nap pin

Nan Nan

nap

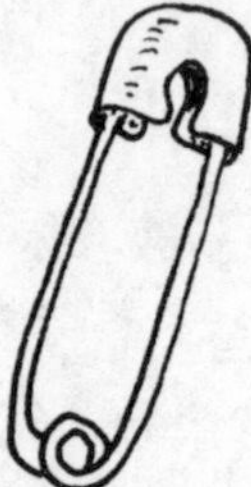

pin

Phonics: Blending /n/*n*
Blend the sounds and say the word. Write the word. Repeat the word.

Name ______________________

Sam and Pam see it.

High Frequency Words: ***and***
Read the book aloud to a partner. Reread for fluency.

The Map

Sam and Pam draw.

Copyright © The McGraw-Hill Companies, Inc.

Sam and Pam  it.

read

Sam and Pam  .

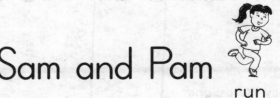

run

Name ______________________________

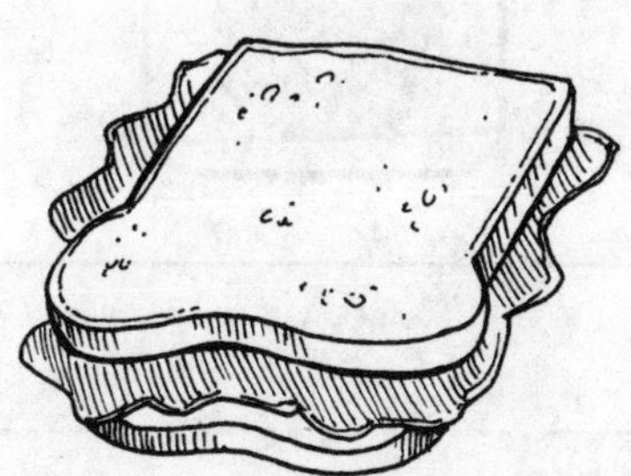

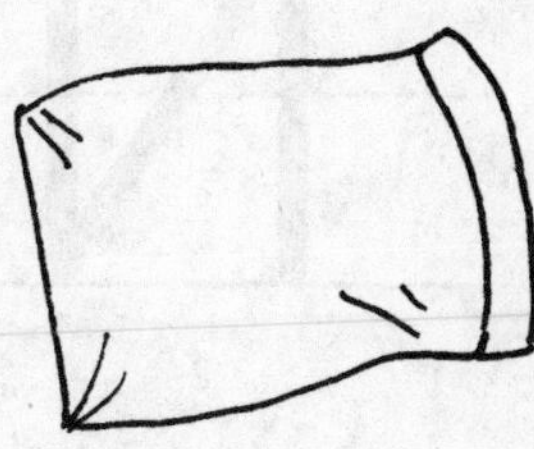

Category Words: Sound Words
Tell about each picture. Put a marker on each picture if it shows an object that makes a sound.

Name ______________________________

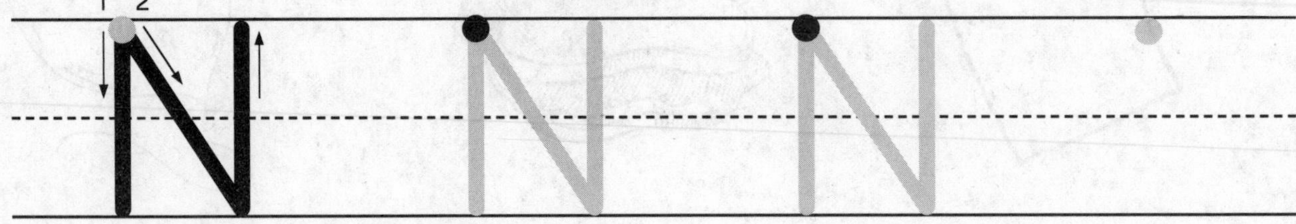

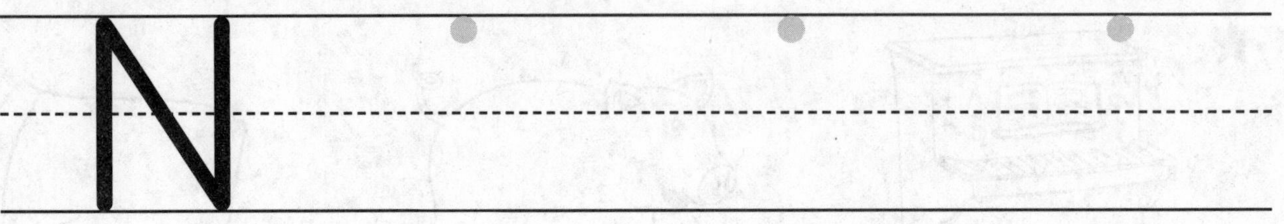

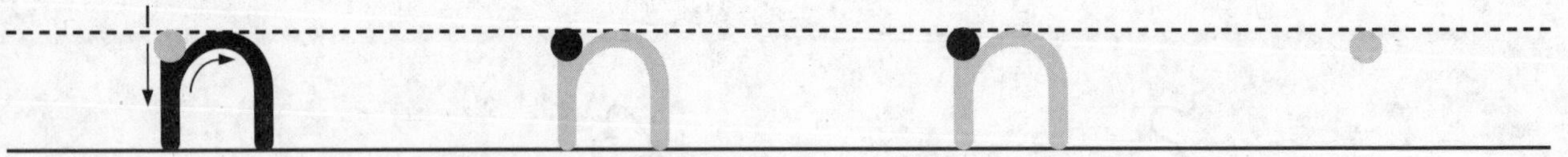

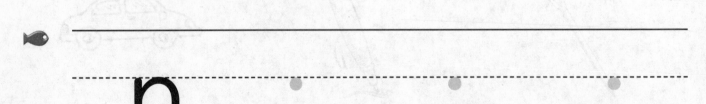

Handwriting: *Nn*
Trace and write each capital letter *N*. Then trace and write each lowercase letter *n*.

Name ____

Phonemic Awareness: /k/

Say the name of each picture. Circle each item if its name begins with the /k/ sound.

Write

Name ______________________________

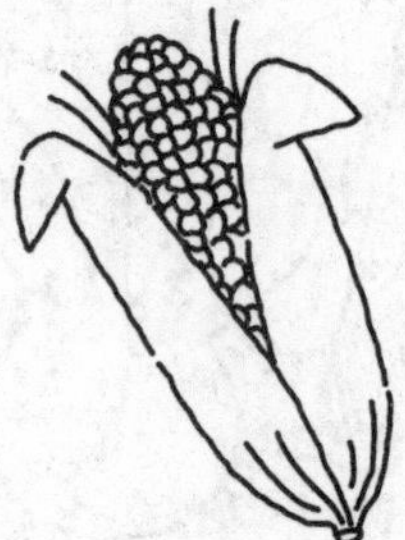

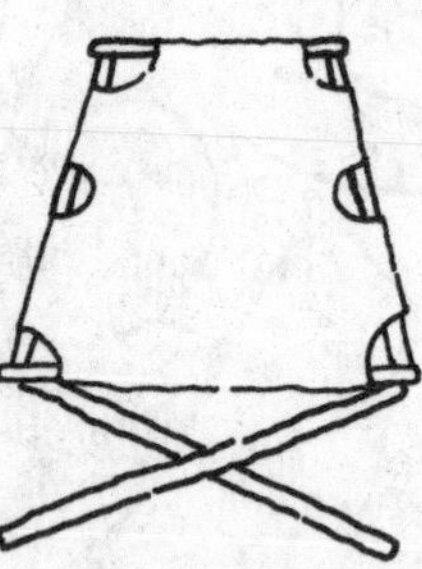

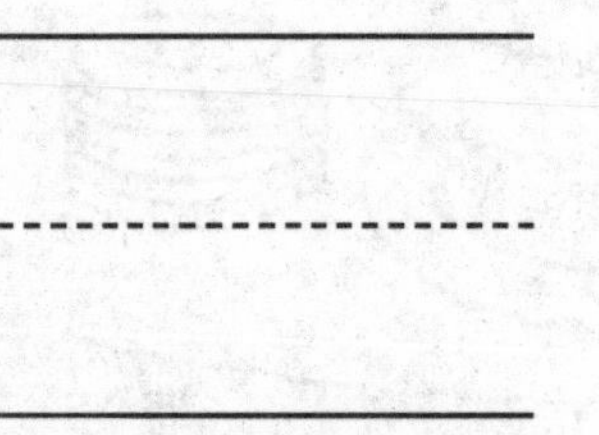

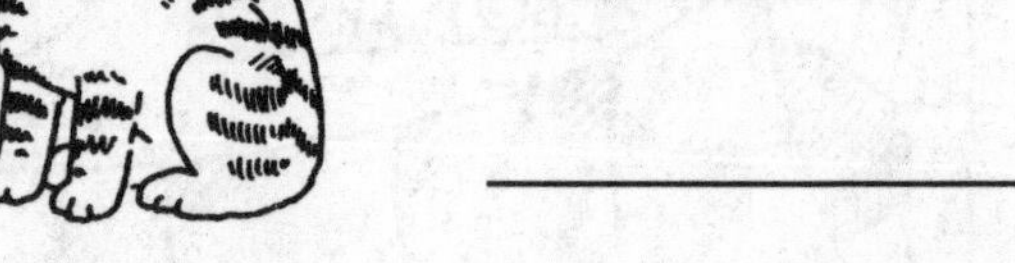

Phonics: /k/c
Say the name of each picture. Write the letter *c* next to each picture whose name begins with the /k/ sound.

Name ____

Comprehension: Character, Setting, Events

Look at the pictures about the story *Please Take Me for a Walk*.

Circle the picture that shows a character from the story.

★Circle the picture that shows the setting.

Circle the picture that shows the character and the setting.

Name ______________________________

cap can cat

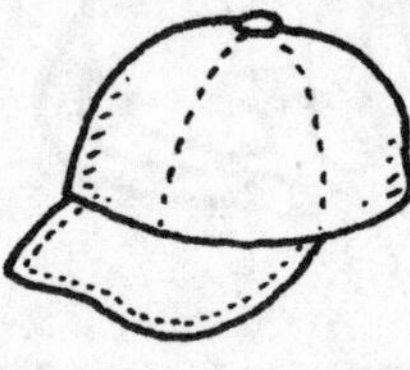

cap

cap

can

cat

Phonics: Blending /k/c
Blend the sounds and say the word. Write the word. Repeat the word.

Name ______________________

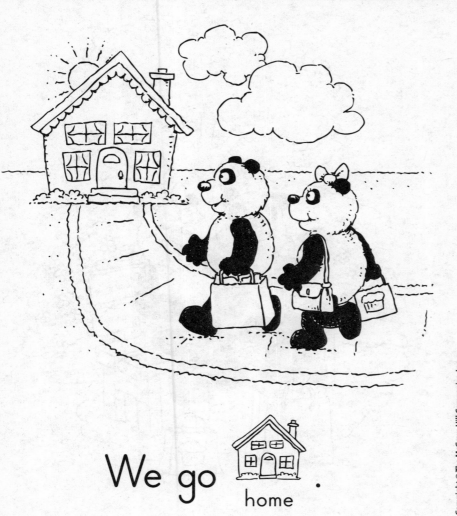

We go  home.

High Frequency Words: ***go***
Read the book aloud to a partner. Reread for fluency.

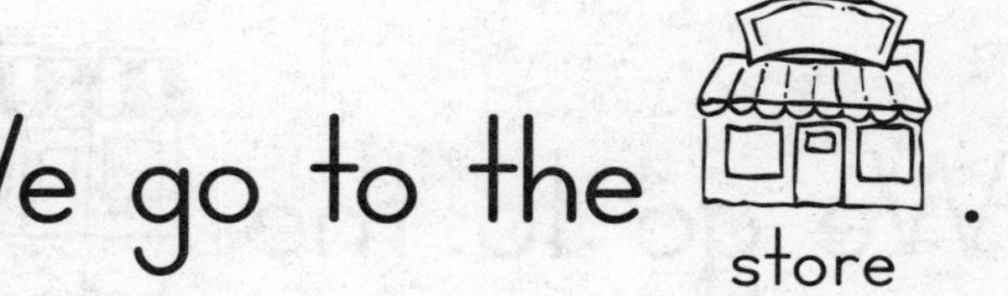
We go to the  store.

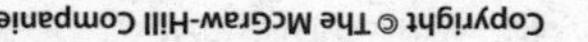

We go to the   bakery .

We go to the 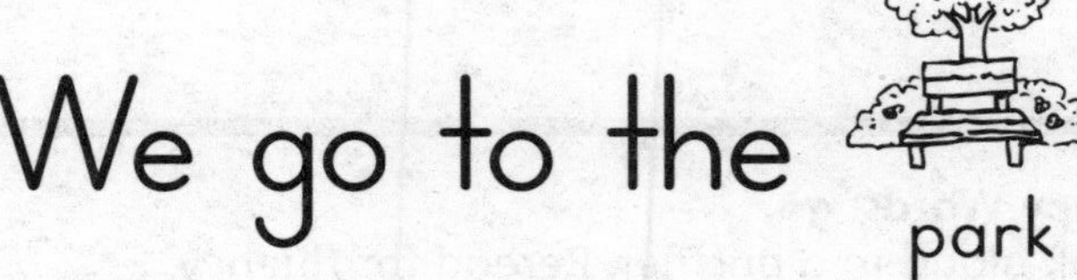 park .

Write

Name ____________________

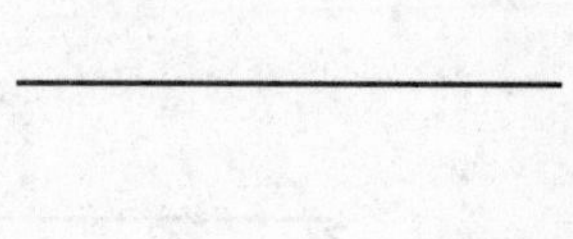

Category Words: Sequence Words
Look at the three pictures. Write 1, 2, and 3 to show what happened first, next, and last. Use the words first, next, and last.

Name

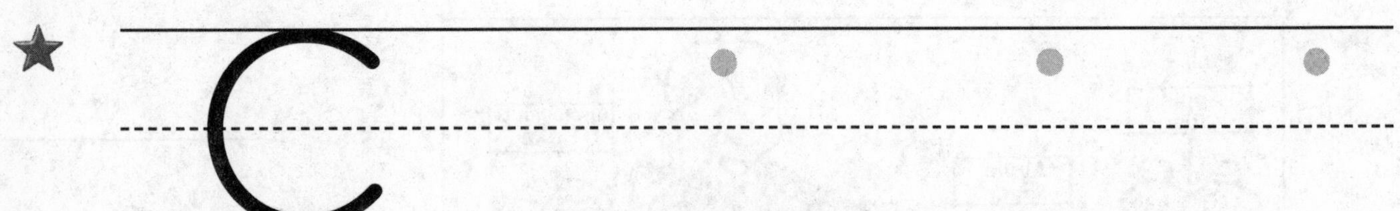

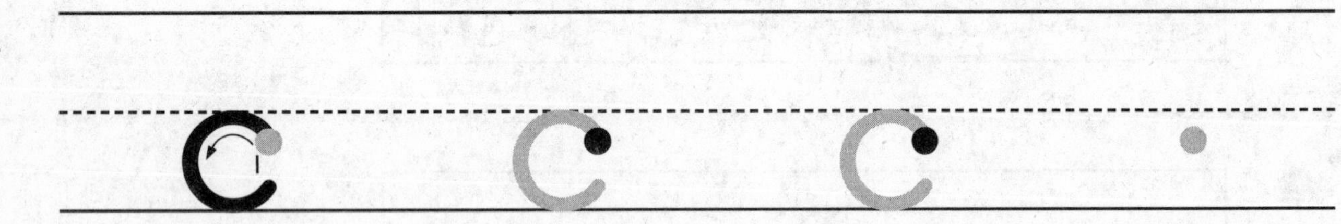

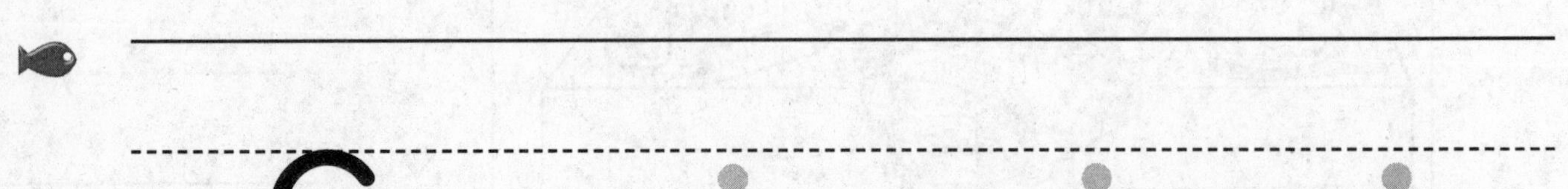

Handwriting: *Cc*
Trace and write each capital letter *C*. Then trace and write each lowercase letter *c*.

Name ____

ON

Phonemic Awareness: /o/
Say the name of each picture. Put a marker on each picture if its name begins with the /o/ sound.

Name

1.

2.

3.

4.

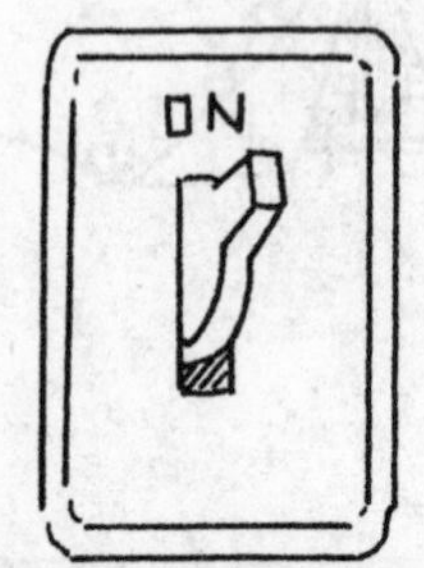

Phonics: /o/o
Say the name of each picture. Write the letter *o* next to each picture whose name begins with the /o/ sound.

Name ______________________________

1.

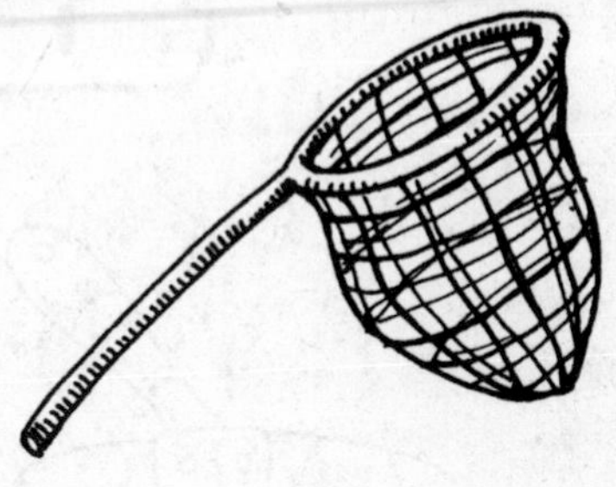

2.

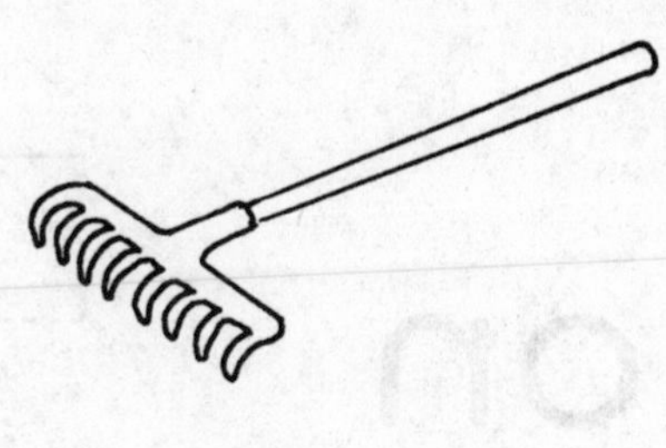

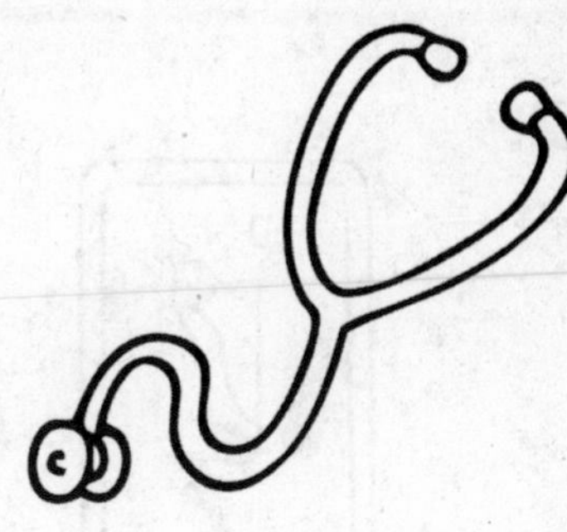

3.

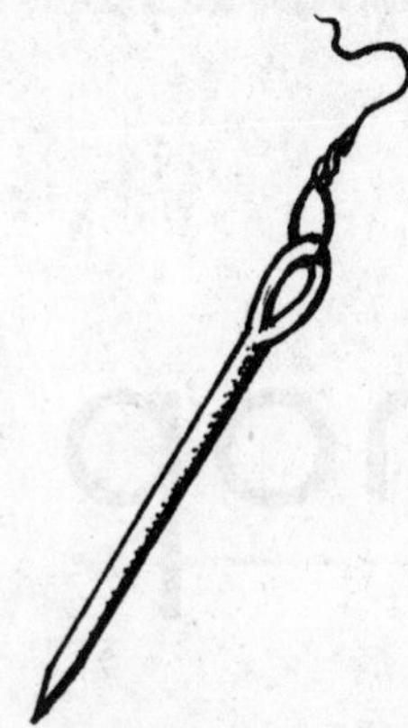

Comprehension: Key Details
Name each worker. Tell what you know about each worker. Circle the picture that shows the tool each worker would use. Tell a partner why you circled each picture.

Name ______________________________

pot on mop

I. 

pot

pot

2. 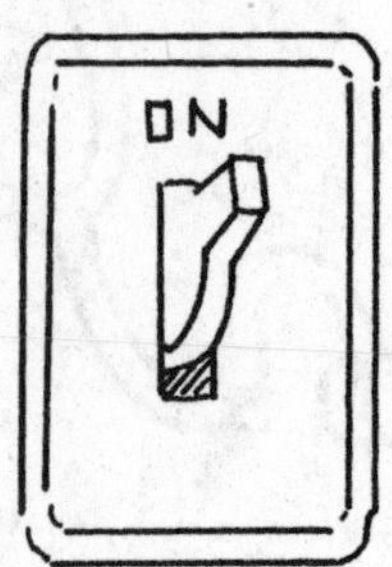

on

3. 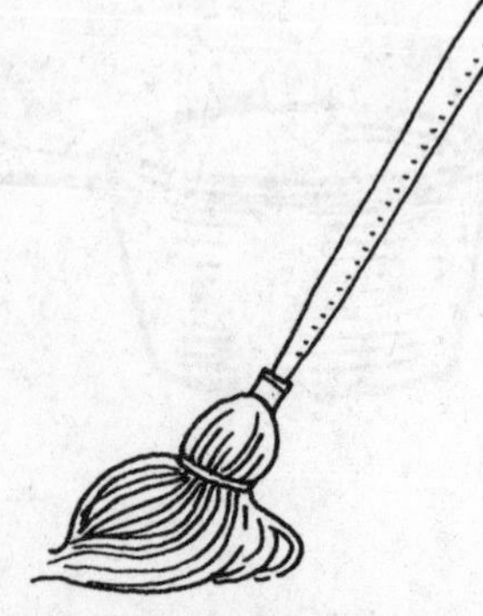

mop

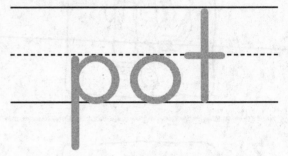

Phonics: Blending *-ot, -on, -op*
Blend the sounds and say the word. Write the word. Repeat the word.

Name ______________________

You and I can pull !

High Frequency Words: ***you***
Read the book aloud to a partner. Reread for fluency.

You and I

You and I can rake .

You and I can dig.

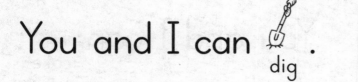

You and I can water.

Name ______________________________

I.

2.

3.

Category Words: Jobs
Look at the pictures in each row. Put a marker on pictures that show someone who does a job. Tell about the job each worker does.

Name ______________________________

1. 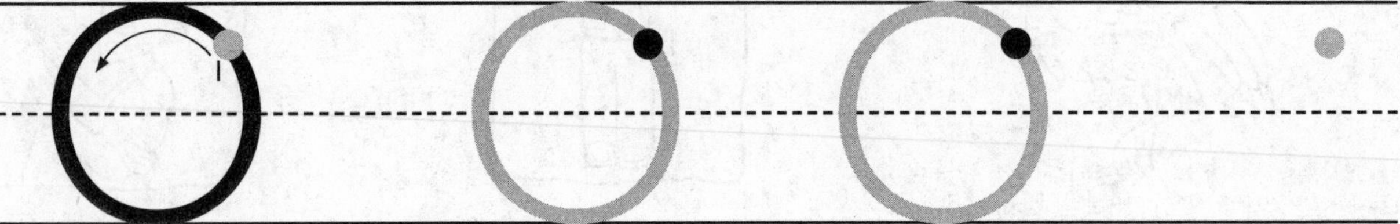

2. 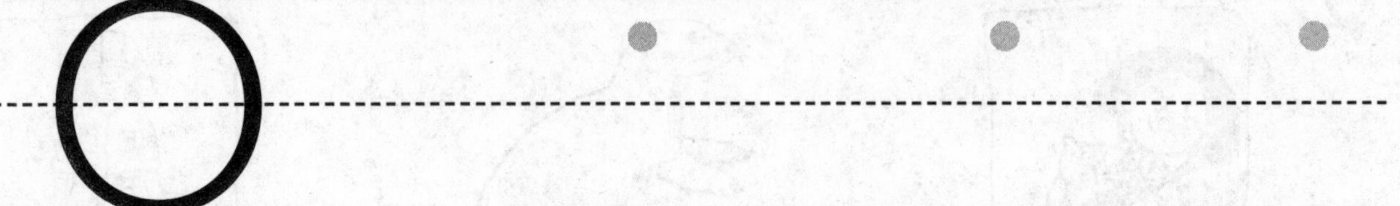

3. 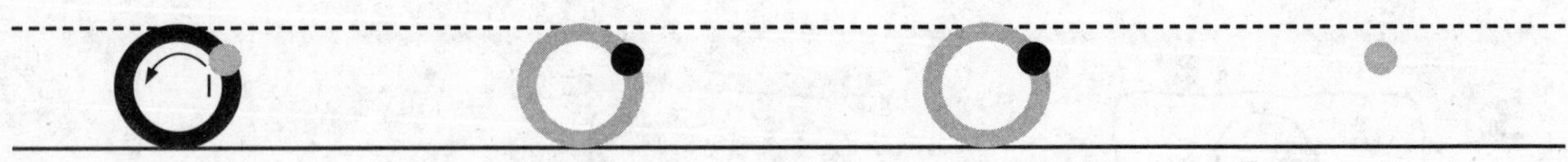

4. 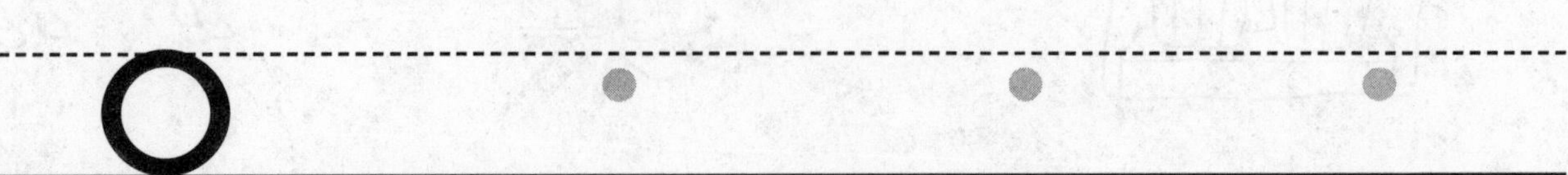

Handwriting: *Oo*
Trace and write each capital letter *O.* Then trace and write each lowercase letter *o.*

Name ______________________________

ON

Phonemic Awareness: /d/

Say the name of each picture. Put a marker on each picture if its name begins with the /d/ sound.

Name ______________________________

1.  d 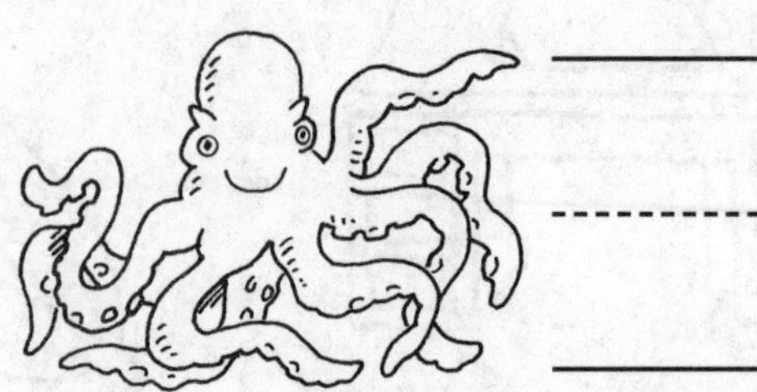

2.  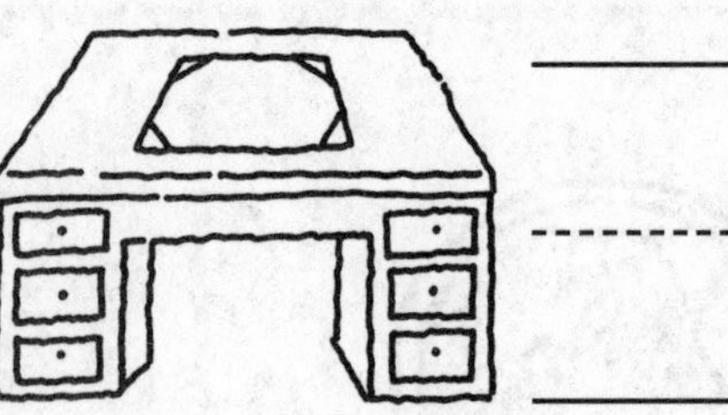

3. 

4. 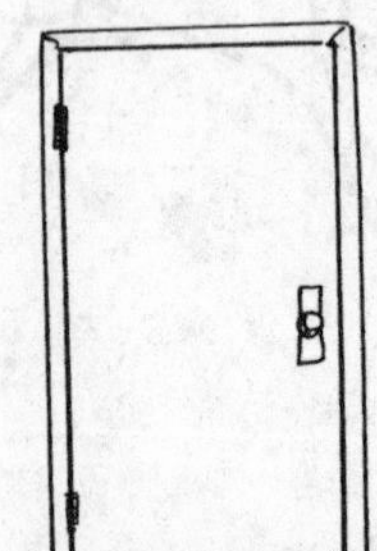 

Phonics: /d/*d*
Say the name of each picture. Write the letter *d* next to each picture whose name begins with the /d/ sound.

Name ______________________________

I.

2.

3.

Comprehension: Character, Setting, Events

Look at the pictures about the story *What Can You Do with a Paleta?*

1. Circle the picture that shows Mama.
2. Circle the picture that shows the setting from the story.
3. Circle the picture that shows an event from the story.

Name ____________________

Dan dot sad

1. 

Dan

Dan

2. 

dot

3. 

sad

Phonics: Blending /d/*d*
Blend the sounds and say the word. Write the word. Repeat the word.

Name ______________________

I do!

High Frequency Words: ***do***
Read the book aloud to a partner. Reread for fluency.

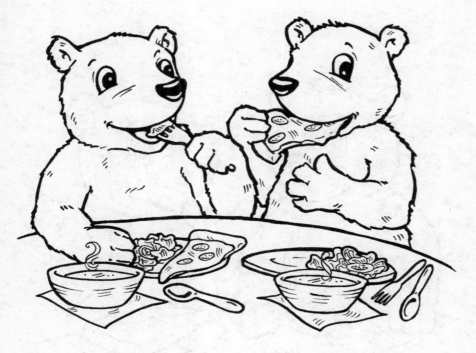

Do You?

Do you like salad?

Do you like soup ?

Do you like pizza ?

Name ______________________________

1.

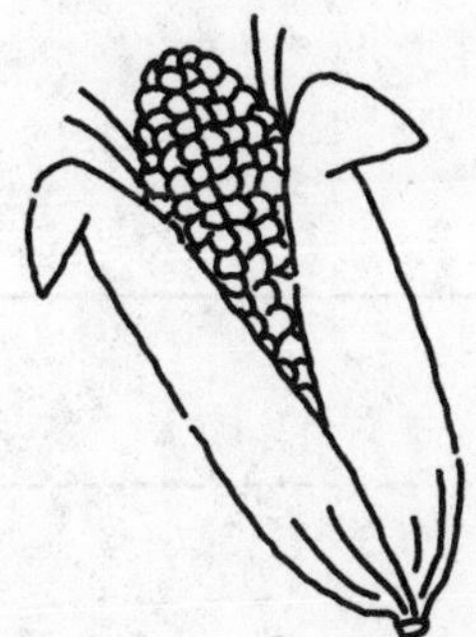

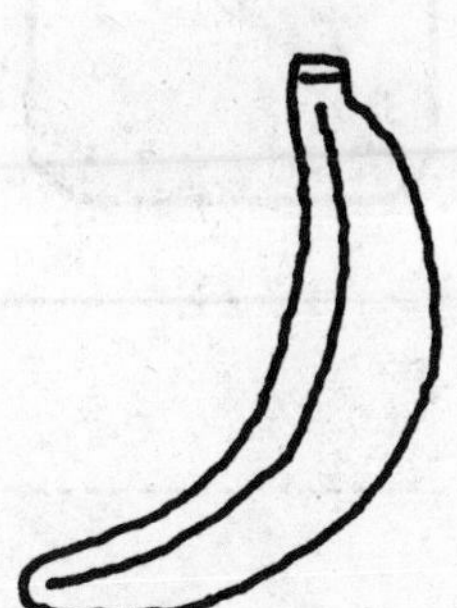

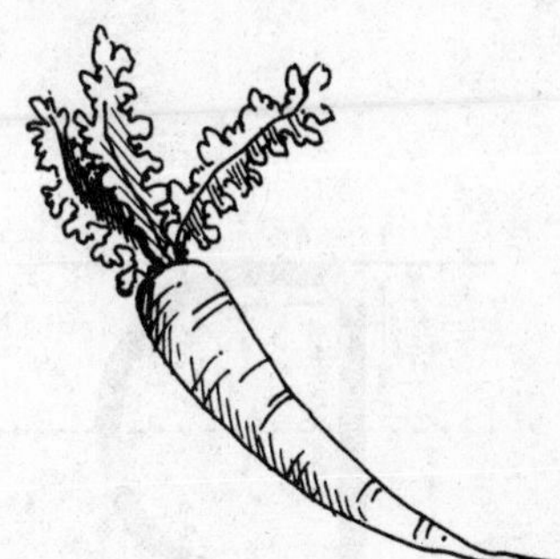

2.

3.

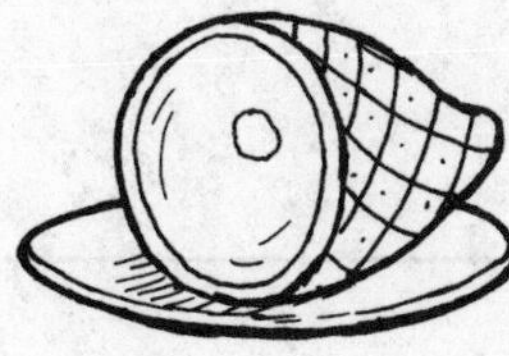

Category Words: Kinds of Foods

1. Put a marker on pictures of vegetables.
2. Put a marker on pictures of fruits.
3. Put a marker on pictures of meats.

What other kinds of foods are shown? Tell about them.

Name ______________________________

1. 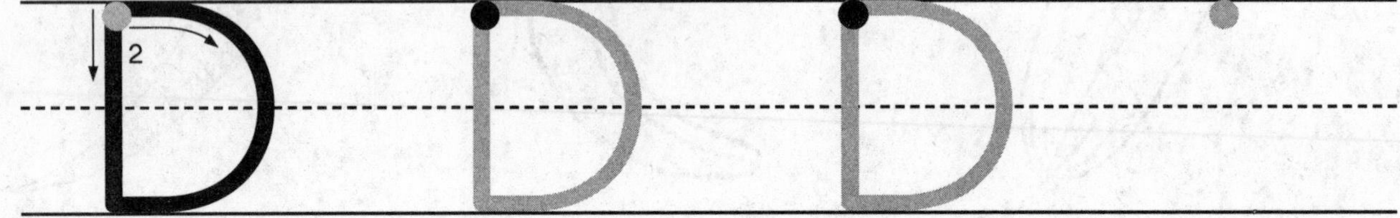

2. 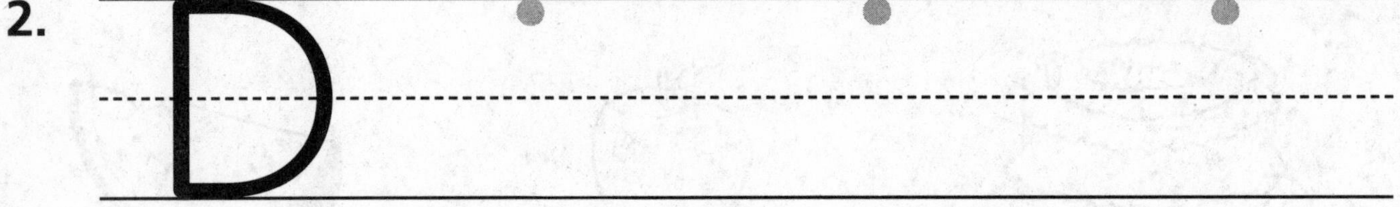

3. 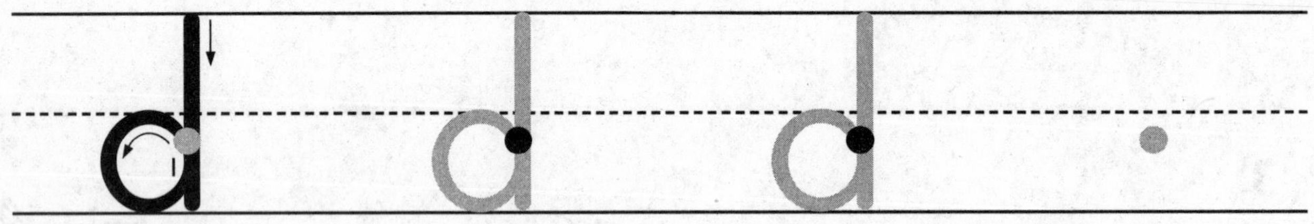

4. 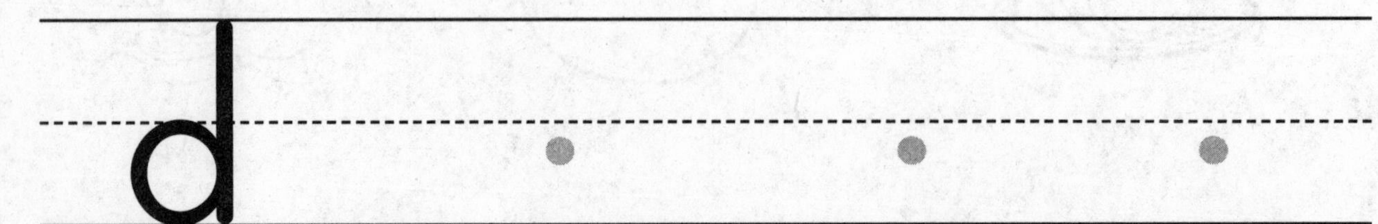

Handwriting: *Dd*
Trace and write each capital letter *D*. Then trace and write each lowercase letter *d*.

Name ________________________________

1.

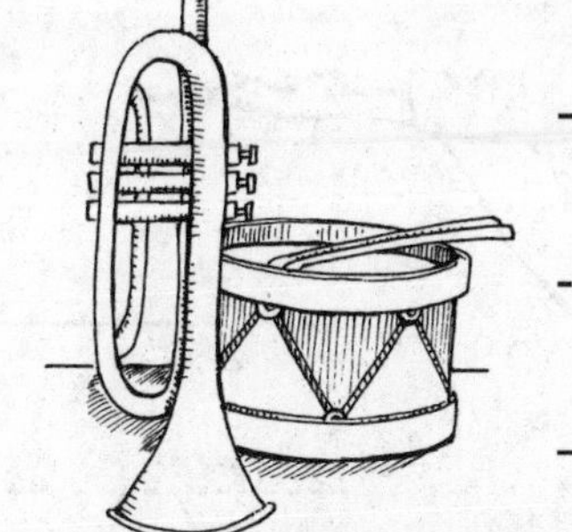

i

2.

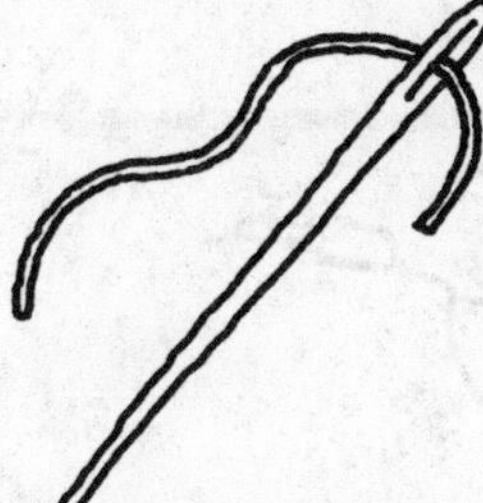

3.

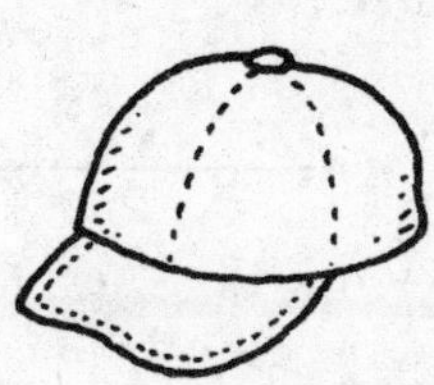

4.

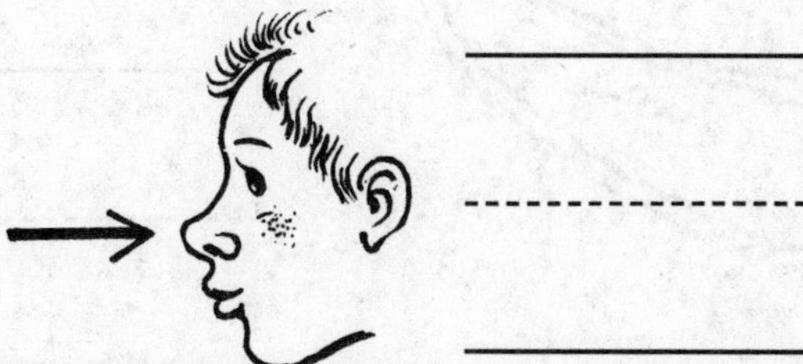

Review Phonics: /i/i, /n/n, /k/c
Say the name of each picture. Write the letter *i, n, or c* next to each picture whose name begins with the /i/, /n/, or /k/ sound.

Name ______________________________

I.

2.

3.

Comprehension: Key Details
Look at the pictures about the story *Roadwork*. Tell what happened in each picture. Then write *I, 2,* and *3* to show what happened first, next, and last.

Name ____________________

NEWS

ON

To:
PARTY
RSVP:

Phonics Review Game: /i/*i*, /n/*n*, /k/*c*, /o/*o*, /d/*d*
Say the name of each item and the letter it begins with. Then cut out each picture.

Name ______________________________

Phonics Review Game: /i/*i*, /n/*n*, /k/*c*, /o/*o*, /d/*d*

Place the picture cards face-down onto a desk or table. Flip two cards over and say the names of the pictures. Have children say the letter that stands for each beginning sound. If the pictures begin with the same letter, you have made a match. Continue playing until all cards have been matched.

Name ______________________

You and I can do it!

Review High Frequency Words: ***to, and, go, you, do***
Read the book aloud to a partner. Reread for fluency.

You and I

We can go to the  park!

We can do a puzzle.

Can we do it?

Name ______________________________

1.

2.

3.

Category Words: Position Words
Put a marker on each picture that shows a position word. Name the position shown in each picture.

Name

on nod cap

1.

on

on

2.

nod

3.

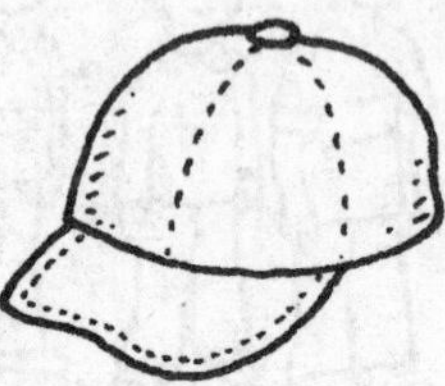

cap

Review Phonics: Blending
Blend the sounds and say the word. Write the word. Repeat the word.

Name ______________________________

cot in dip

1\. 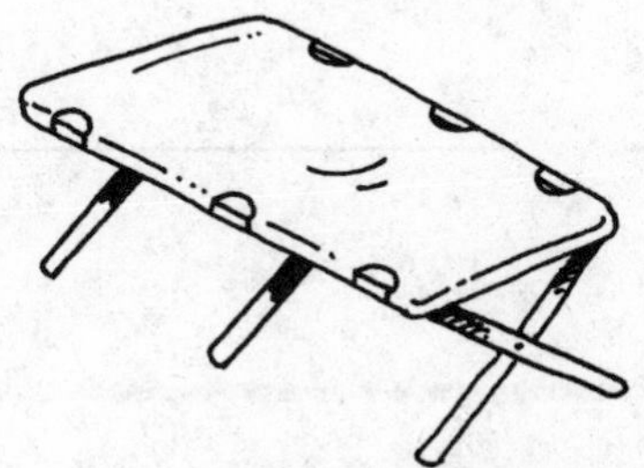 cot

cot

2\. 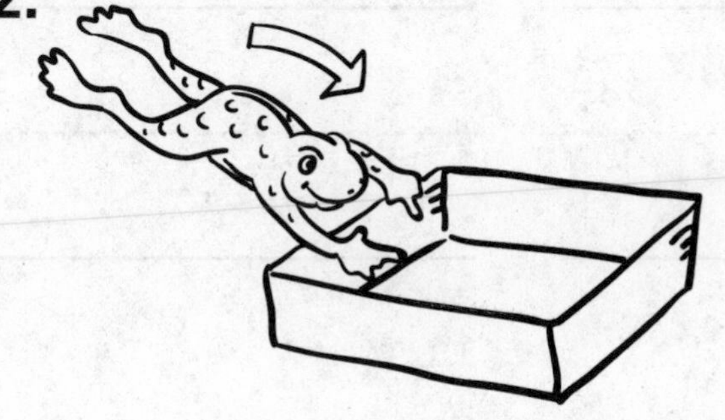 in

3\.  dip

Review Phonics: Blending
Blend the sounds and say the word. Write the word. Repeat the word.

Write

Name ___________________________

1.

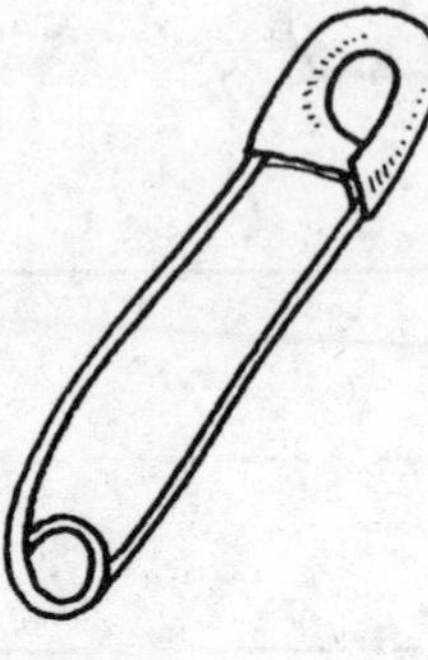

pin

2.

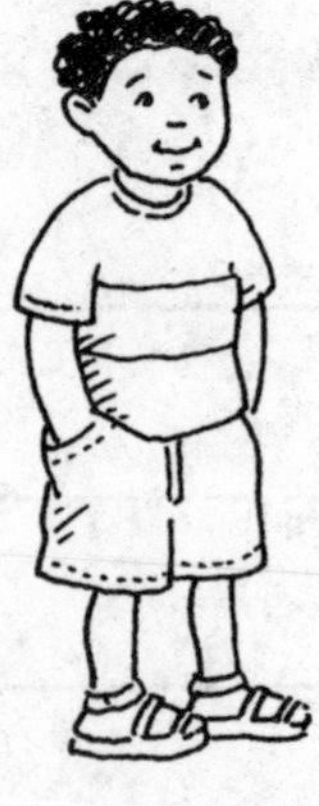

Don

3.

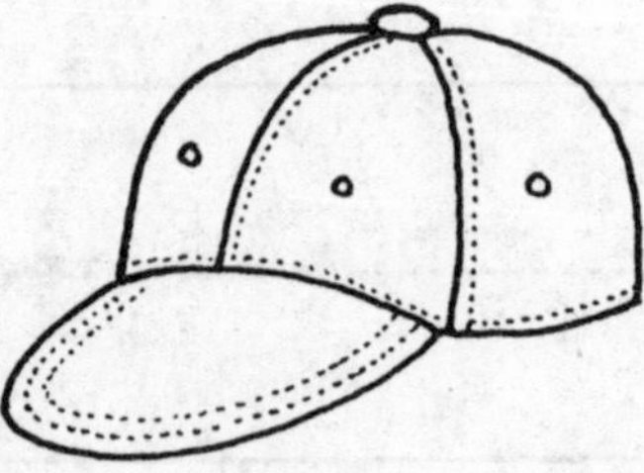

cap

Handwriting Review
Say each word as you trace it and write it. Then read each word to a partner.

Play

Name ______________________________

Phonemic Awareness: /h/
Say the name of each picture. Put a marker on each picture if its name begins with the /h/ sound.

Name ______________________________

1.

h

2.

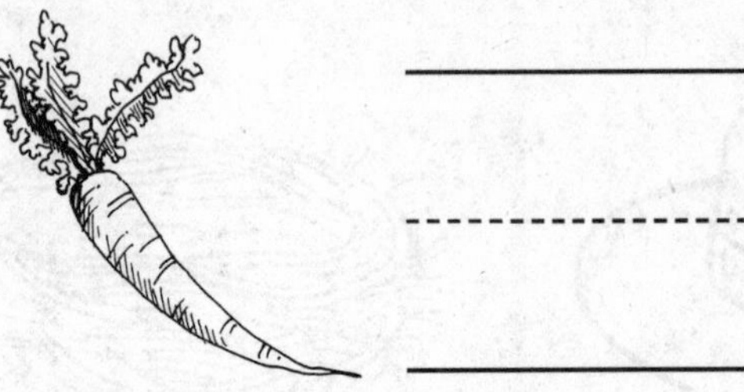

3.

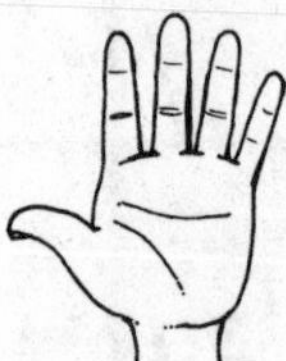

4.

Phonics: /h/*h*
Say the name of each picture. Write the letter *h* next to each picture whose name begins with the /h/ sound.

Name ______________________________

I.

2.

Comprehension: Character, Setting, Events
I. Circle the picture that shows the main character from *My Garden*.
2. Circle the illustration that shows the setting from the story.
Turn to a partner and talk about an event from the story.

Write

Name ___

hat hot hop

I.

hat hat

2.

hot

3.

hop

Phonics: Blending /h/*h*
Blend the sounds and say the word. Write the word. Repeat the word.

Name ____________________

We do not see my cat.

High Frequency Words: ***my***
Read the book aloud to a partner. Reread for fluency.

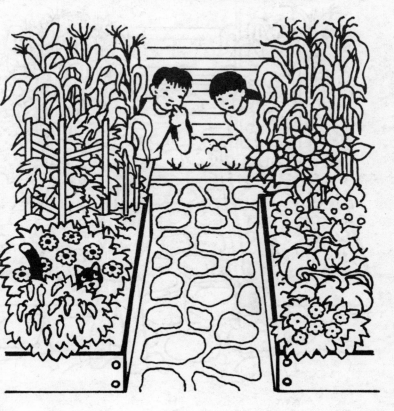

We See It!

Tam and I see my cat.

My cat and I see Tam.

Tam and I do not see.

Name ______________________________

I.

2.

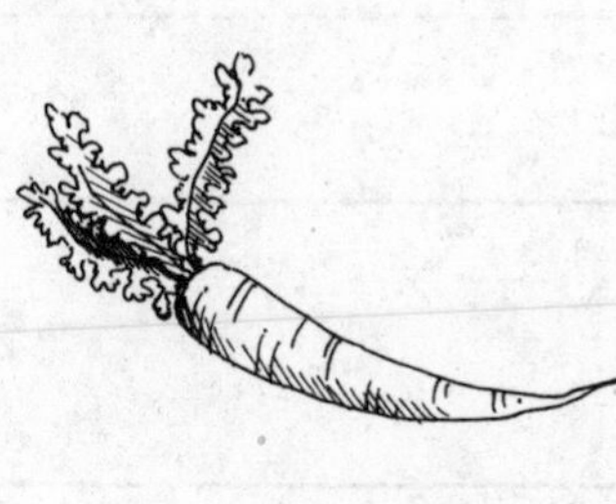

3.

Category Words: Size Words

I. Put a marker on the picture that shows something big.
2. Put a marker on the picture that shows something small.
3. Put a marker on the picture that shows something tall.

Name ______________________________

1. 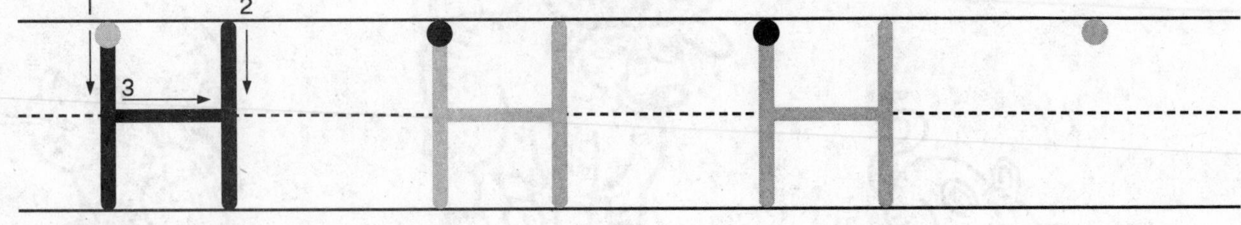

2. 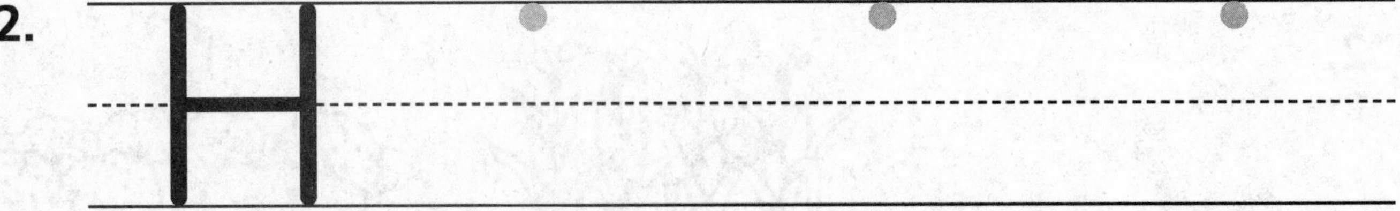

3. 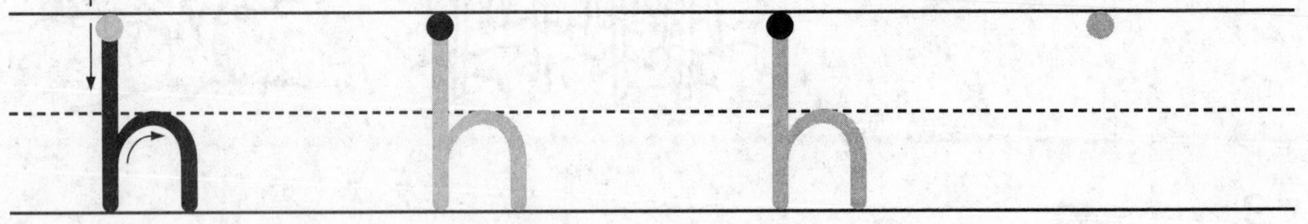

4. 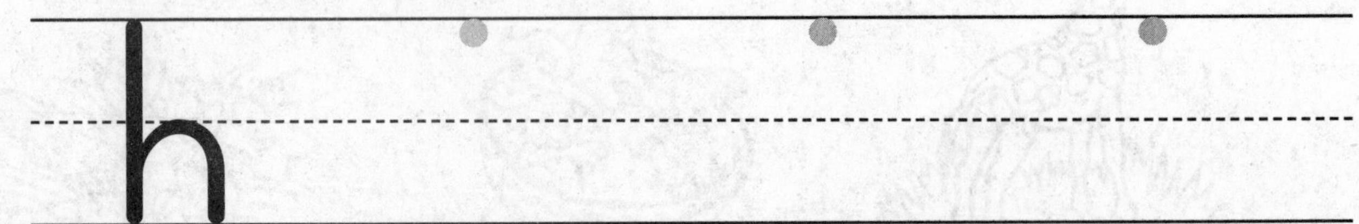

Handwriting: ***Hh***
Trace and write each capital letter *H*. Then trace and write each lowercase letter *h*.

Name ______________________________

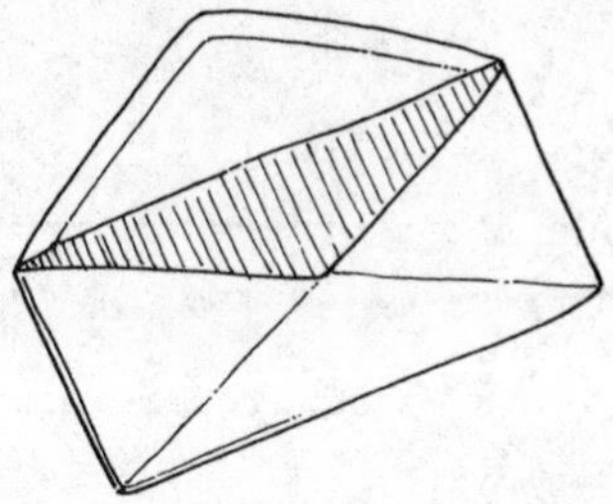

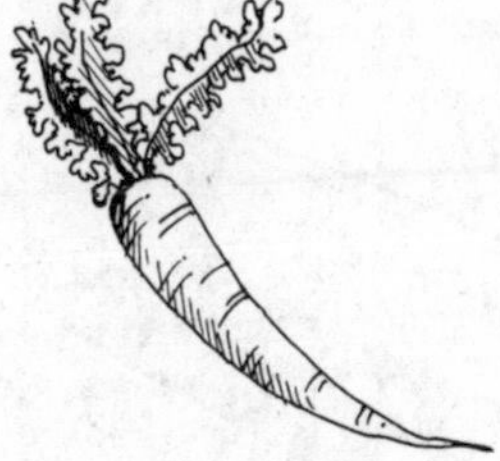

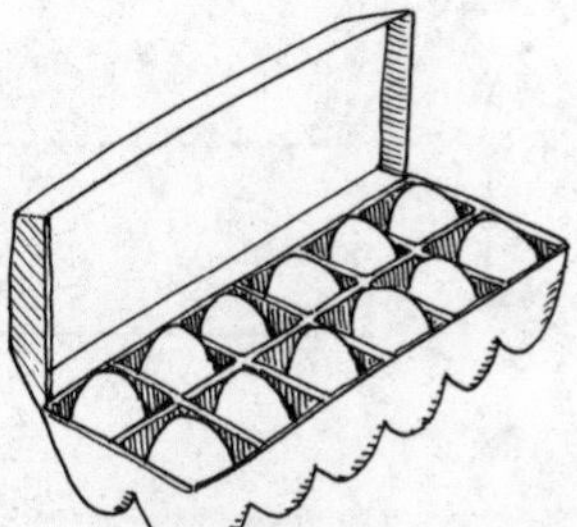

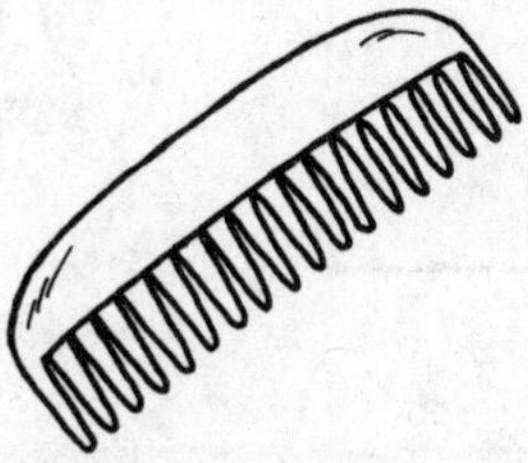

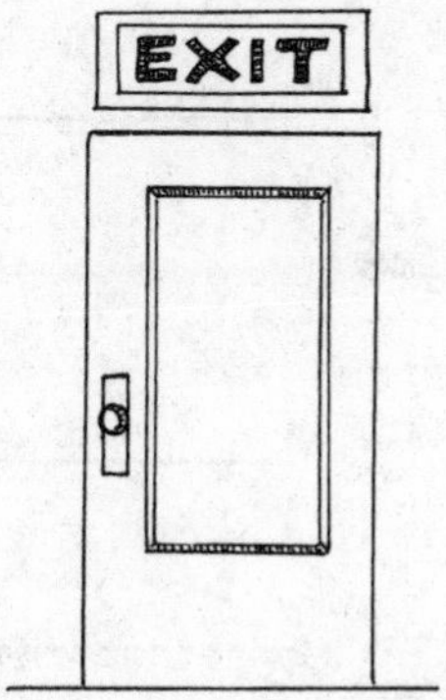

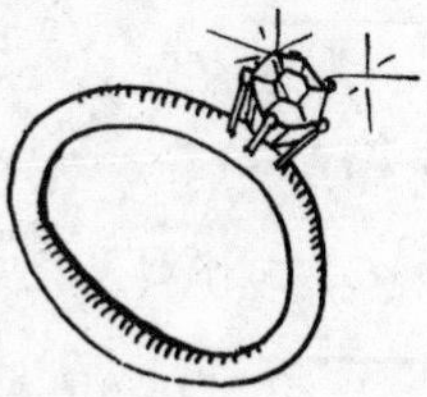

Phonemic Awareness: /e/
Say the name of each picture. Put a marker on each picture if its name begins with the /e/ sound.

Name ______________________

Ee

1.

e

2.

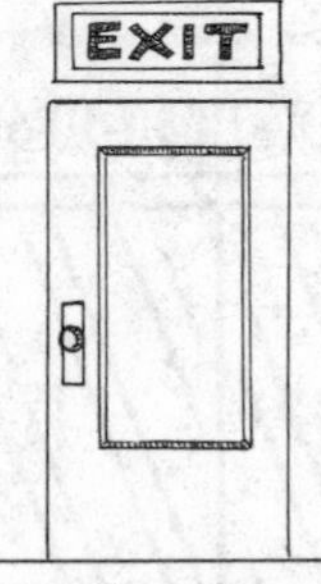

3.

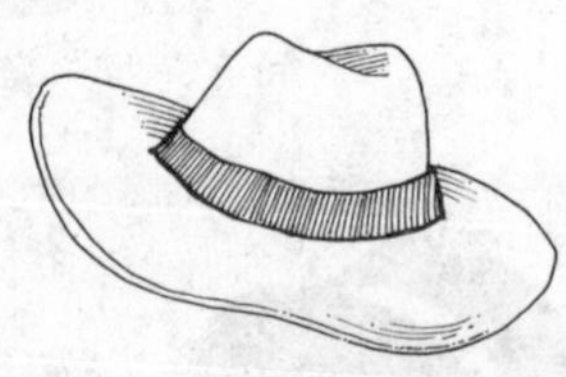

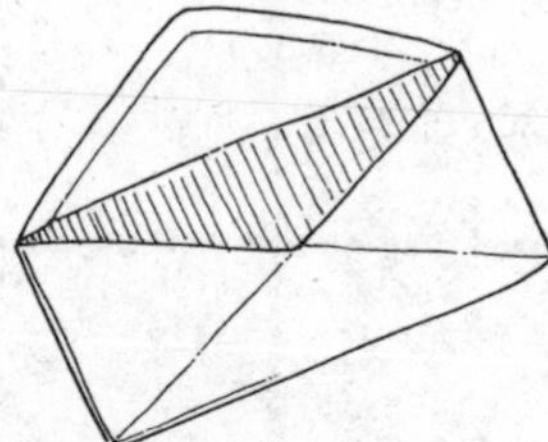

4.

Phonics: /e/e
Say the name of each picture. Write the letter *e* next to each picture whose name begins with the /e/ sound.

Name ______________________________

1.

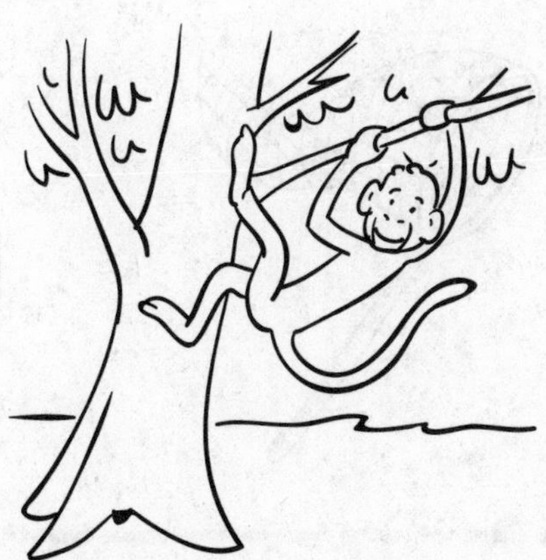

2.

Comprehension: Main Topic and Key Details
Talk to a partner about the main topic of *A Grand Old Tree*.

1. Circle the picture that shows a detail about the tree.
2. Circle the picture that shows another detail about the tree.

Write

Name ___________________________

net Ed hen

1.

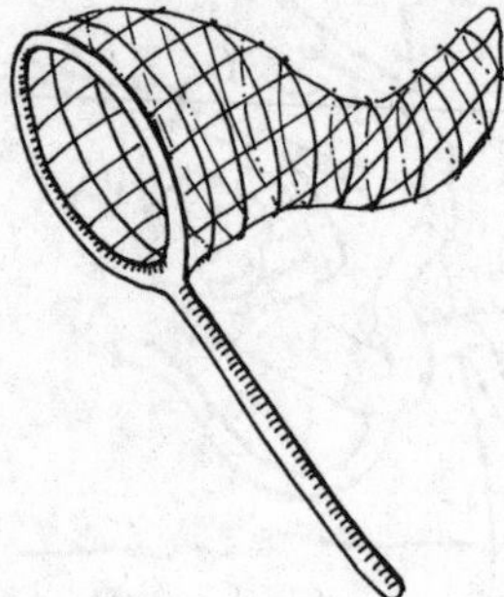

net

net

2.

Ed

3.

hen

Phonics: Blending *-et, -ed, -en*
Blend the sounds and say the word. Write the word. Repeat the word.

Name ______________________

We are not sad.

We can hop!

High Frequency Words: ***are***
Read the book aloud to a partner. Reread for fluency.

Are You Hot?

Are you hot?

Are you sad?

Copyright © The McGraw-Hill Companies, Inc.

We can go!

We are not hot.

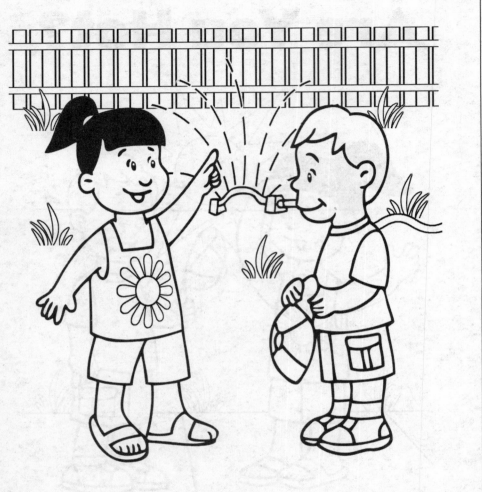

Name ______________________________

1.

2.

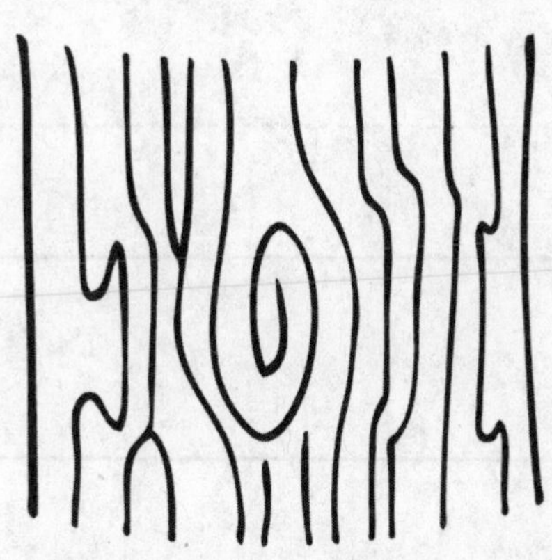

3.

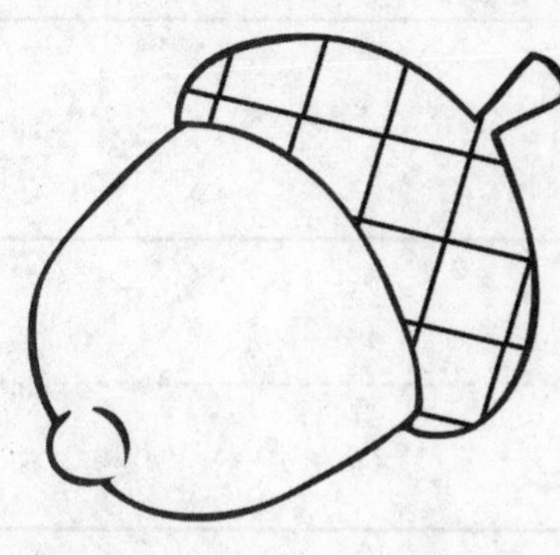

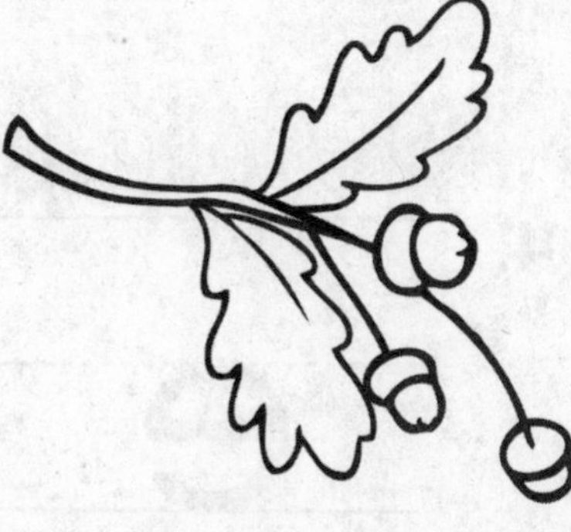

Category Words: Tree Parts
Look at each picture. Tell about it. Put a marker on each picture that shows a tree part. Say the name of each tree part.

Write

Name

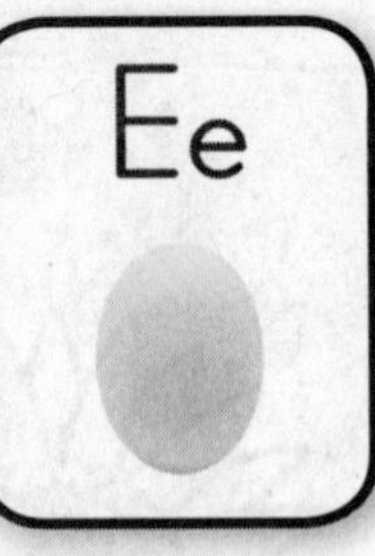

I.

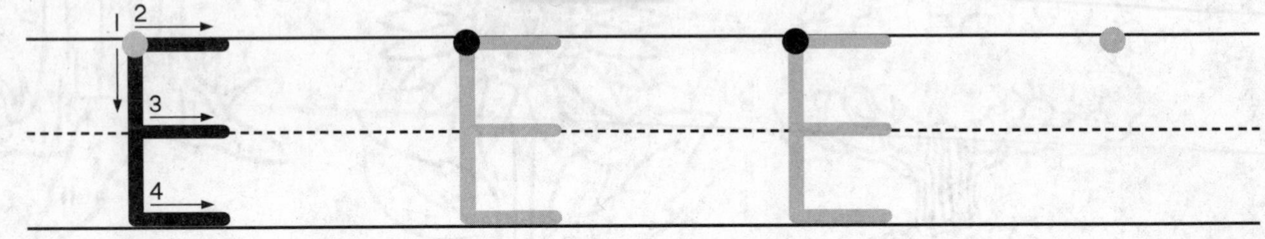

2.

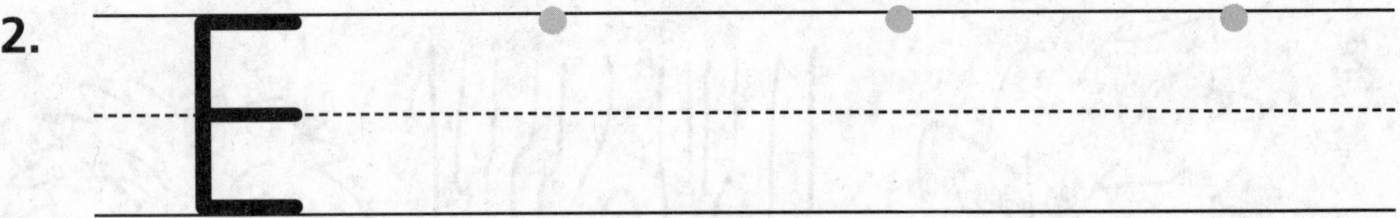

3.

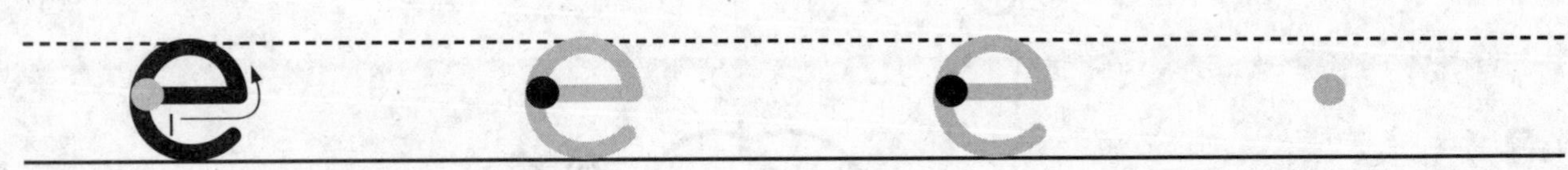

4.

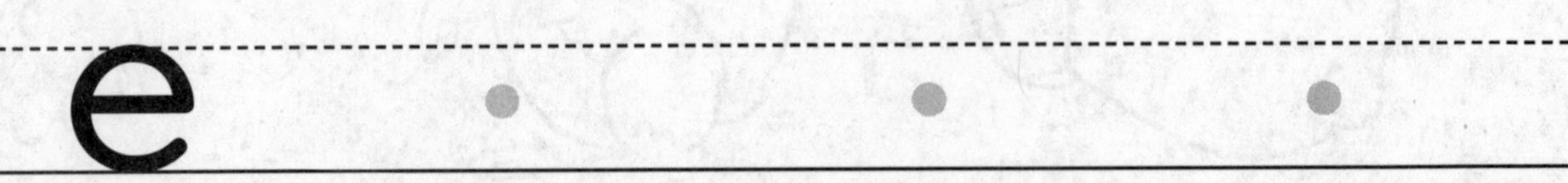

Handwriting: *Ee*
Trace and write each capital letter *E*. Then trace and write each lowercase letter *e*.

Name ______________________________

Phonemic Awareness: /f/
Say the name of each picture. Put a marker on each picture if its name begins with the /f/ sound.

Play

Name ______________________________

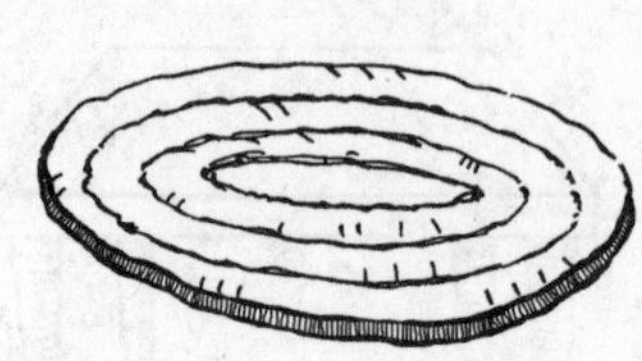

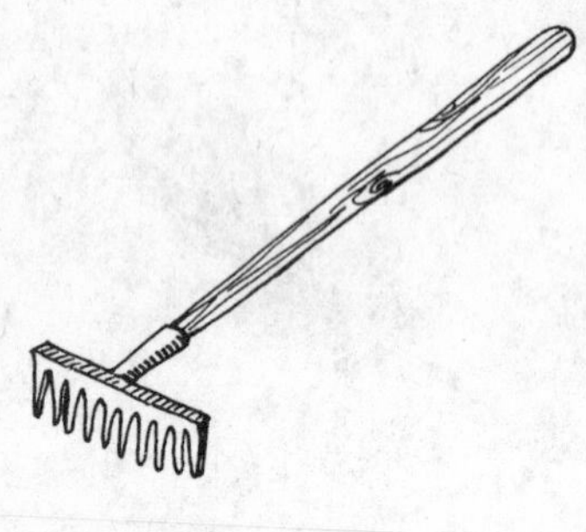

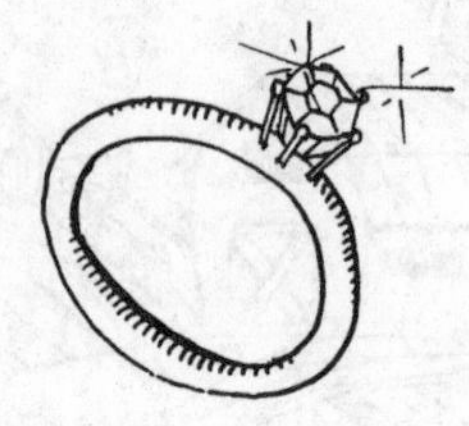

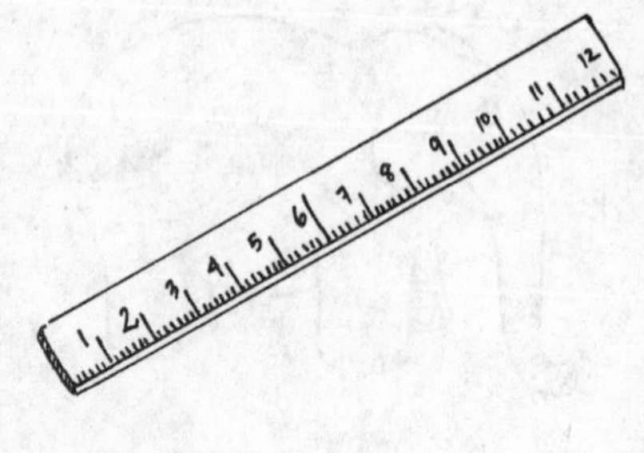

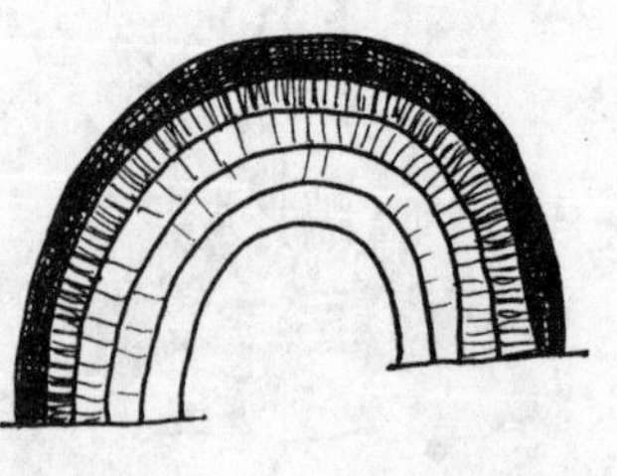

Phonemic Awareness: /r/
Say the name of each picture. Put a marker on each picture if its name begins with the /r/ sound.

Name ______________________

1. 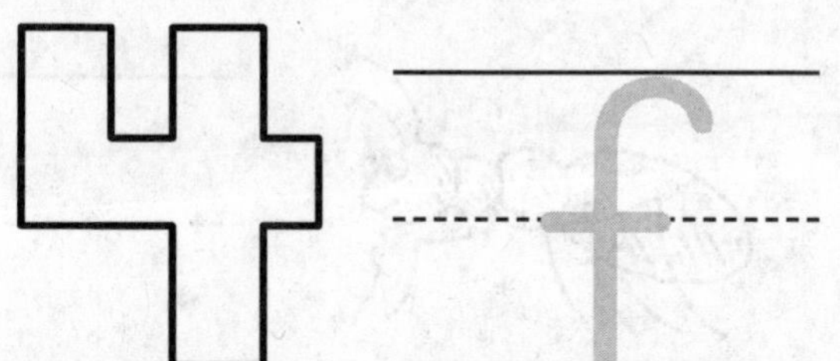

2. 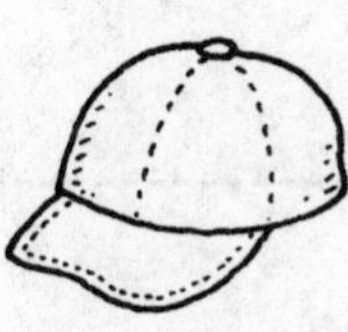 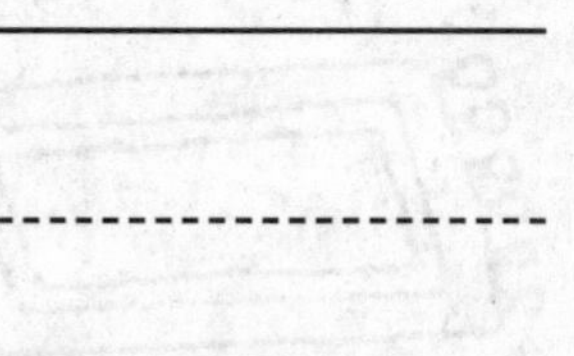 

3. 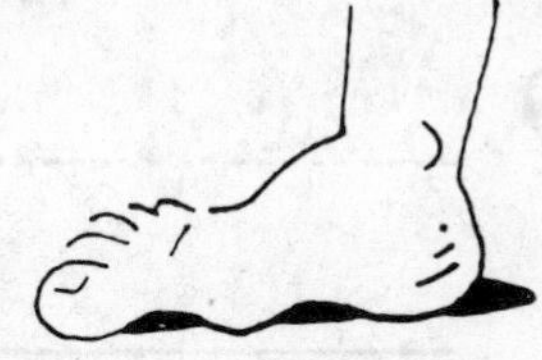 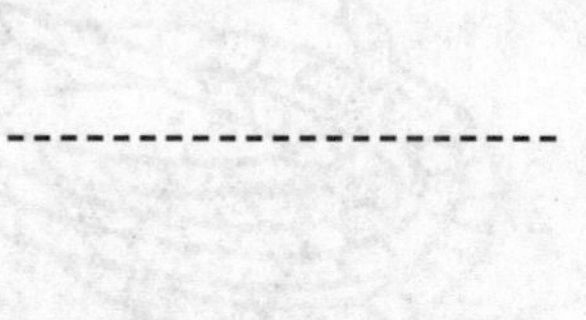 

4.  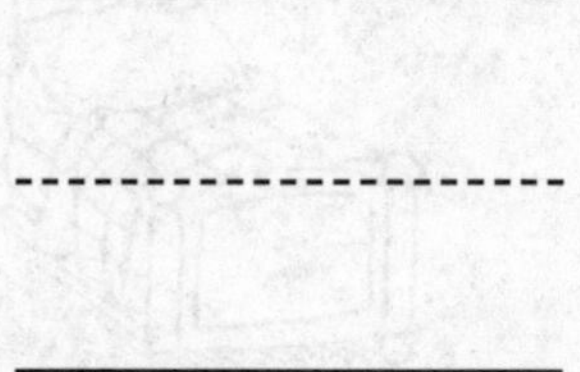 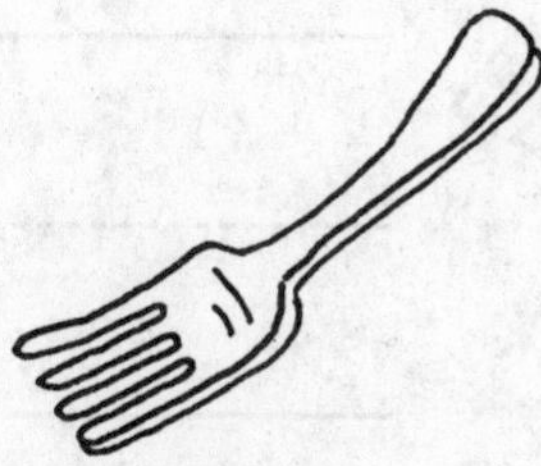

Phonics: /f/*f*
Say the name of each picture. Write the letter *f* next to each picture whose name begins with the /f/ sound.

Name ____________________

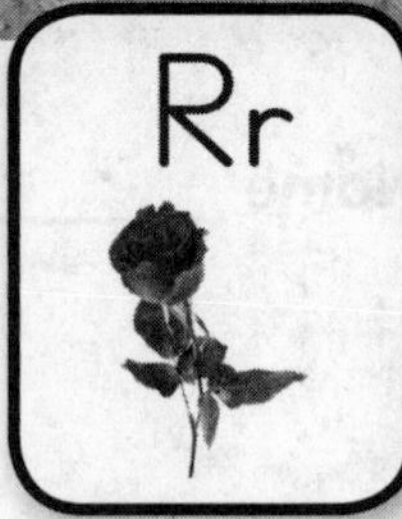

1.  r 

2. 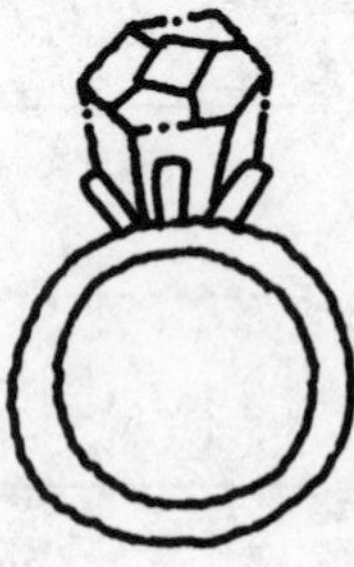 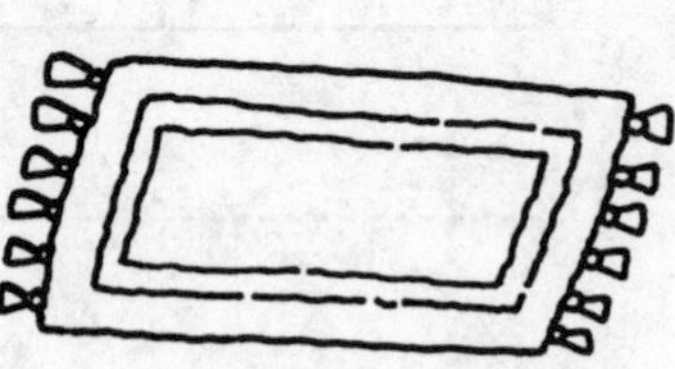

3.  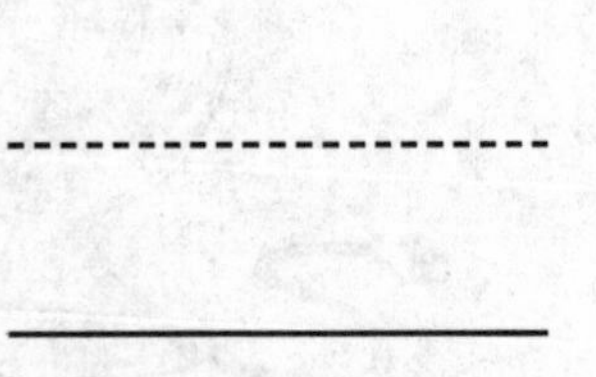 

4. 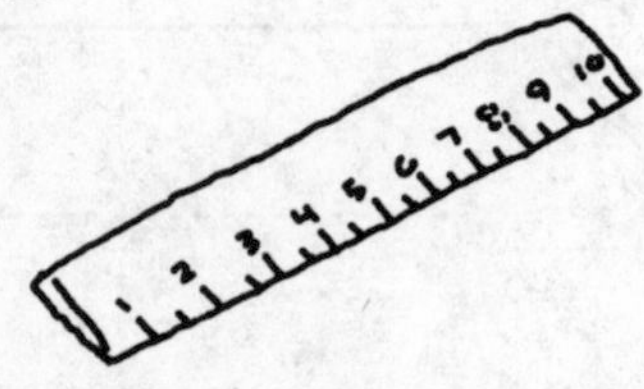 

Phonics: /r/r
Say the name of each picture. Write the letter *r* next to each picture whose name begins with the /r/ sound.

Name ____

1.

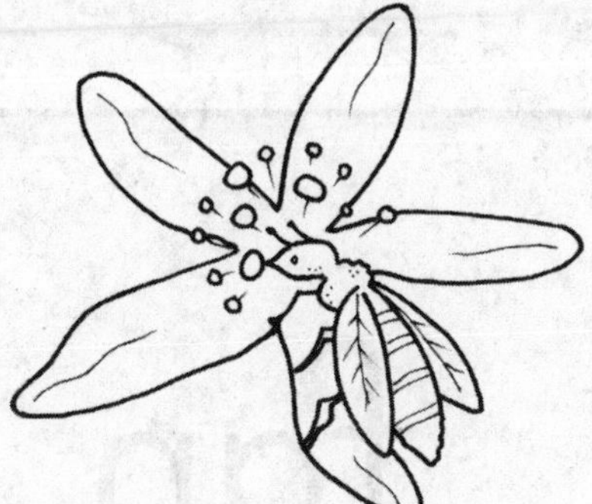

2.

3.

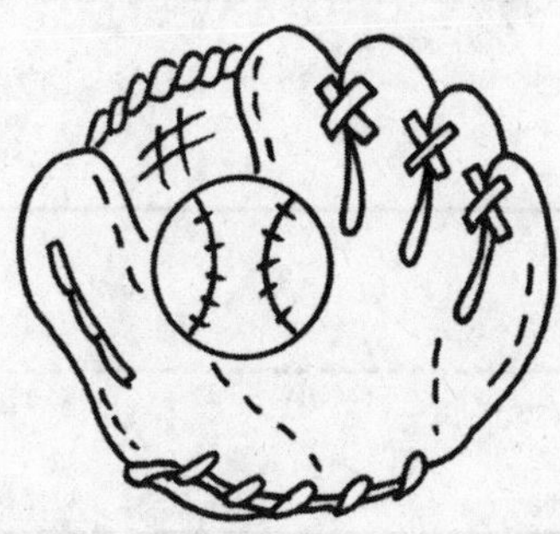

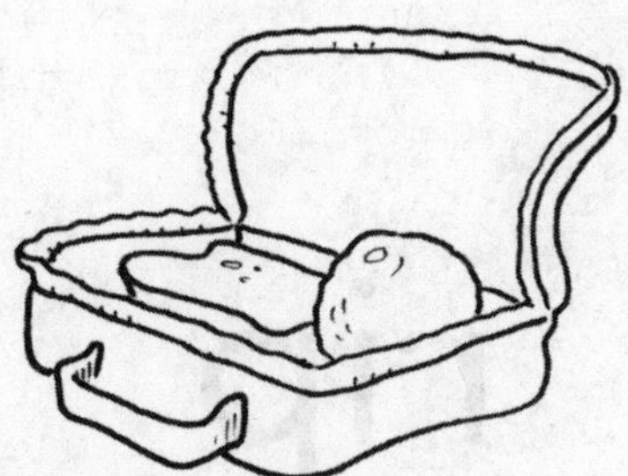

Comprehension: Main Topic and Key Details
Circle the pictures that show a detail about the selection *An Orange in January.* Talk to a partner about the details in each picture that you circled. Then talk about the main topic of the story.

Name ______________________________

fan red rip

1.

fan

2.

red

3.

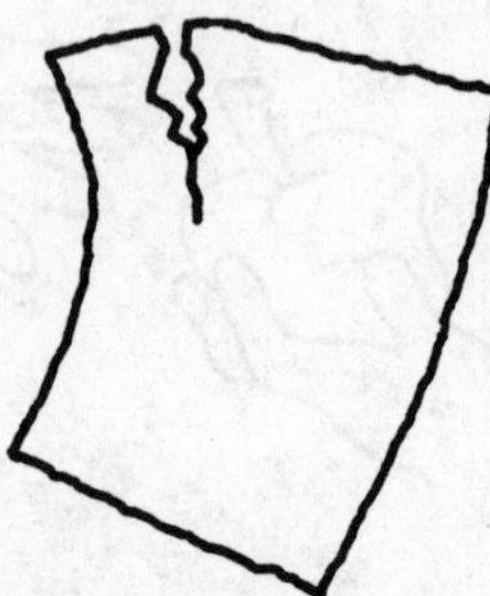

rip

Phonics: Blending /f/f, /r/r
Blend the sounds and say the word. Write the word. Repeat the word.

Name ____________________

He sat with mom.

Mom fed him!

High Frequency Words: ***he, with***
Read the book aloud to a partner. Reread for fluency.

Tim

He fed the hen.

He sat with the cat.

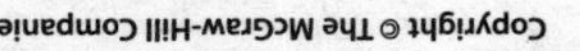

He fed the cat.

He sat with Nat.

Name ________________________________

1.

2.

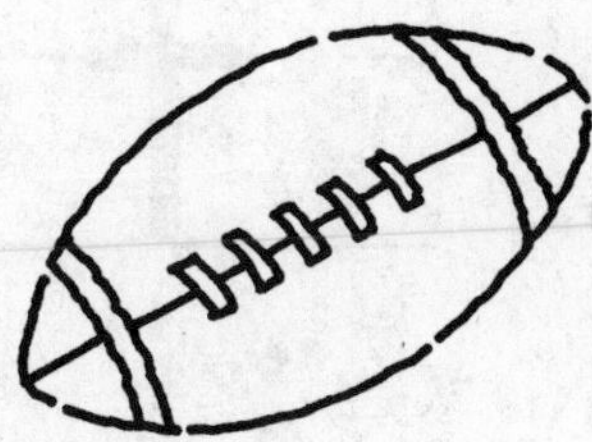

3.

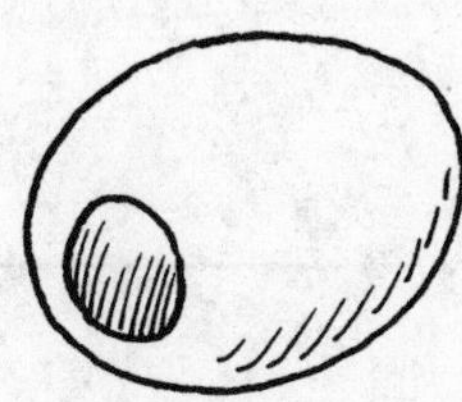

Category Words: Foods
Put a marker on each picture that shows food. Say the name of each food. Tell which pictures do not show foods.

Name ________________________________

1. 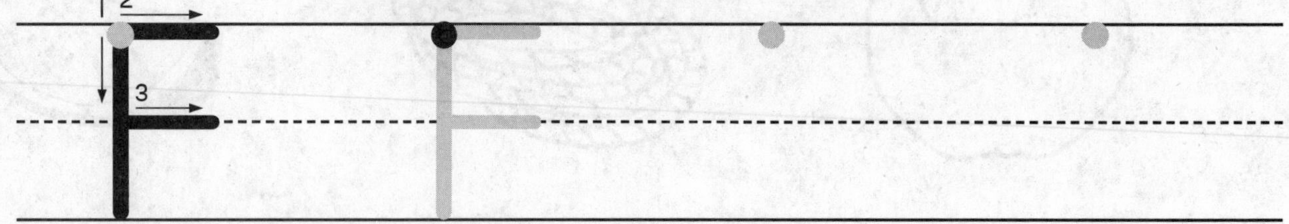

2. 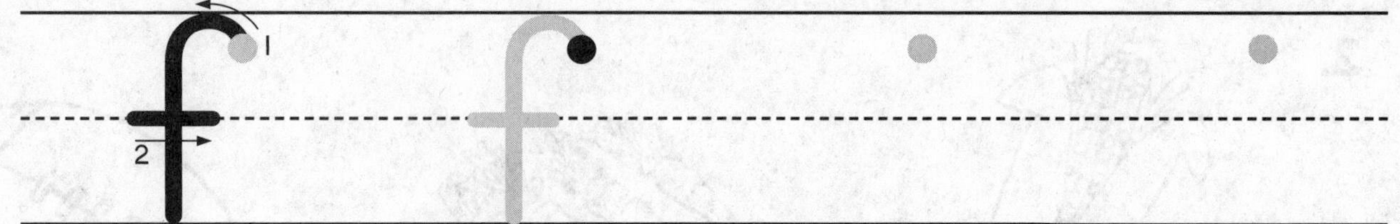

3. 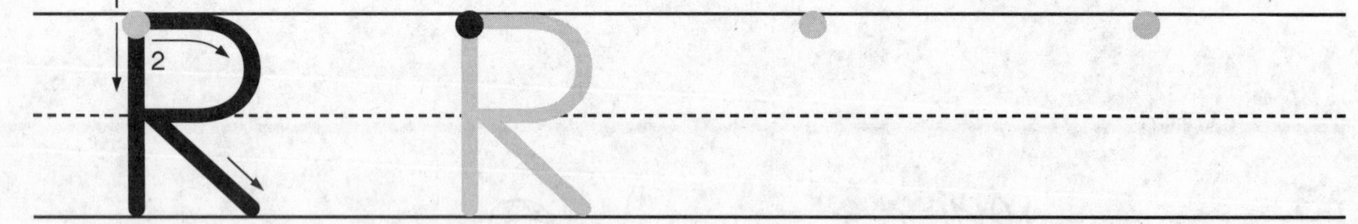

4. 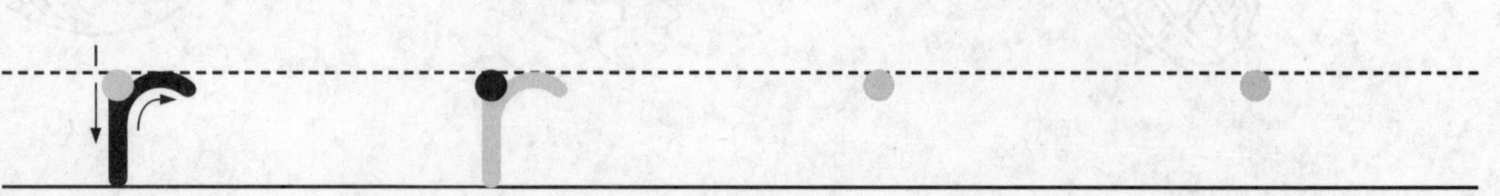

Handwriting: *Ff, Rr*
Trace and write each capital letter *F* and each lowercase letter *f*. Then trace and write each capital letter *R* and each lowercase letter *r*.

Name ____________________

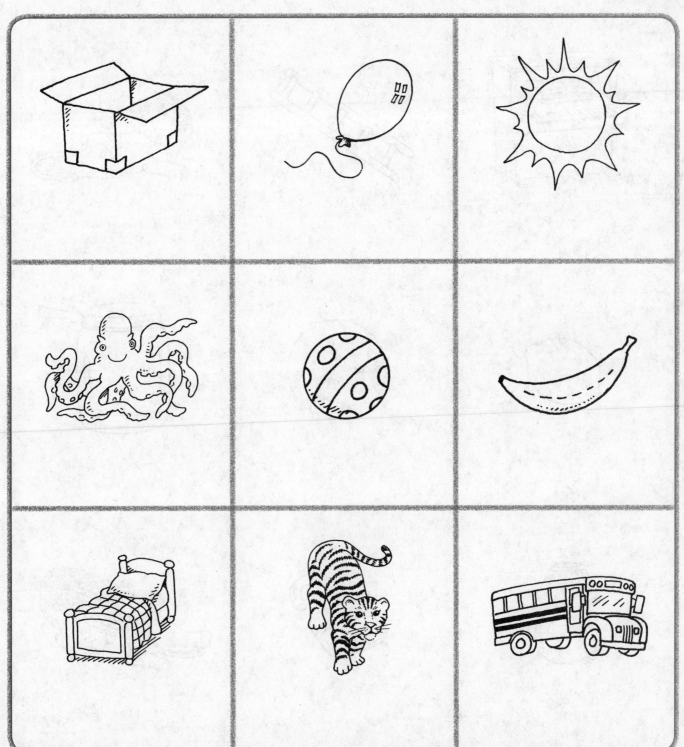

Phonemic Awareness: /b/

Say the name of each picture. Put a marker on each picture if its name begins with the /b/ sound.

Play

Name ______________________________

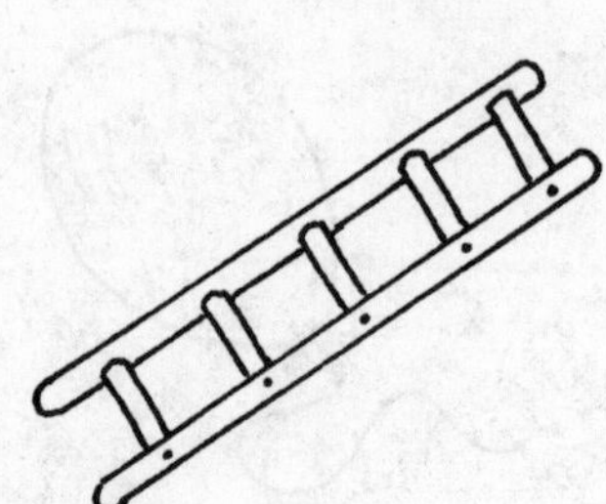

Phonemic Awareness: /l/
Say the name of each picture. Put a marker on each picture if its name begins with the /l/ sound.

Name ___

I.

b

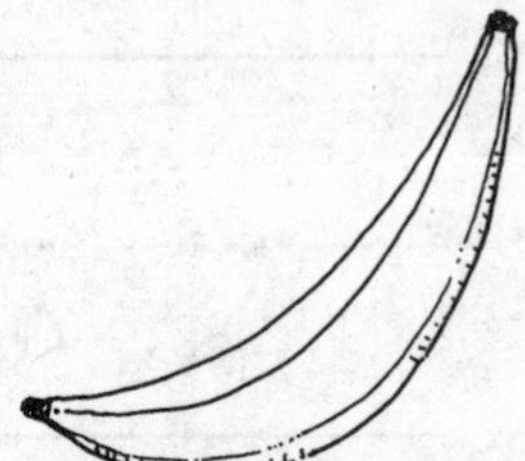

2.

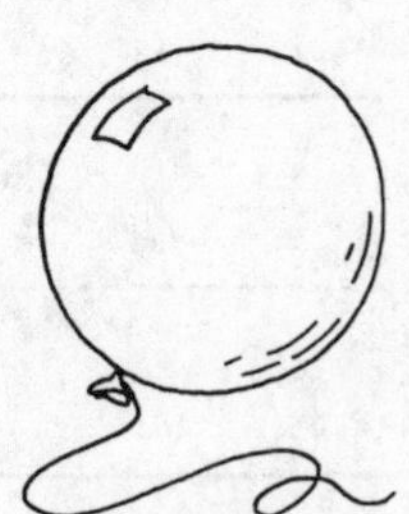

3.

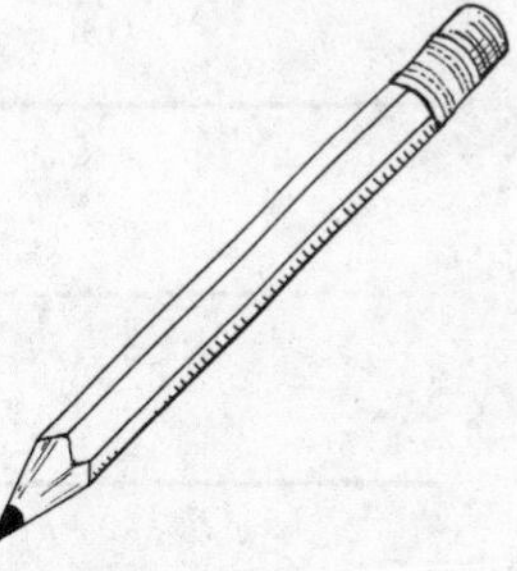

4.

Phonics: /b/*b*

Say the name of each picture. Write the letter *b* next to each picture whose name begins with the /b/ sound.

Name ______________________________

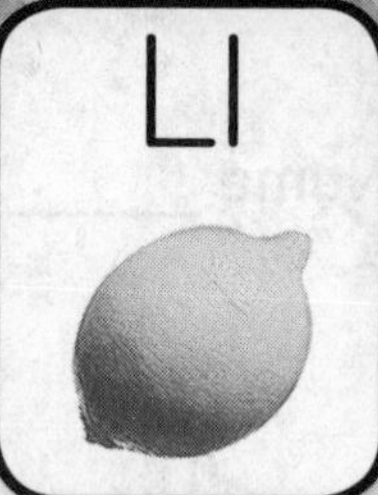

1.

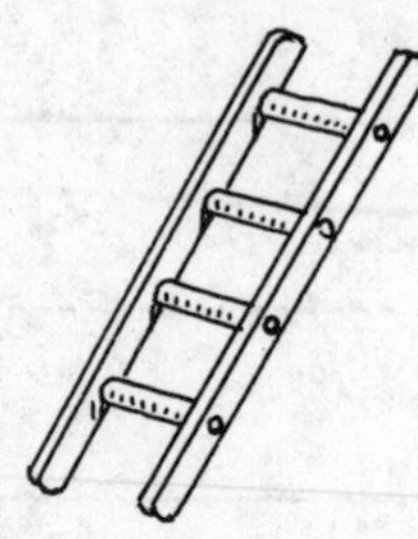

2.

3.

4.

Phonics: /l/
Say the name of each picture. Write the letter *l* next to each picture whose name begins with the /l/ sound.

Name ________________________________

1.

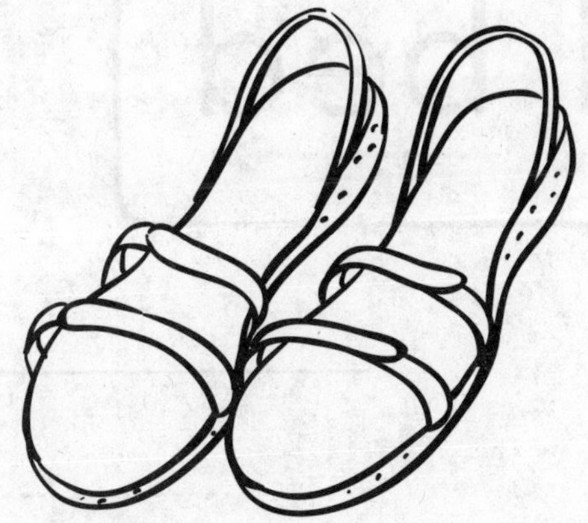

2.

3.

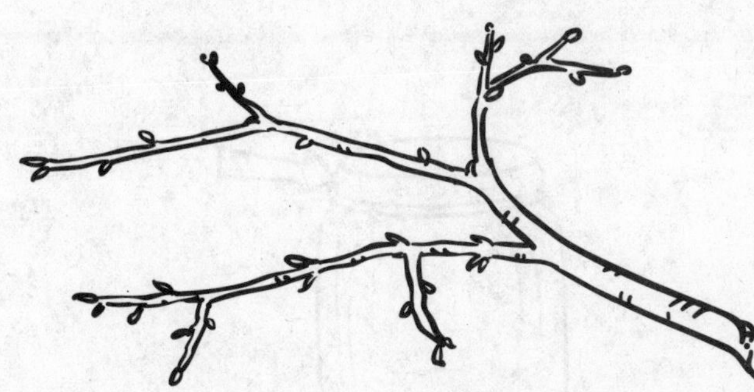

Comprehension: Key Details
Look at the pictures about the story *Mama, Is It Summer Yet?*

1. Put a marker on the picture that shows what happened first.
2. Put a marker on the picture that shows what happened next.
3. Put a marker on the picture that shows what happened last.

Name ______________________________

bib lid bed

1.

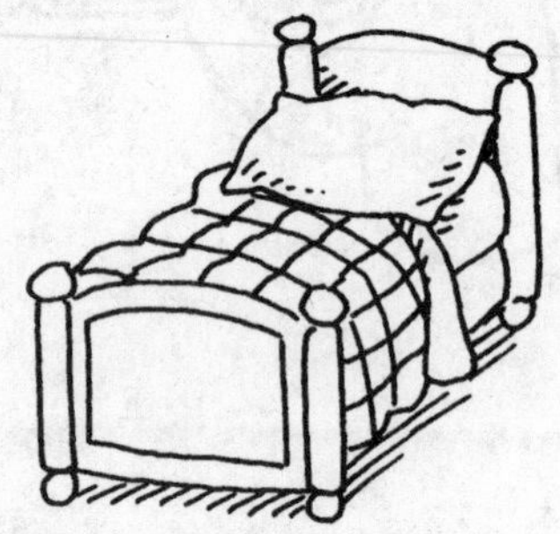

bed

2.

3.

Phonics: Blending /b/*b*, /l/*l*
Blend the sounds and say the word. Write the word. Repeat the word.

Name ________________________

Deb can sit on it!

It is big!

High Frequency Words: ***is, little***
Read the book aloud to a partner. Reread for fluency.

Little and Big

Deb can see it.

It is little.

Deb can pat it in.

It is not little.

Name ____

I.

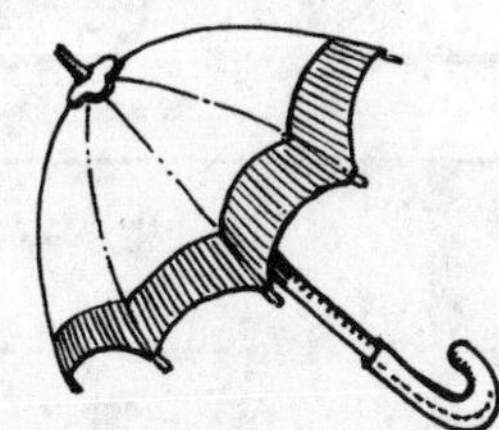

2.

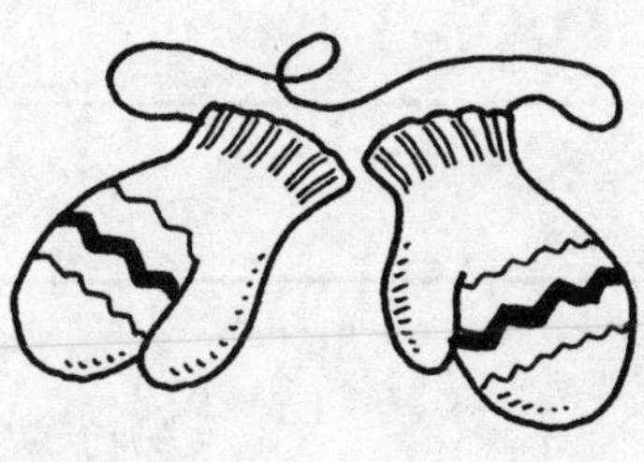

3.

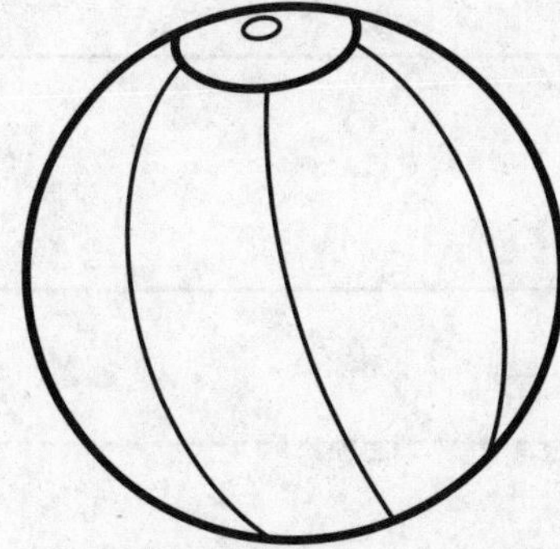

Category Words: Seasons
Put a marker on each picture that shows something from the winter season. Repeat for summer, spring, and fall. Tell a partner about your favorite season.

Name ________________________________

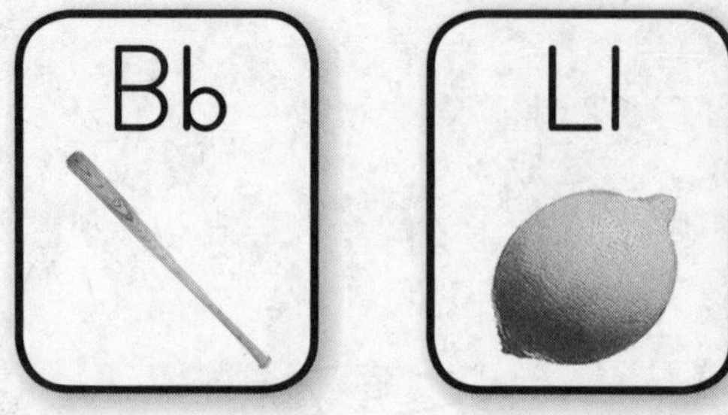

1. 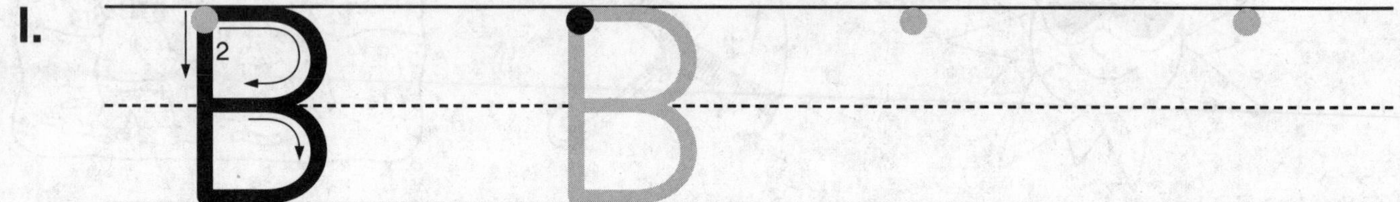

2. 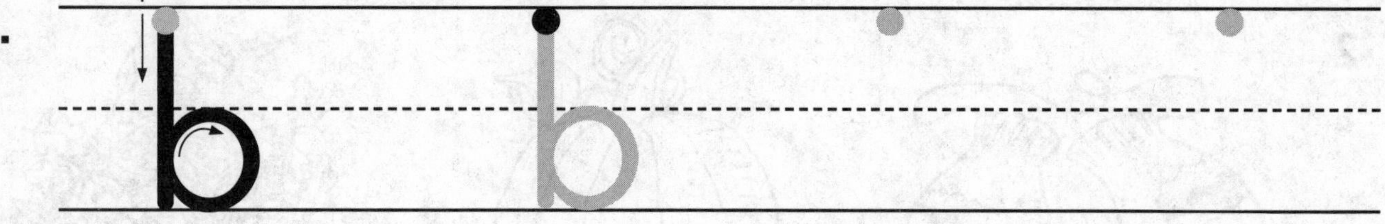

3. 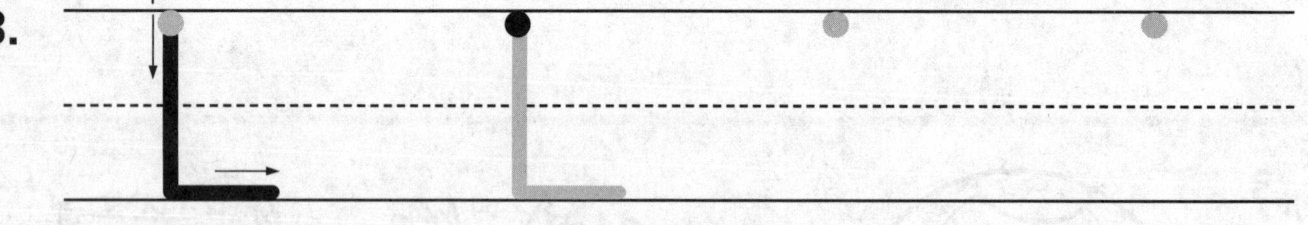

4. 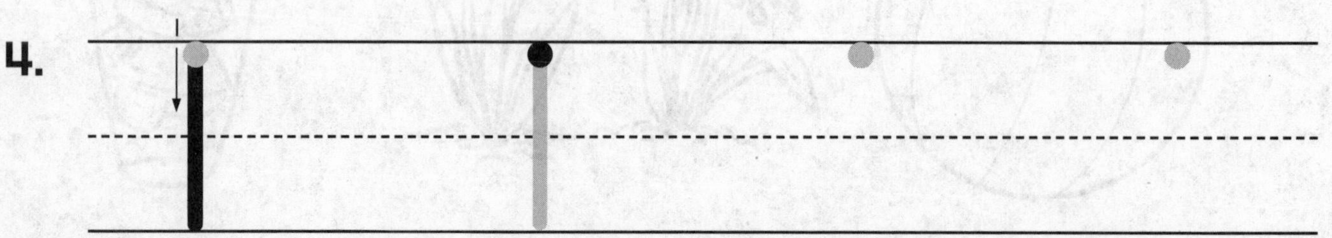

Handwriting: *Bb, Ll*
Trace and write each capital letter *B* and each lowercase letter *b*. Then trace and write each capital letter *L* and each lowercase letter *l*.

Play

Name ____________________

Phonemic Awareness: /k/
Say the name of each picture. Put a marker on each picture if its name begins with the /k/ sound.

Play

Name ____________________

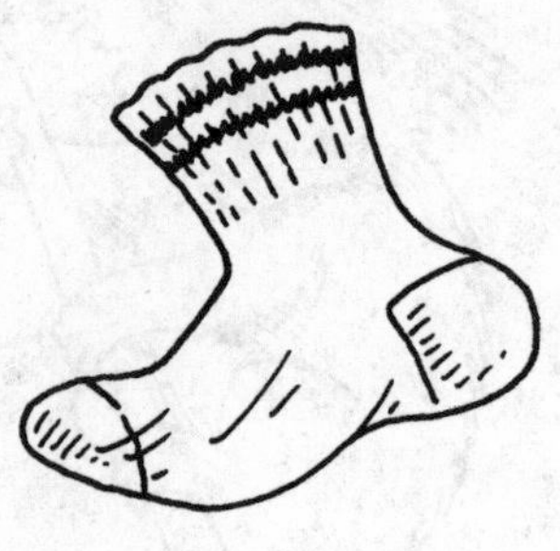

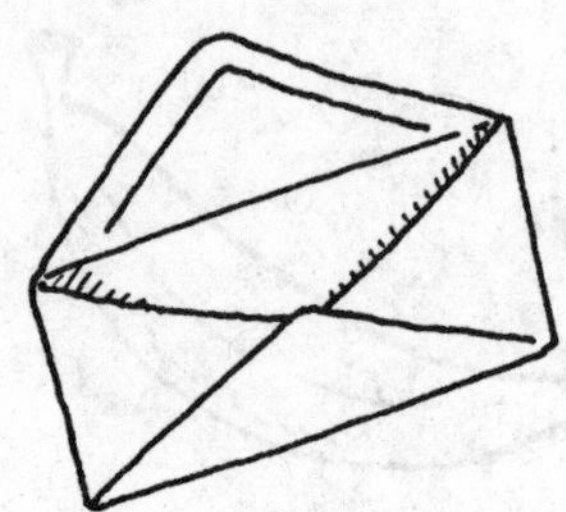

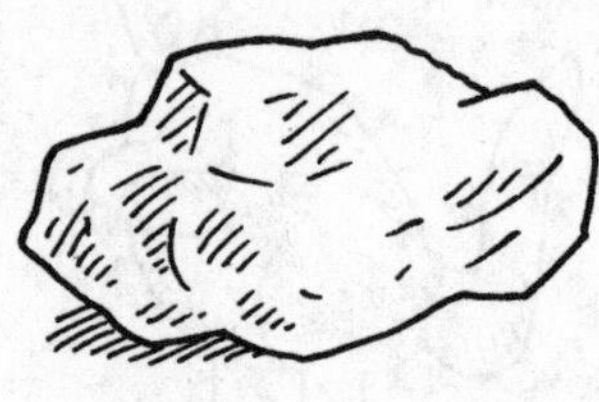

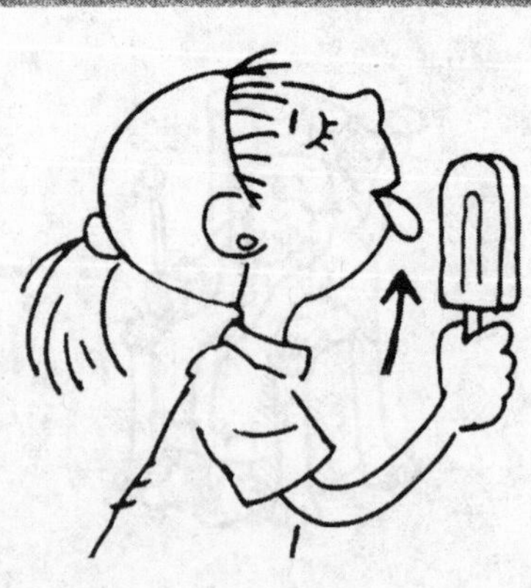

Phonemic Awareness: /k/
Say the name of each picture. Put a marker on each picture if its name ends with the /k/ sound.

Name ______________________

1.

k

2.

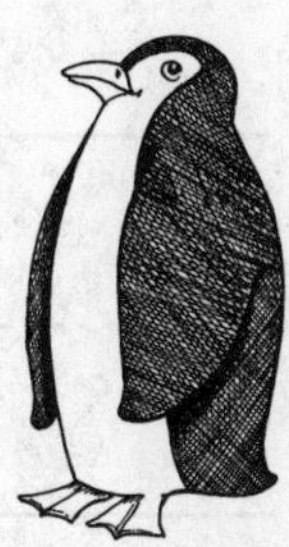

3.

4.

Phonics: /k/*k*
Say the name of each picture. Write the letter *k* next to each picture whose name begins with the /k/ sound.

Name ___

1.  ck 

2. 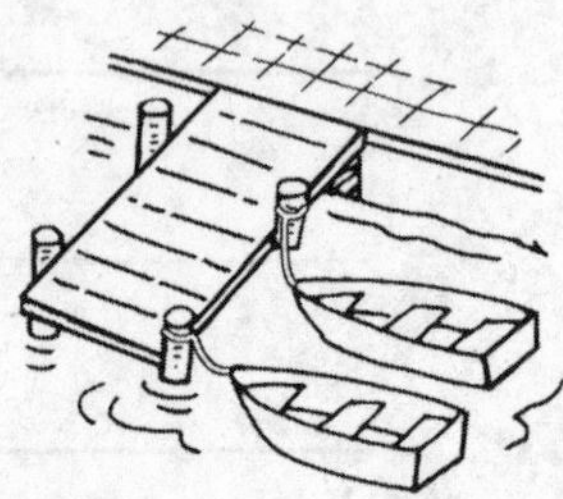 

3.  

4.  

Phonics: /k/*ck*
Say the name of each picture. Write the letters *ck* next to each picture whose name ends with the /k/ sound.

Name ______________________

I.

2.

3.

Comprehension: Key Details
Look at the pictures from the story *Rain*. Tell what happened in each picture. Then write *I, 2,* or *3* to show what happened first, next, and last.

Name

neck kick kid

1.

neck

2.

3.

Phonics: Blending /k/*k*, /k/*ck*
Blend the sounds and say the word. Write the word. Repeat the word.

Name ______________________

Dad is back.

She can sip and nap.

High Frequency Words: ***she, was***
Read the book aloud to a partner. Reread for fluency.

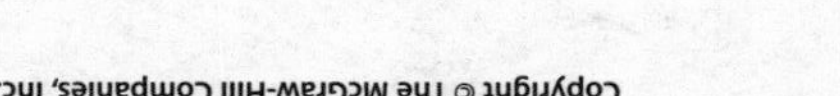

Dad is Back

She was sad.

Dad sat on the bed.
She was hot.

She was sick.

Name ______________________________

I.

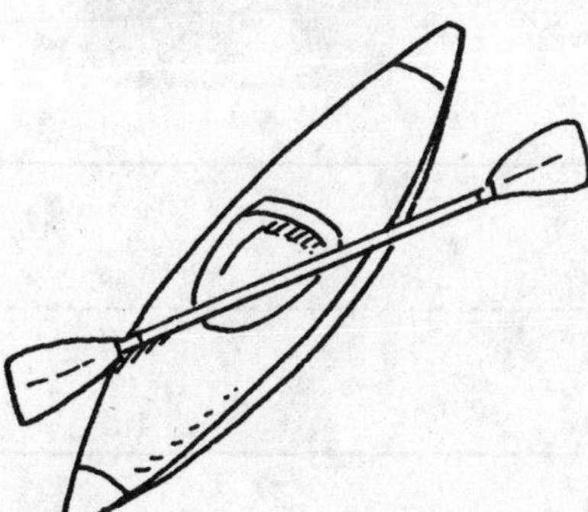

2.

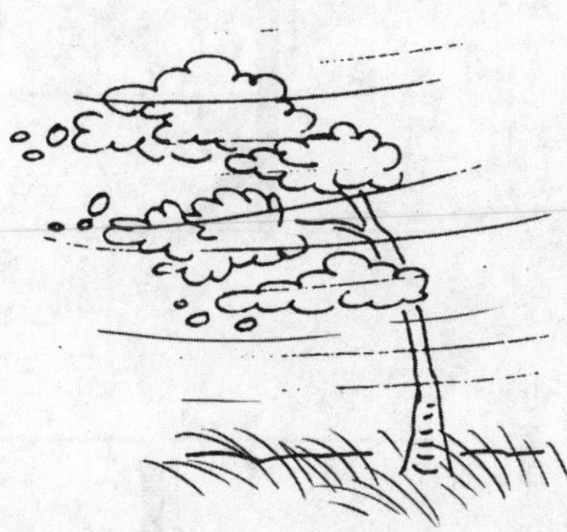

3.

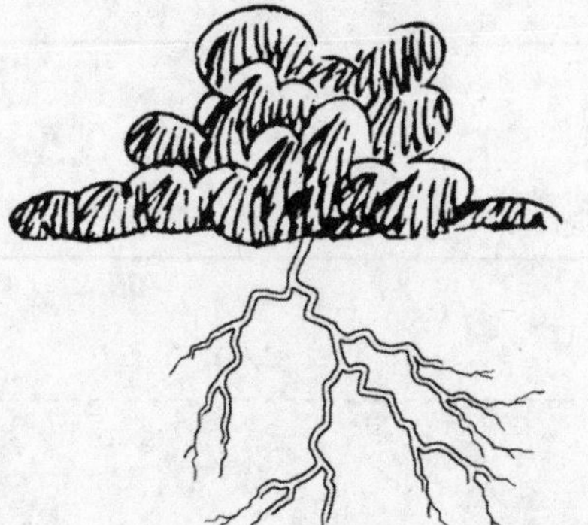

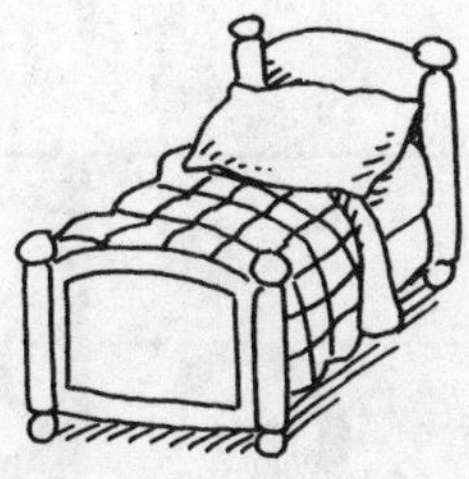

Category Words: Weather Words
Put a marker on pictures that show different kinds of weather. Talk to a partner about the kinds of weather that are shown. Then talk about your favorite kind of weather.

Name ____________________

1. 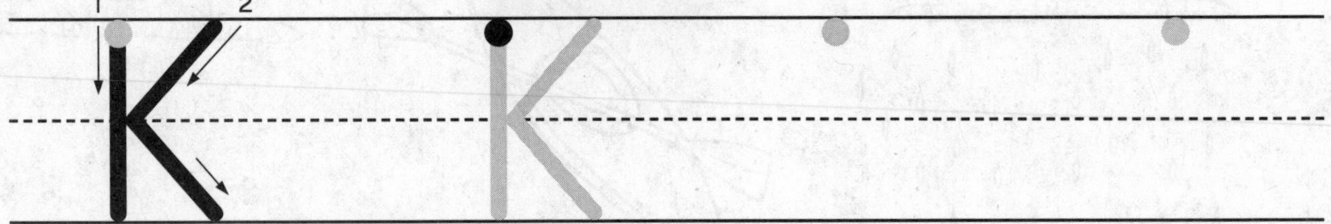

2. 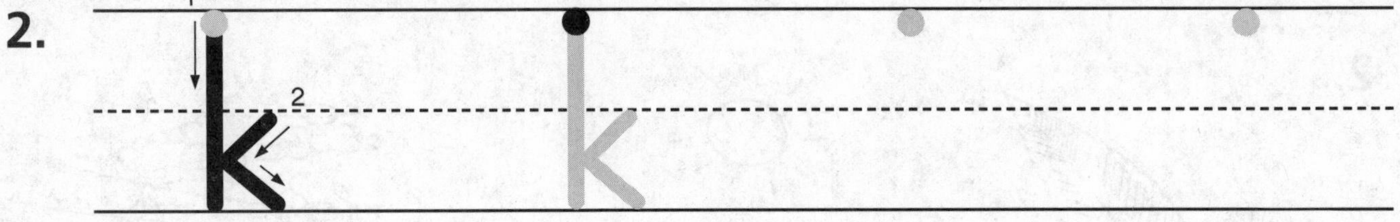

3. 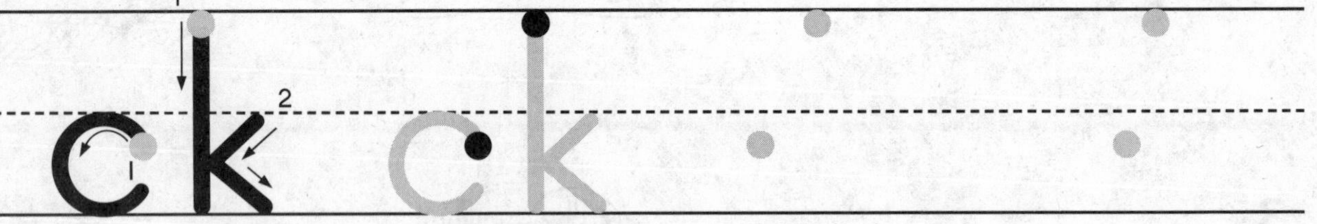

4. 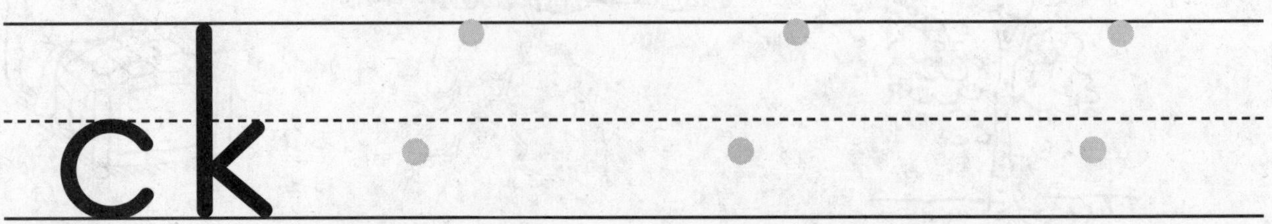

Handwriting: *Kk, ck*
Trace and write each capital letter *K* and each lowercase letter *k*.
Then trace and write the letters *ck*.

Name ____________________

I. 5  

2. 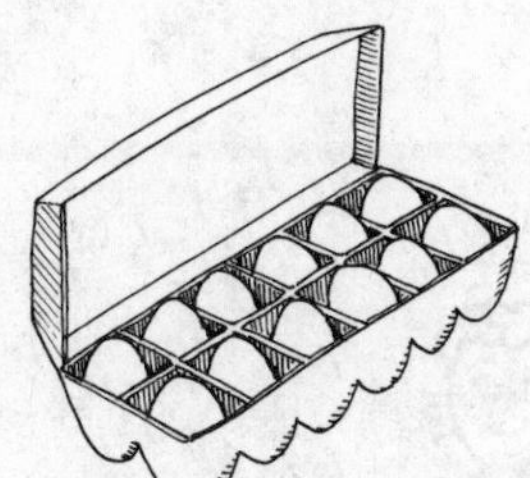 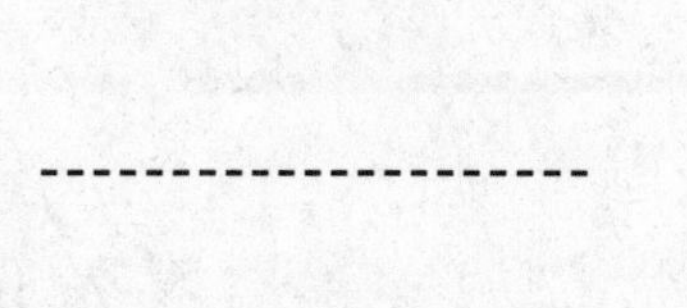 

3.   

4.  

Review Phonics: /h/*h*, /e/*e*, /f/*f*
Say the name of each picture. Write the letter *h, e,* or *f* next to each picture whose name begins with the /h/, /e/, or /f/ sound.

Circle

Name ______________________________

1.

2.

3.

Comprehension: Key Details

Look at the pictures about the story *Waiting Out the Storm*.

1. Circle the picture that shows how the animals stay safe when it rains.
2. Circle the picture that shows how the people stay safe when it rains.
3. Circle the picture that shows how the birds stay safe when it rains.

Name

1.

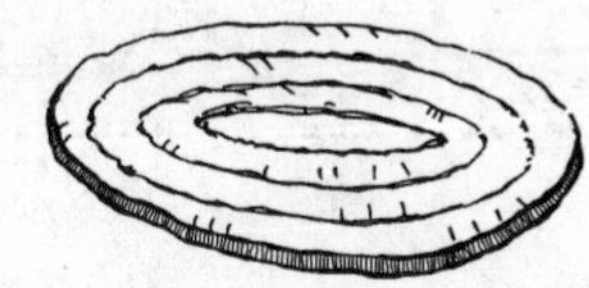

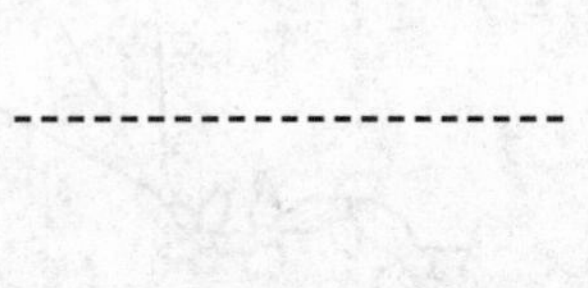

2.

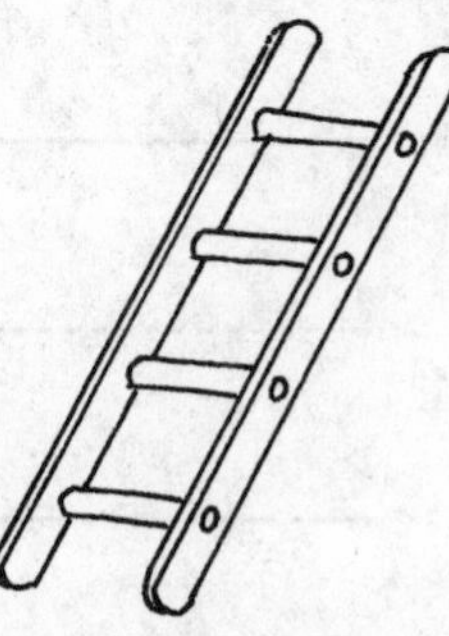

3.

4.

Review Phonics: /r/*r*, /b/*b*, /l/*l*
Say the name of each picture. Write the letter *r, b,* or *l* next to each picture whose name begins with the /r/, /b/, or /l/ sound.

Write

Name

1. 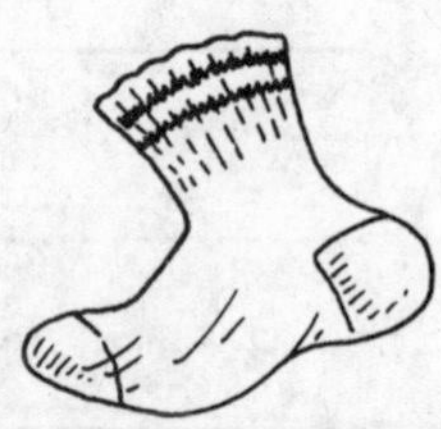

ck

2. 

3. 

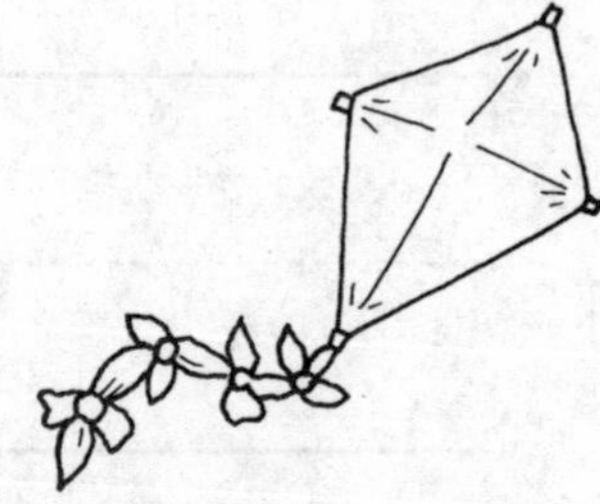

4. 

Review Phonics: /k/*k*, /k/*ck*
Say the name of each picture. Write the letter *k* next to each picture whose name begins with the /k/ sound. Then write the letters *ck* next to each picture whose name ends with the /k/ sound.

Play

Name ______________________________

Phonics Review Game: /h/h, /e/e, /f/f, /r/r, /b/b, /l/l

Place a marker on "Start." Move your marker from square to square. When you land on a picture, say the name of the picture and the letter it begins with. If you land on a letter, say a word that begins with that letter. When you reach "End," play again and think of new words.

Name ______________________________

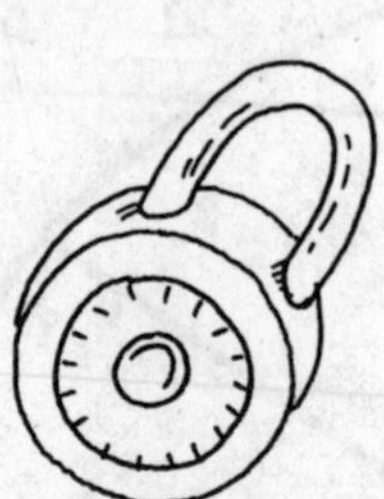

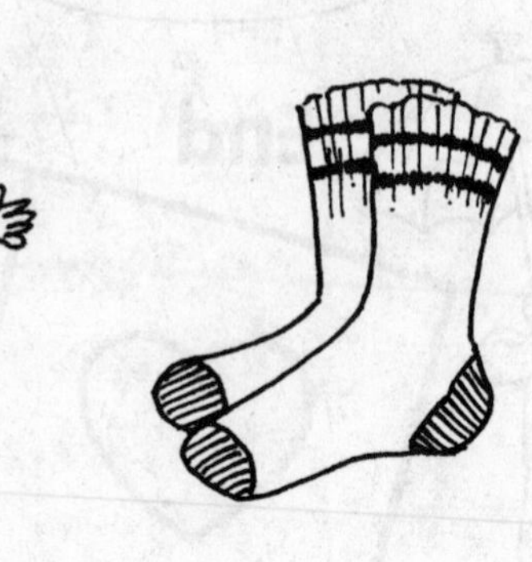

b ck

Phonics Review Game: /b/*b*, /k/*ck*
Say the name of each picture. Draw lines to connect the pictures to the letters they end with.

Name ________________

He is with my little cat!

High Frequency Word Review: ***my, are, he, with, is, little, she, was***
Read the book aloud to a partner. Reread for fluency.

Tip, Tap

Tip, tap on my deck.

We are in.
She was mad!

We sit with my little cat.

Name ______________________________

1.

2.

3.

Category Words: Question Words

1. Circle the picture that shows who a story might be about.
2. Circle the picture that shows what a story might be about.
3. Circle a picture that shows where a story might take place.

Name ______________________

Rob hen bed

I.

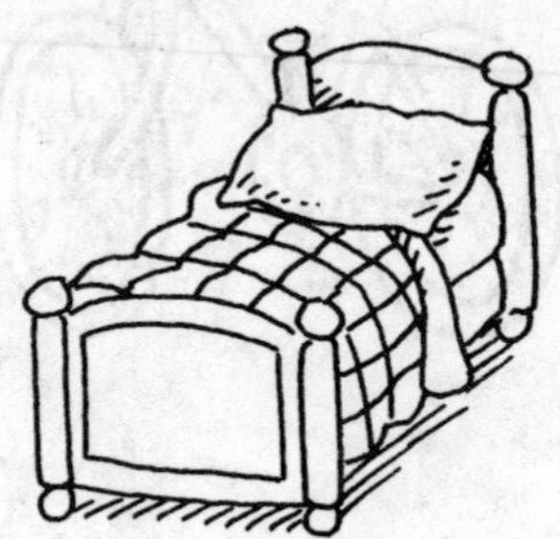

bed

2.

3.

Review Phonics: Blending
Blend the sounds and say the word. Write the word. Repeat the word.

Name

lid kick fan

I.

lid

2.

3.

Review Phonics: Blending
Blend the sounds and say the word. Write the word. Repeat the word.

Write

Name

1.

lock

2.

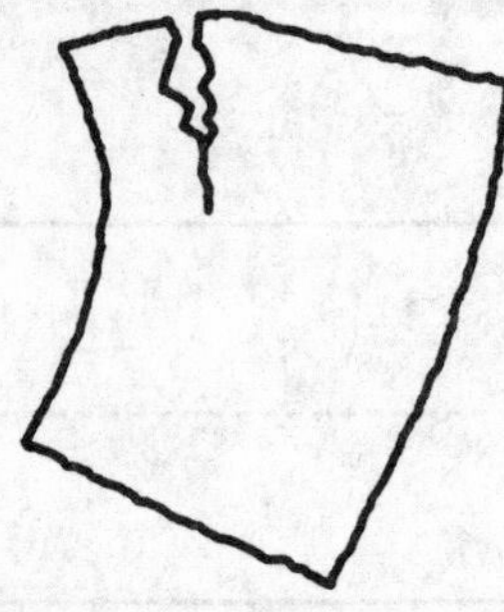

rip

3.

hop

Handwriting Review
Say each word as you trace it and write it. Then read each word to a partner.

Play

Name ________________________________

Phonemic Awareness: /u/
Say the name of each picture. Put a marker on each picture if its name begins with the /u/ sound.

Name ______________________________

1.  

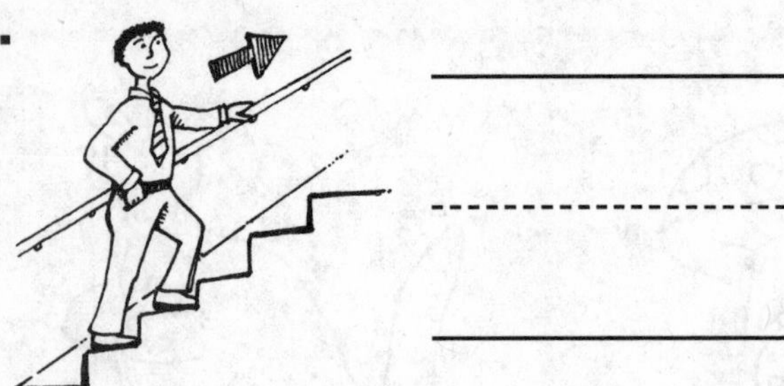

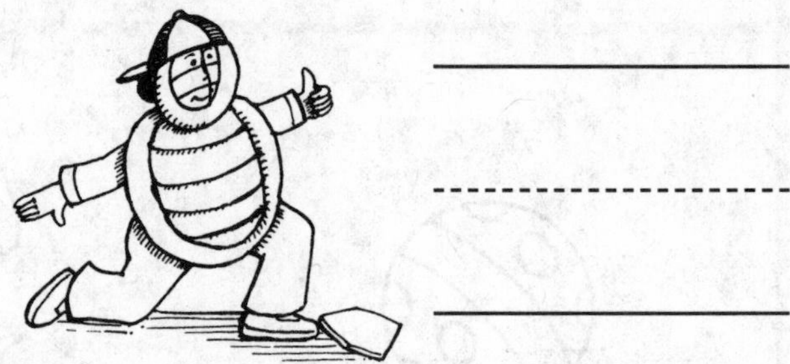

2.

3. 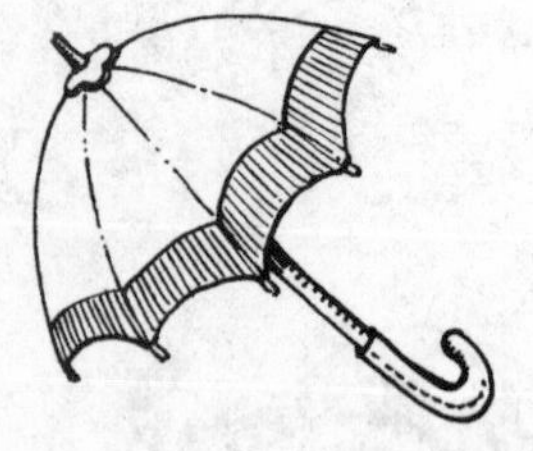 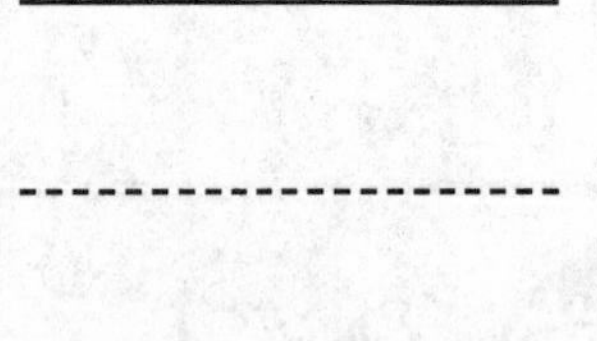 

4. 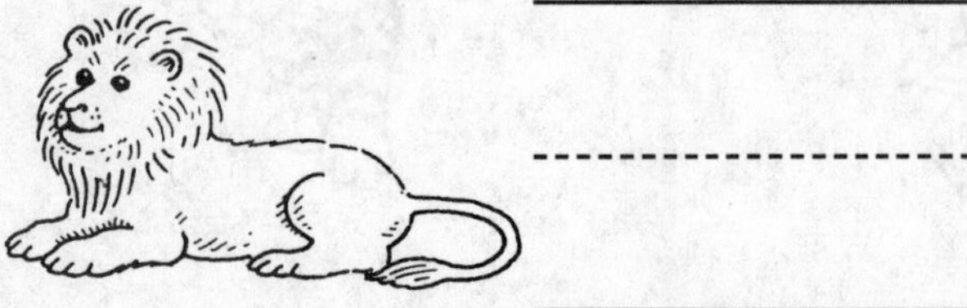 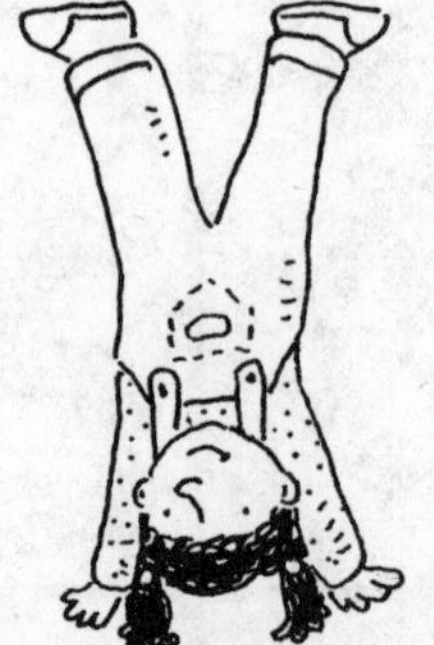

Phonics: /u/*u*
Say the name of each picture. Write the letter *u* next to each picture whose name begins with the /u/ sound.

Name ______________________________

1.

2.

3.

Comprehension: Connections Within Text
Tell about each animal. Circle one thing that is the same about the animals in each row. Then talk to a partner about one thing that is different about the animals in each row.

Name ________________________________

bus up sun

I.

sun

2.

3.

Phonics: Blending *-un, -us, -up*
Blend the sounds and say the word. Write the word.
Repeat the word.

Name ______________________

The pup is for you.

You have a pet!

High Frequency Words: ***for, have***
Read the book aloud to a partner. Reread for fluency.

For You

You have a little duck.

It can hop for Mom!

You have a little pig.

It can rub the mud.

Copyright © The McGraw-Hill Companies, Inc.

You have a little pup!

It can have fun.

Name ____

1.

2.

3.

Category Words: Animal Parts
Name each animal. Point to the ears, eyes, mouth, and nose on two of the animals.

1. Put a marker on the animals that have wings.
2. Put a marker on the animals that have fur.
3. Put a marker on the animals that have tails.

Name

1.

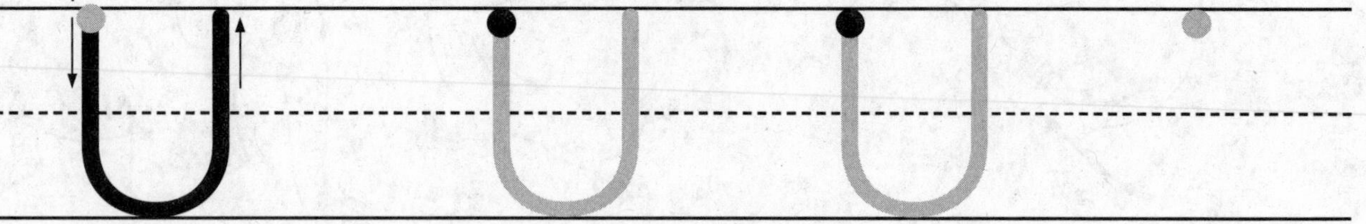

2.

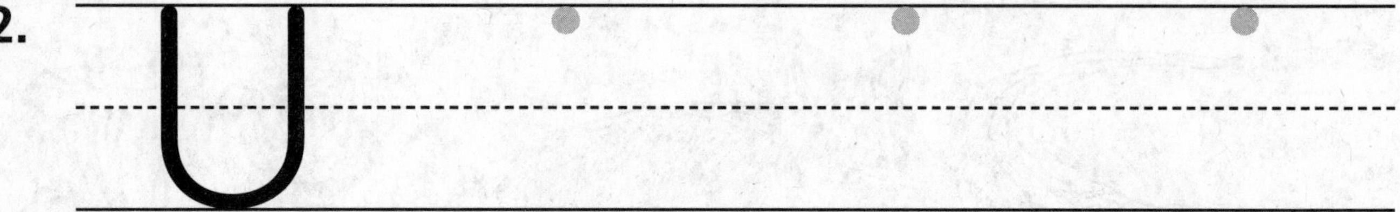

3.

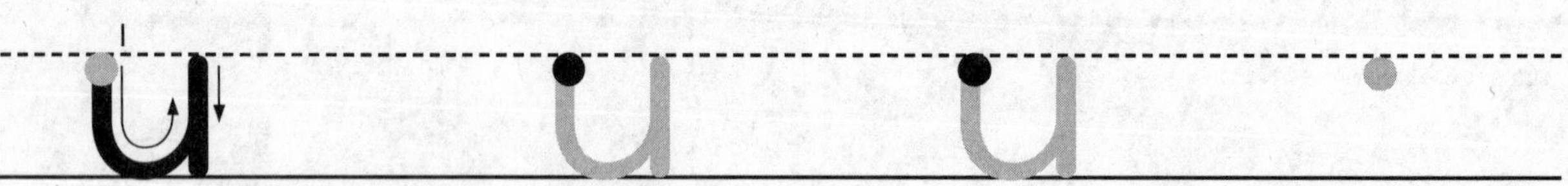

4.

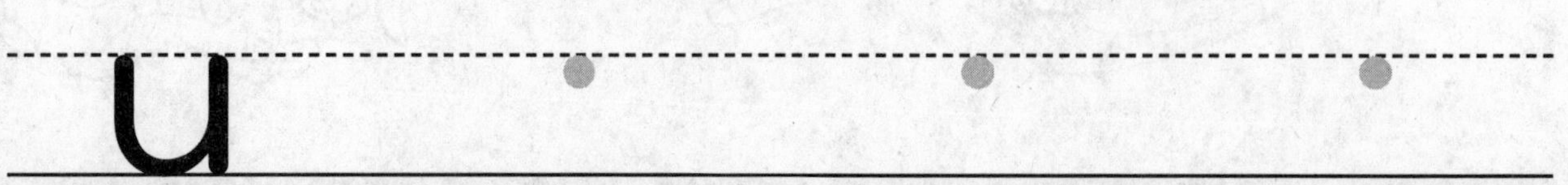

Handwriting: *Uu*
Trace and write each capital letter *U*. Then trace and write each lowercase letter *u*.

Name ______________________________

Gum
YUM YUM GUM

Phonemic Awareness: /g/
Say the name of each picture. Put a marker on each picture if its name begins with the /g/ sound.

Play

Name ______________________________

Phonemic Awareness: /w/
Say the name of each picture. Put a marker on each picture if its name begins with the /w/ sound.

Name ______________________________

1. 

g

2. 

3. 

4. 

Phonics: /g/*g*

Say the name of each picture. Write the letter *g* next to each picture whose name begins with the /g/ sound.

Name ______________________

1. 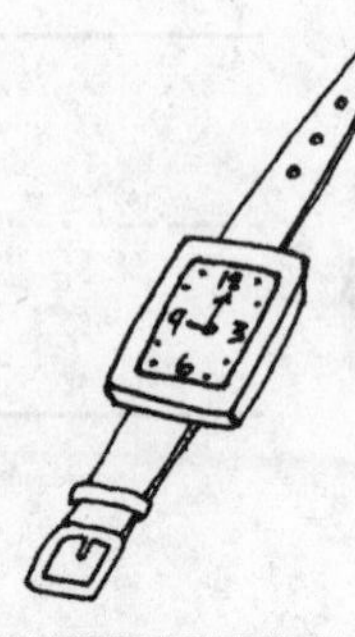 w 

2.  

3. 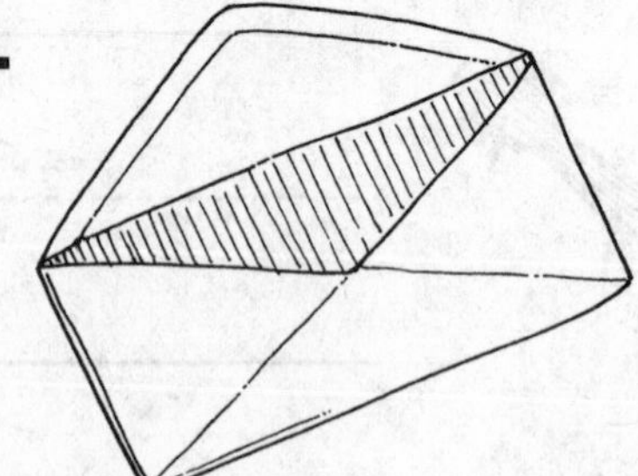 

4.  

Phonics: /w/*w*
Say the name of each picture. Write the letter *w* next to each picture whose name begins with the /w/ sound.

Name ______________________________

1.

2.

3.

Comprehension: Character, Setting, Plot

1. Circle the pets that are characters in the story *The Birthday Pet.*
2. Circle the settings from the story.
3. Circle Danny's favorite pet.

Name ______________________

wig gum web

1.

wig

2.

3.

Phonics: Blending /g/*g*, /w/*w*
Blend the sounds and say the word. Write the word. Repeat the word.

Name ____________________

They do not nap.

They have a lot of fun!

High Frequency Words: ***they, of***
Read the book aloud to a partner. Reread for fluency.

A Lot of Fun!

They like to tug.

They have a lot of fun!

They have a pen.
They hop and hop!

Copyright © The McGraw-Hill Companies, Inc.

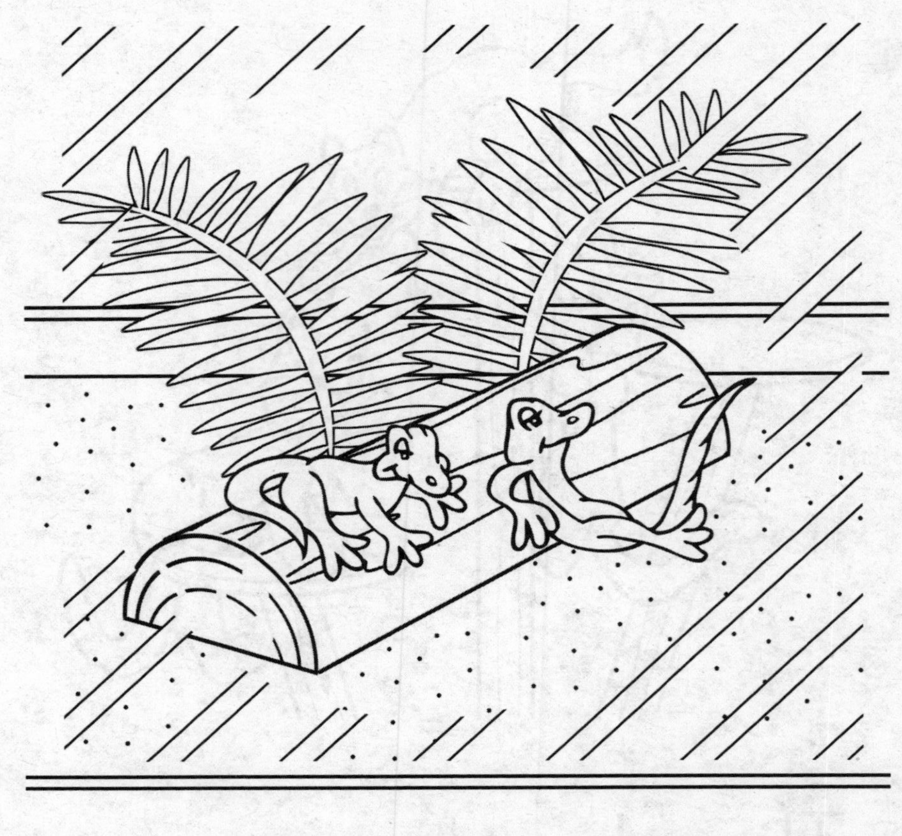

They have a log.
They like to nap a lot.

Name ______________________________

1.

2.

3.

Category Words: Pets

Put a marker on each picture that shows a pet.

1. Tell which animal would not make a good pet.
2. Tell which pet likes milk.
3. Tell which pet needs to live in water.

Name ____________________

1.

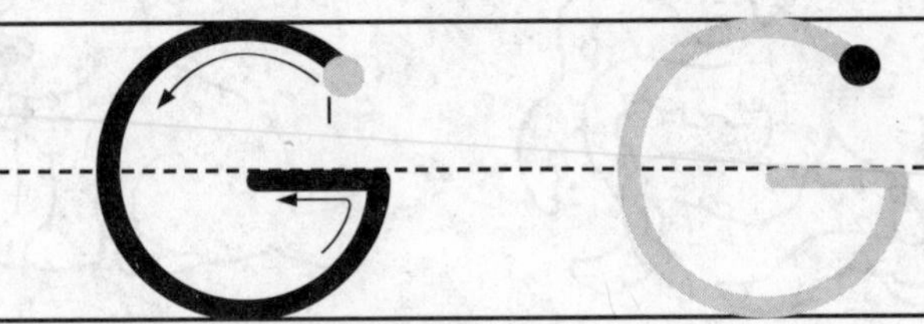

2.

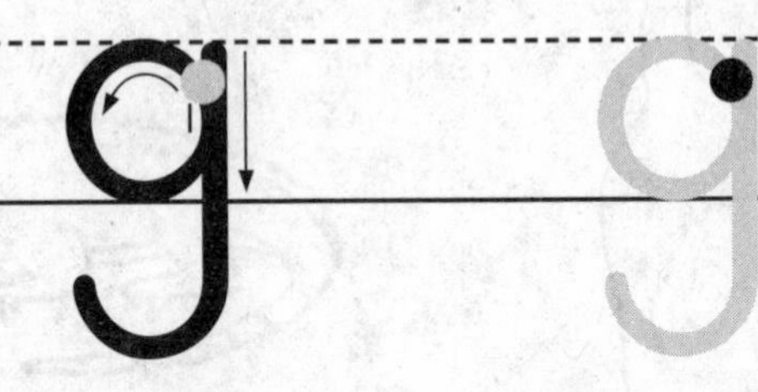

3.

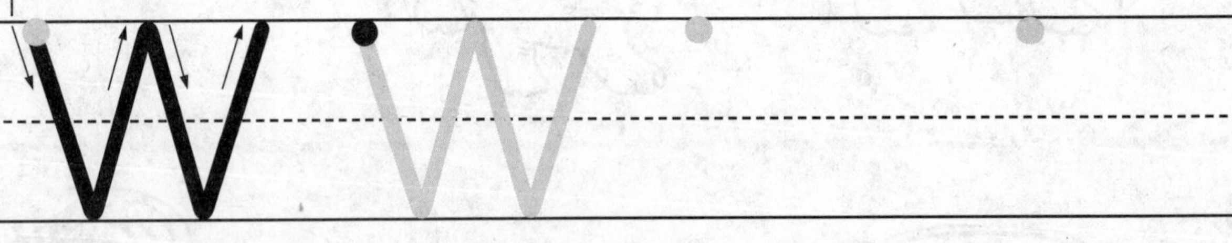

4.

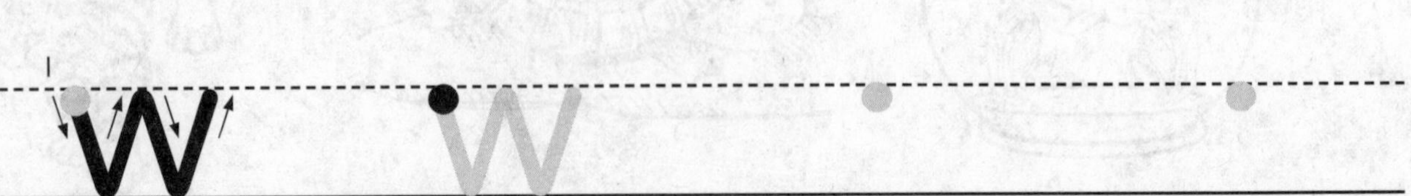

Handwriting: *Gg, Ww*
Trace and write each capital letter *G* and each lowercase letter g. Then trace and write each capital letter *W* and each lowercase letter *w*.

Name ______________________________

Phonemic Awareness: /ks/
Say the name of each picture. Put a marker on each picture if its name ends with the /ks/ sound.

Play

Name ______________________________

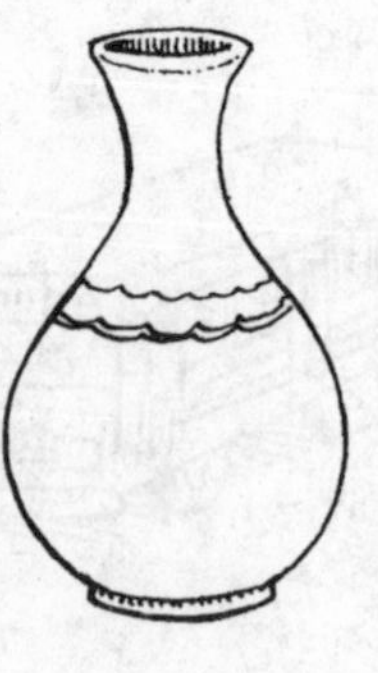

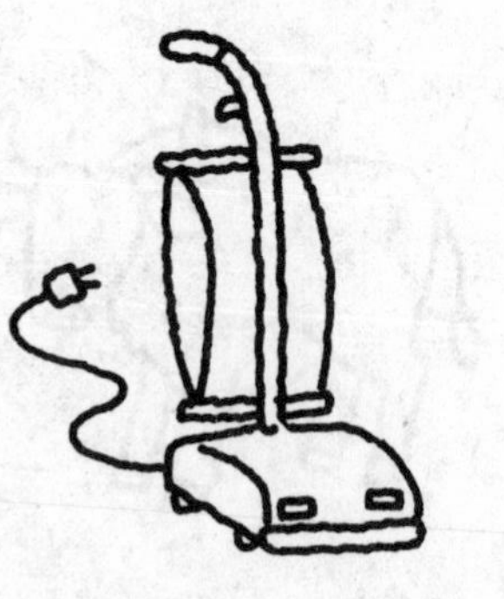

Phonemic Awareness: /v/
Say the name of each picture. Put a marker on each picture if its name begins with the /v/ sound.

Name ________________________________

1.

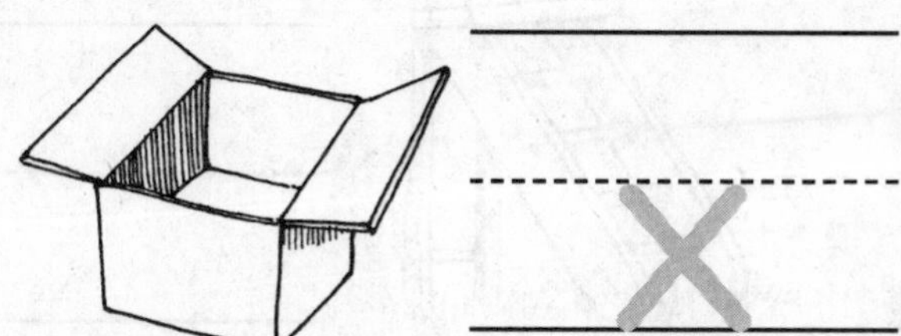

2.

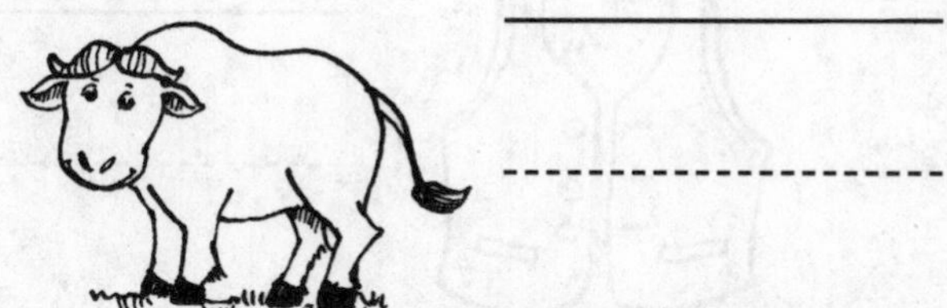

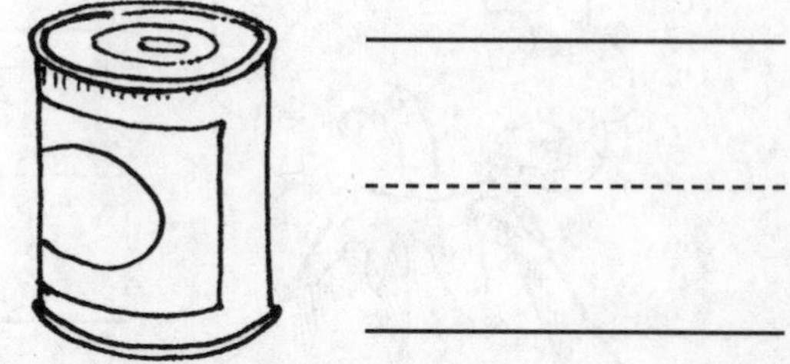

3.

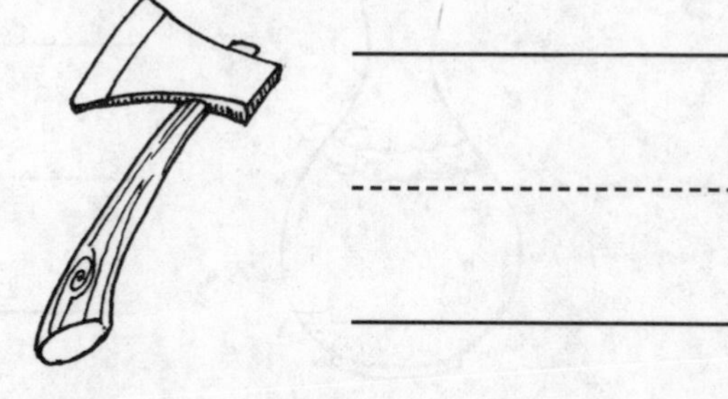

4.

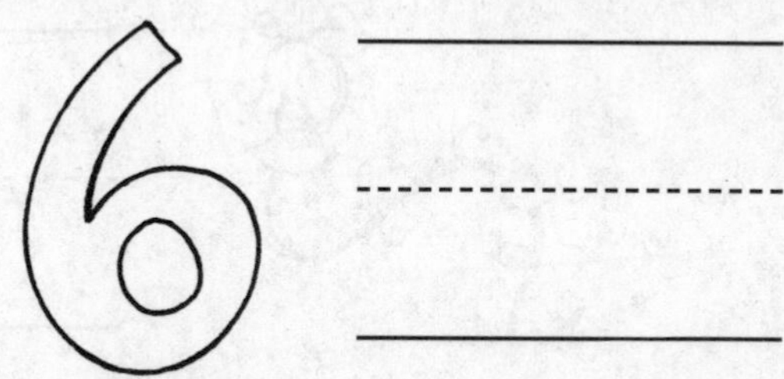

Phonics: /ks/x

Say the name of each picture. Write the letter *x* next to each picture whose name ends with the /ks/ sound.

Name ______________________

1.  v 

2.  

3.  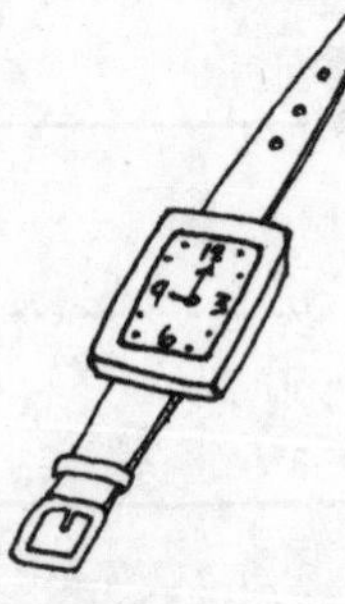

4.  

Phonics: /v/v
Say the name of each picture. Write the letter *v* next to each picture whose name begins with the /v/ sound.

Name ______________________________

1.

2.

3.

Comprehension: Character, Setting, Plot

1. Circle the picture that shows a character from the story *Bear Snores On*.
2. Circle the picture that shows the setting from the story.
3. Circle the picture that shows what caused Bear to wake up.

Name ______________________________

six van box

1.

box

2.

3.

Phonics: Blending /ks/x, /v/v
Blend the sounds and say the word. Write the word. Repeat the word.

Name ________________

"I do fit," said Fox.

"I want to nap!"

High Frequency Words: ***said, want***
Read the book aloud to a partner. Reread for fluency.

A Bed for Fox

"I see a bed," said Fox.

"I want to nap."

"Mud!" said Fox.

"I do not like mud."

"I see a den!" said Fox.

"I want to fit."

Copyright © The McGraw-Hill Companies, Inc.

Name ______________________________

1.

2.

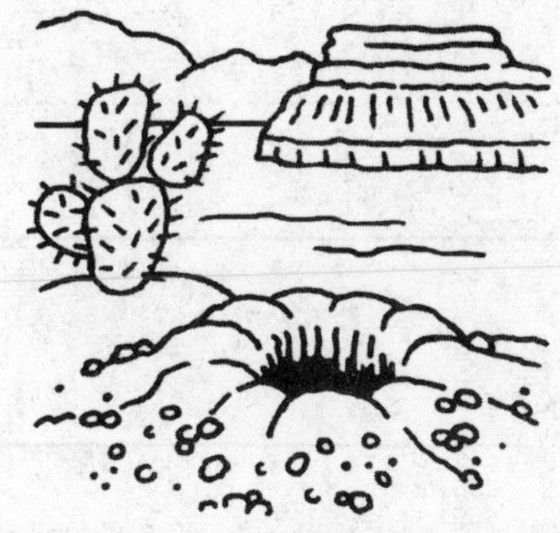

3.

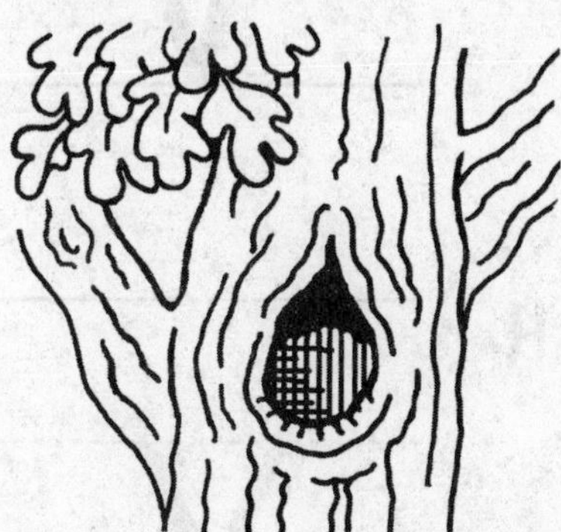

Category Words: Animal Homes
Put a marker on each picture that shows an animal home.
1. Tell about the picture that shows where a bird lives.
2. Tell about the picture that shows where a bee lives.
3. Tell about the picture that shows where a squirrel lives.

Name ____________________

1. 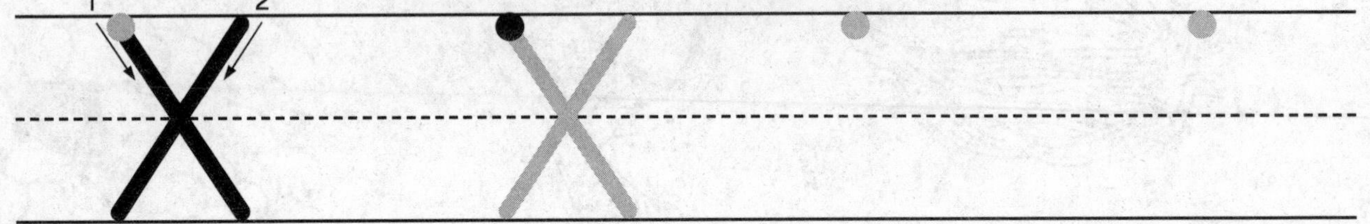

2. 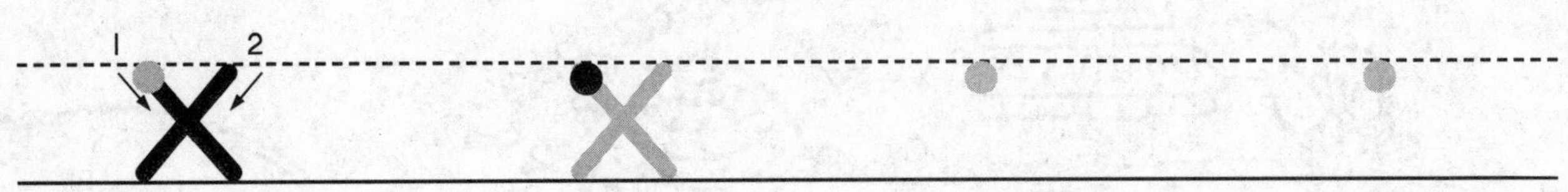

3. 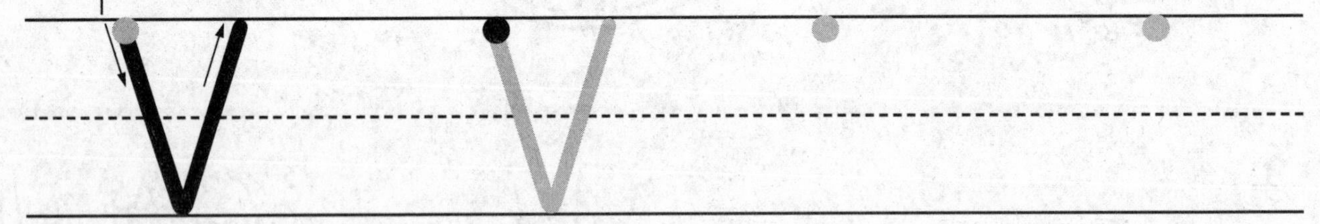

4. 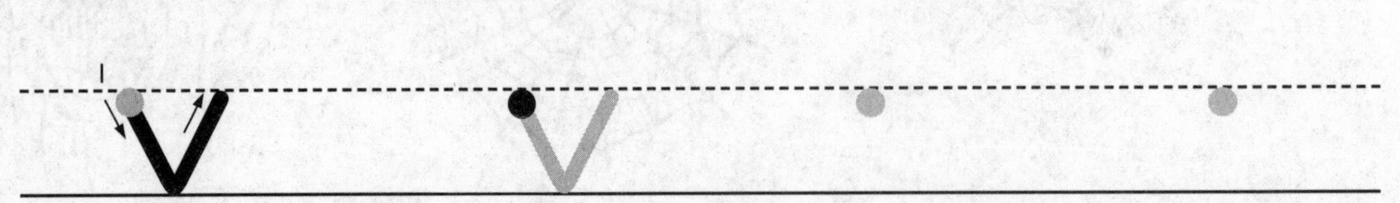

Handwriting: *Xx, Vv*
Trace and write each capital letter *X* and each lowercase letter *x*. Then trace and write each capital letter *V* and each lowercase letter *v*.

Name ____

Phonemic Awareness: /j/
Say the name of each picture. Put a marker on each picture if its name begins with the /j/ sound.

Play

Name ____________________

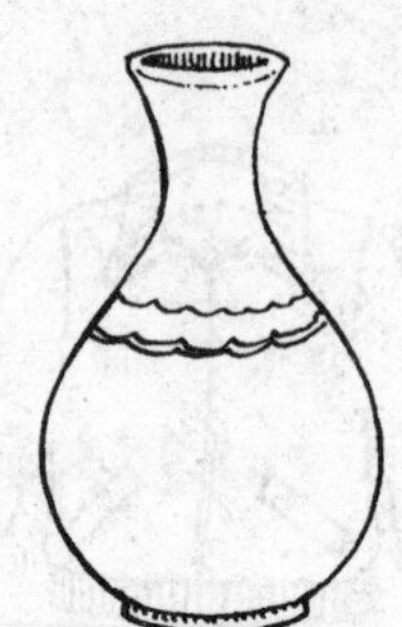

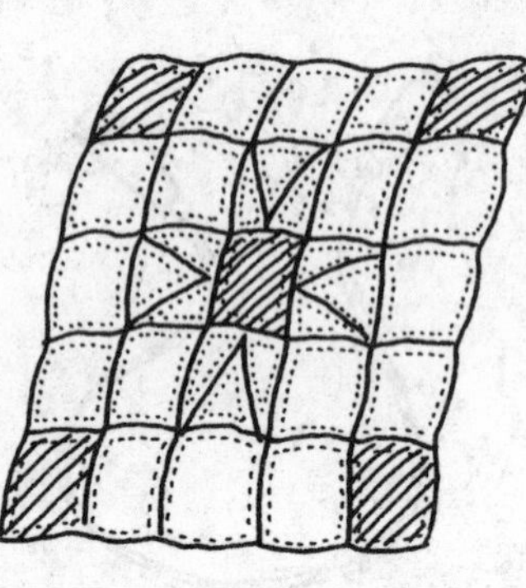

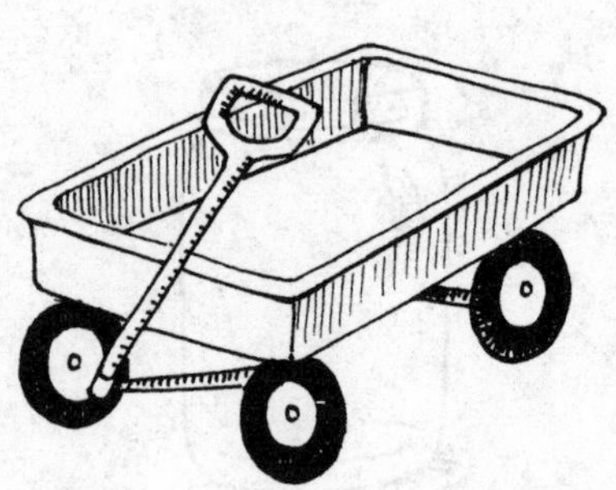

Phonemic Awareness: /kw/
Say the name of each picture. Put a marker on each picture if its name begins with the /kw/ sound.

Name ______________________________

1.

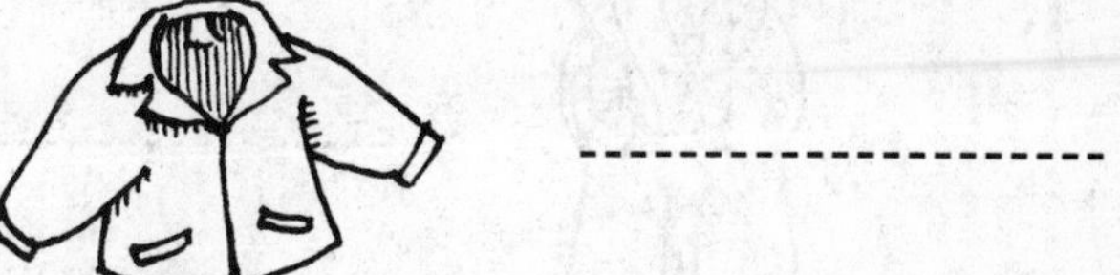

2.

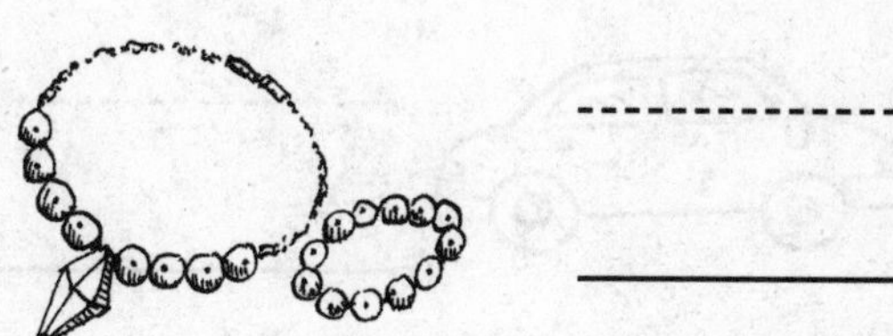

3.

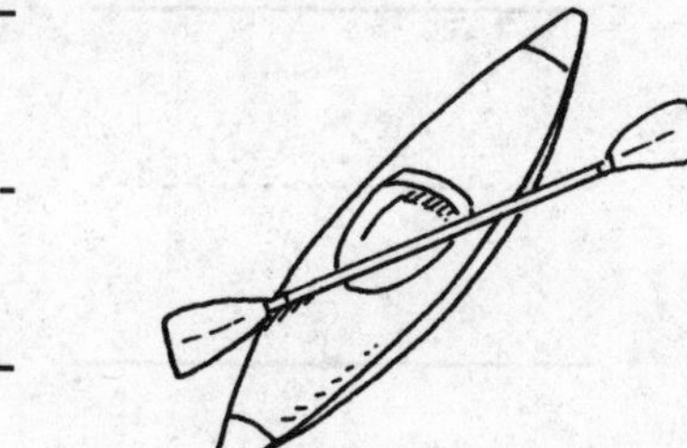

4.

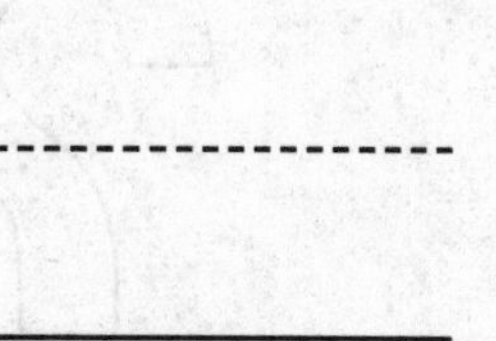

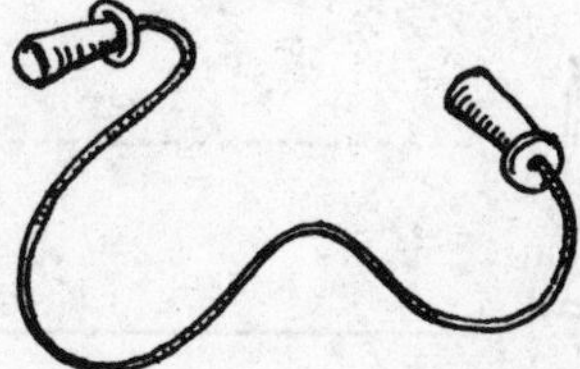

Phonics: /j/*j*

Say the name of each picture. Write the letter *j* next to each picture whose name begins with the /j/ sound.

Name ______________________

1.  

2.  

3.  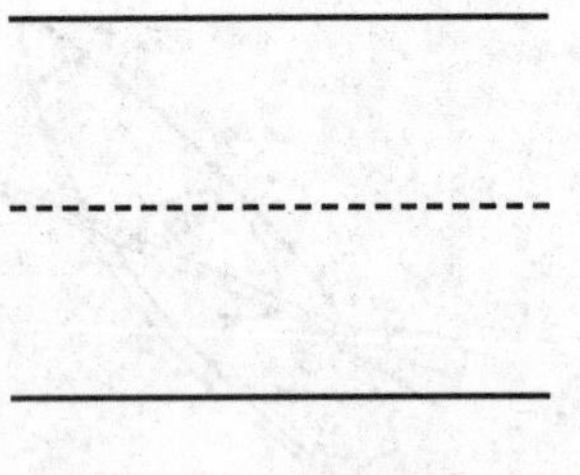 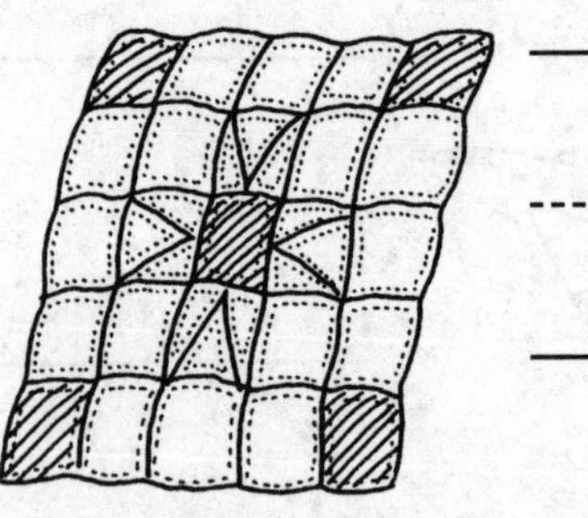

4. 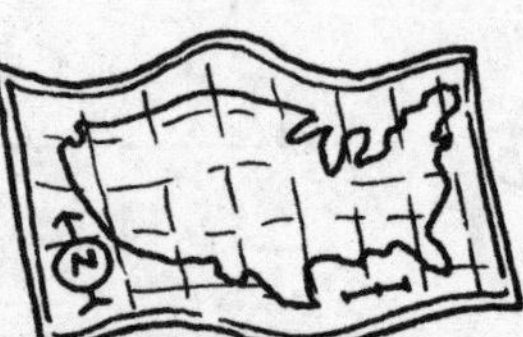 

Phonics: /kw/*qu*
Say the name of each picture. Write the letters *qu* next to each picture whose name begins with the /kw/ sound.

Name ____

1.

2.

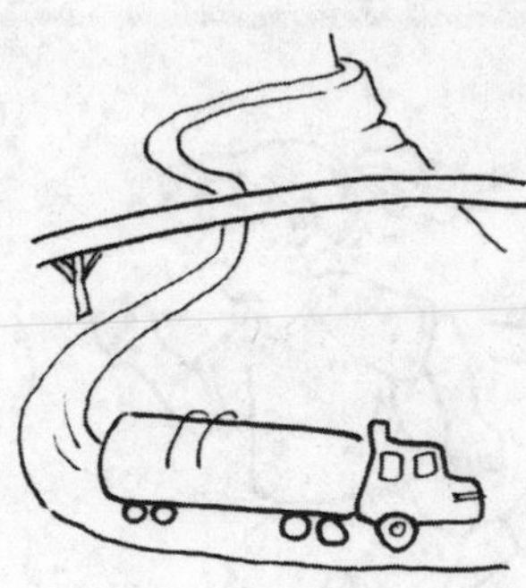

3.

Comprehension: Character, Setting, Plot
Look at the pictures about the story *When Daddy's Truck Picks Me Up.*

1. Circle the character who is picking the boy up from school.
2. Circle the setting that Daddy is in during most of the story.
3. Circle the picture that shows why Daddy was late.

Write

Name ____________________

jug quick quack

I.

jug

2.

3.

Phonics: Blending /j/*j*, /kw/*qu*
Blend the sounds and say the word. Write the word. Repeat the word.

Name ________________________________

Can you see me?

Here I am!

High Frequency Words: ***here, me***
Read the book aloud to a partner. Reread for fluency.

Here I Am!

Can you see me?

Here I am on the bus.

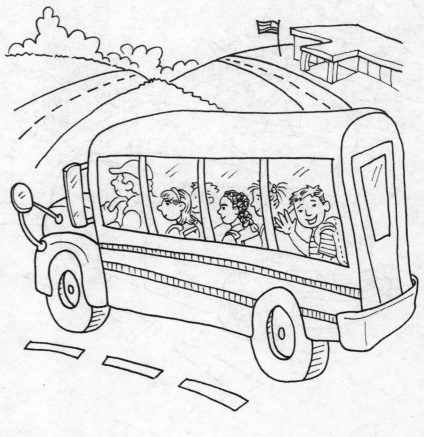

Can you see me?

Here I am in a van.

Can you see me?

Here I am in a jet.

Name ______________________________

1.

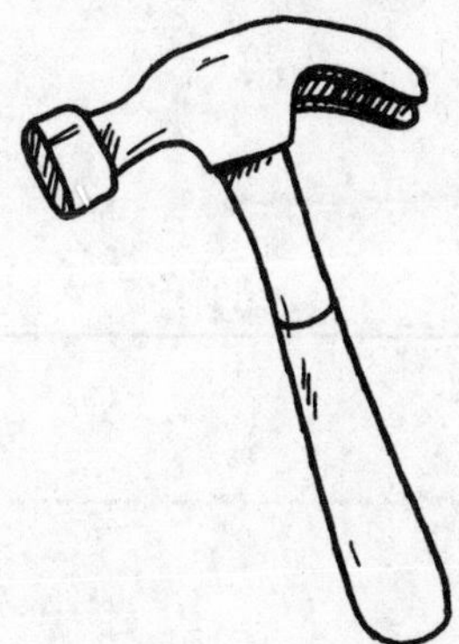

2.

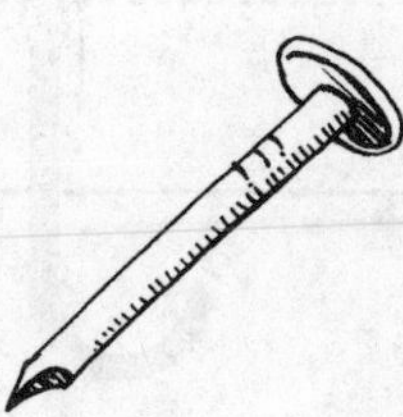

3.

Category Words: Vehicles
Put a marker on each picture that shows a vehicle. Name each vehicle. Tell which ones you have ridden in.

Name ______________________________

1.

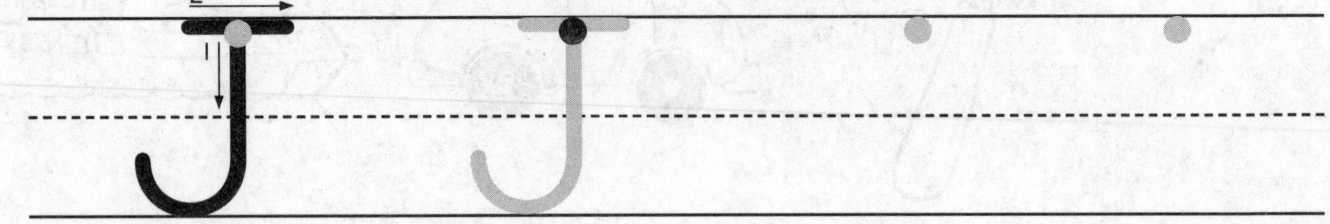

2.

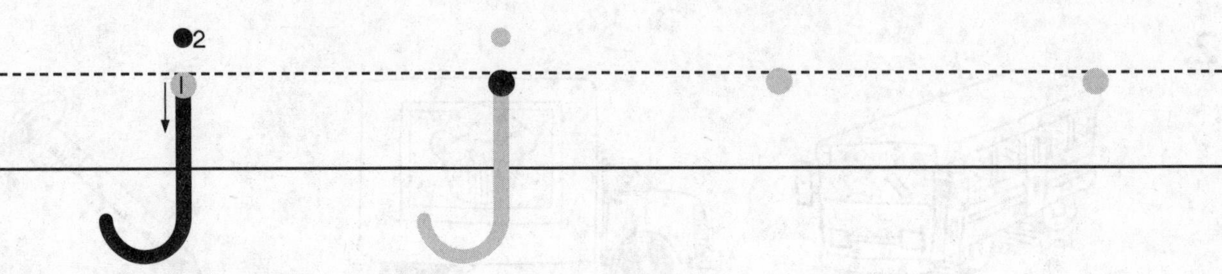

3.

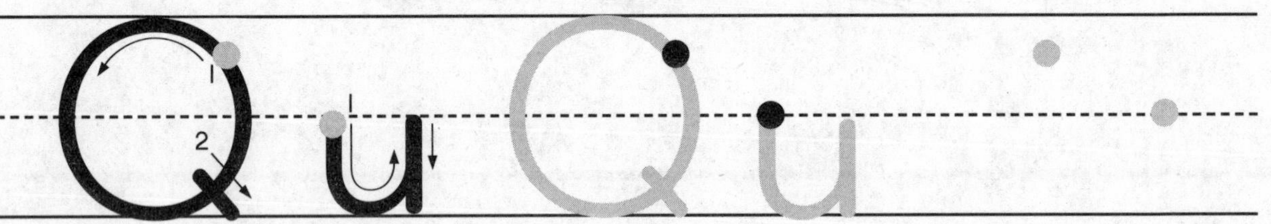

4.

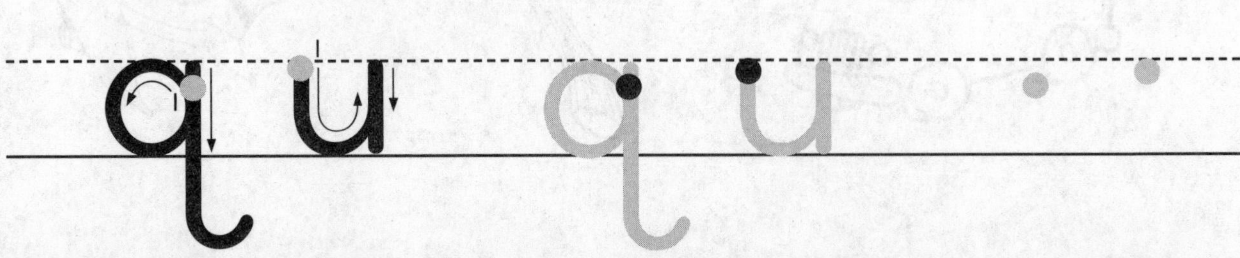

Handwriting: *Jj, Qu, qu*
Trace and write each capital letter *J* and each lowercase letter *j*.
Then trace and write the letters *Qu* and the letters *qu*.

Name ______________________________

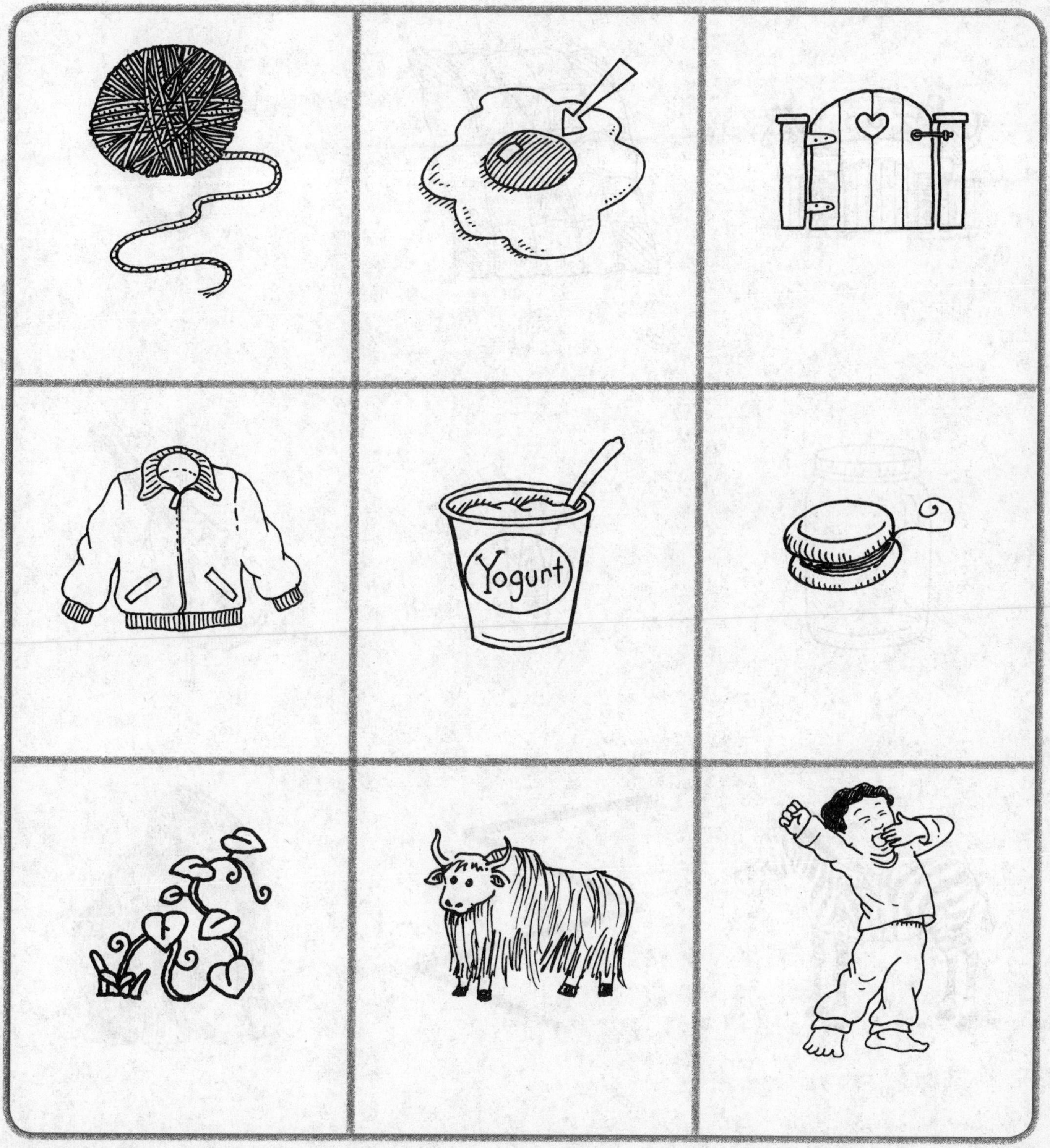

Phonemic Awareness: /y/

Say the name of each picture. Put a marker on each picture if its name begins with the /y/ sound.

Play

Name ___________________________

	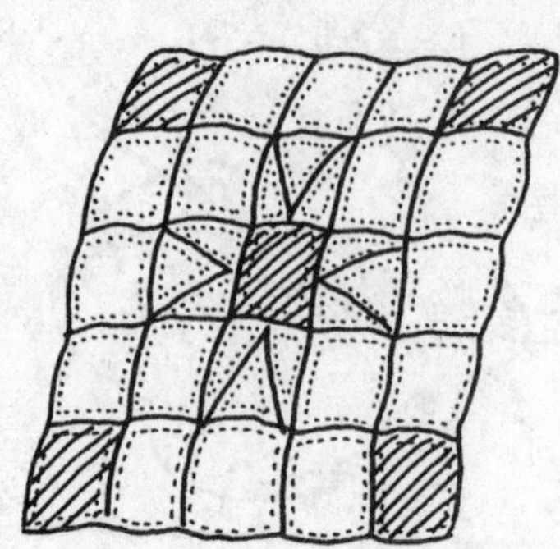	

	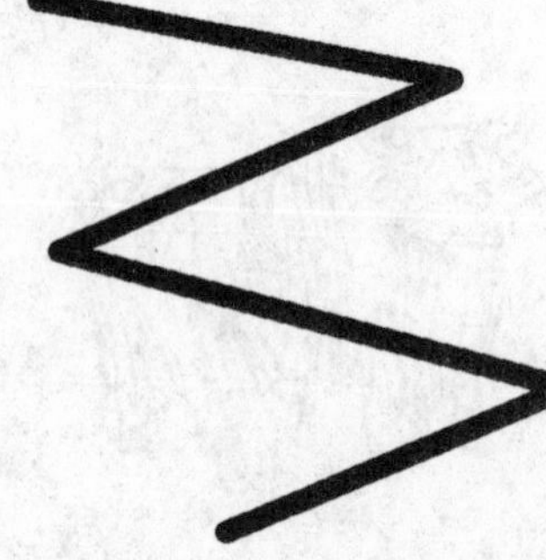	

Phonemic Awareness: /z/
Say the name of each picture. Put a marker on each picture if its name begins with the /z/ sound.

Name ___

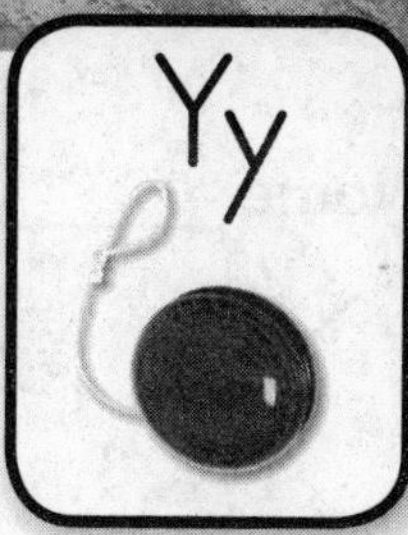

1.

2.

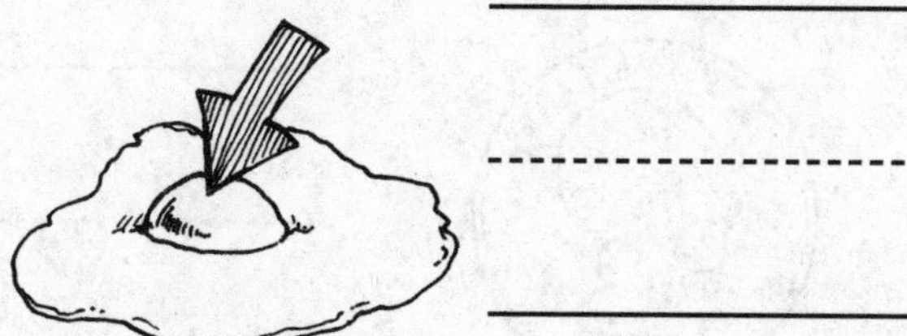

3.

4.

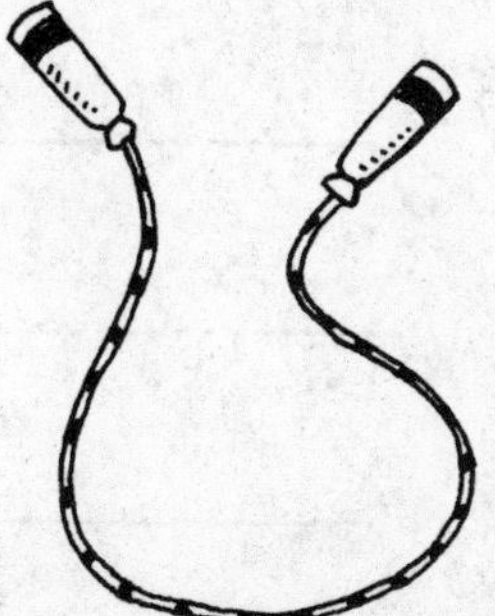

Phonics: /y/*y*
Say the name of each picture. Write the letter *y* next to each picture whose name begins with the /y/ sound.

Write

Name ___

Zz

1. 

2. 

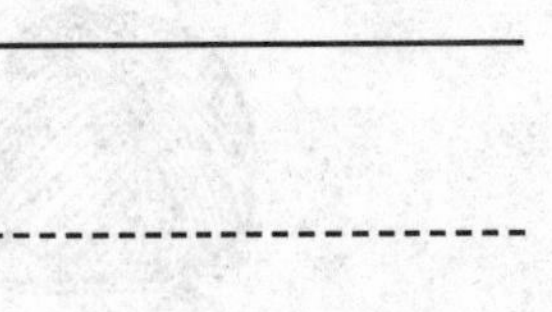

3. 

4. 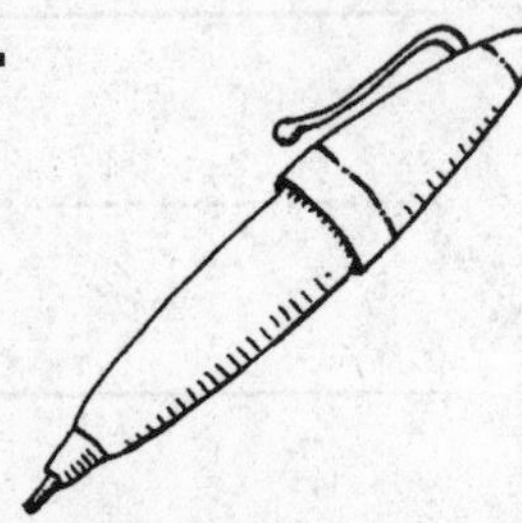

Phonics: /z/z
Say the name of each picture. Write the letter *z* next to each picture whose name begins with the /z/ sound.

Name ______________________________

1.

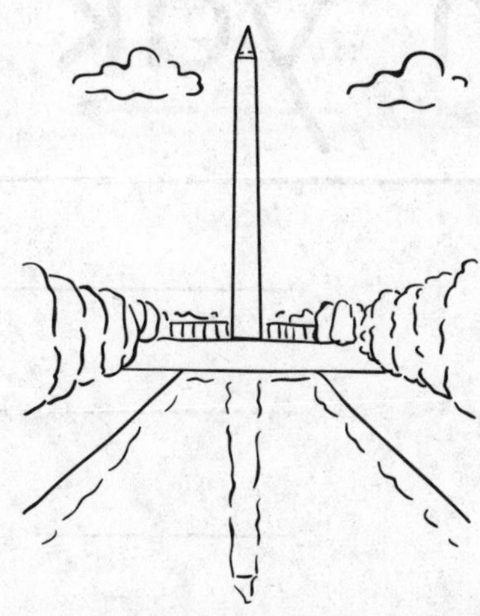

2.

3.

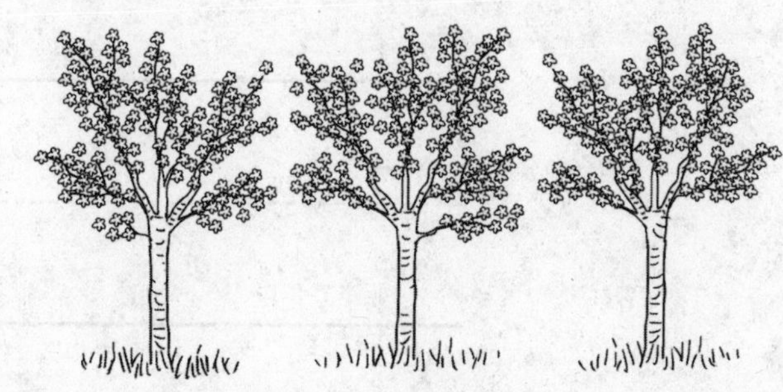

Comprehension: Main Topic and Key Details
Look at the pictures about the selection *Ana Goes to Washington, D.C.* Circle the picture in each row that shows a key detail about the main topic of the selection. Talk with a partner about why you circled each picture.

Name

zip yum yak

1.

yak

2.

3.

Phonics: Blending /y/y, /z/z
Blend the sounds and say the word. Write the word. Repeat the word.

Name ______________________________

"We can do this!"

High Frequency Words: ***this, what***
Read the book aloud to a partner. Reread for fluency.

What Can You Do?

"This is for you."
"What can you do?"

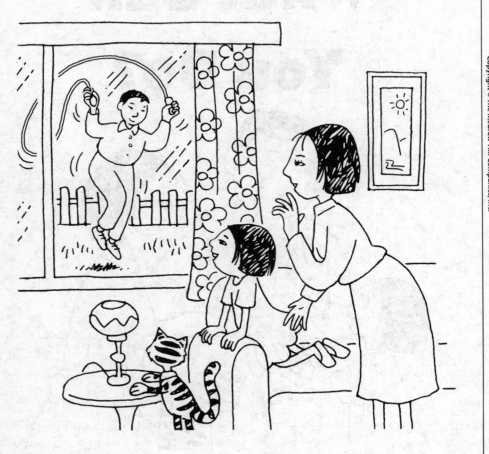

"I can do this," said Dad.

"What can we do?"

Name ______________________________

1\.

2\.

3\.

Category Words: Ordinal Numbers

1. Put a marker on the child in the second location.
2. Put a marker on the vehicle in the fifth location.
3. Put a marker on the bird in the first location.

Tell a partner about why you circled each picture.
Use the words *first, second, third, fourth,* or *fifth.*

Name ______________________________

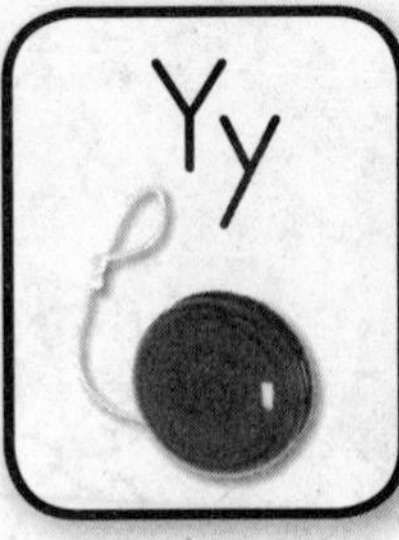

1.

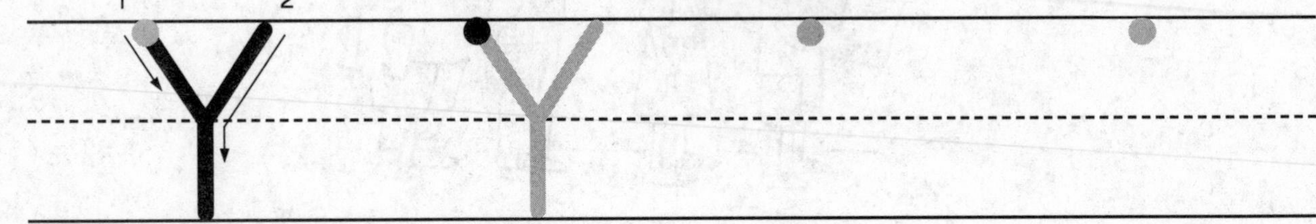

2.

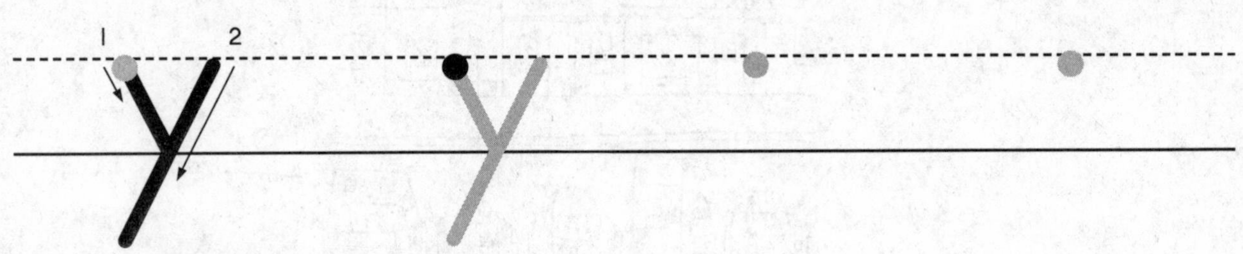

3.

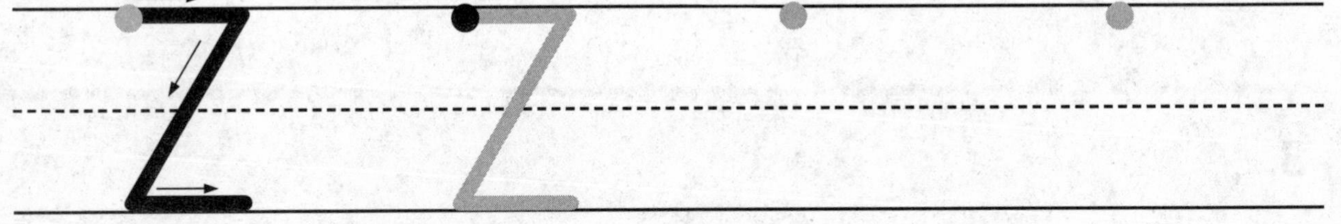

4.

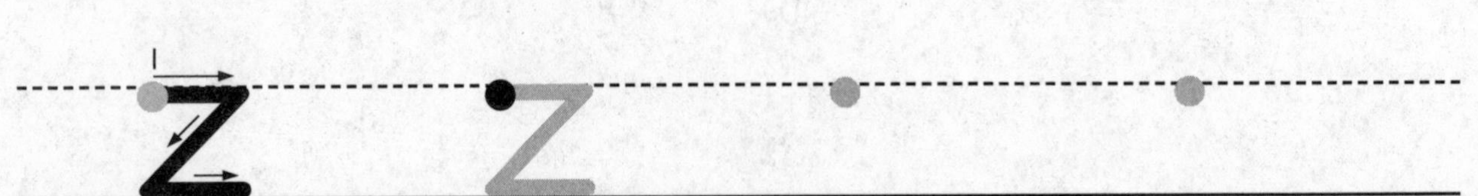

Handwriting: *Yy, Zz*
Trace and write each capital letter *Y* and each lowercase letter *y*.
Then trace and write each capital letter *Z* and each lowercase letter *z*.

Name ___________________________________

Review Phonics: /u/*u*, /g/*g*, /w/*w*
Say the name of each picture. Put a marker on each picture if its name begins with the letter *u*, *g*, or *w*.

Circle

Name ______________________________

I.

2.

3.

Comprehension: Character, Setting, Plot
Look at the pictures about the story *Bringing Down the Moon*.
1. Circle the picture that shows the character who wants the moon.
2. Circle the picture that shows the setting from the story.
3. Circle the picture that shows what Mole used to pull down the moon.

Name ________________________________

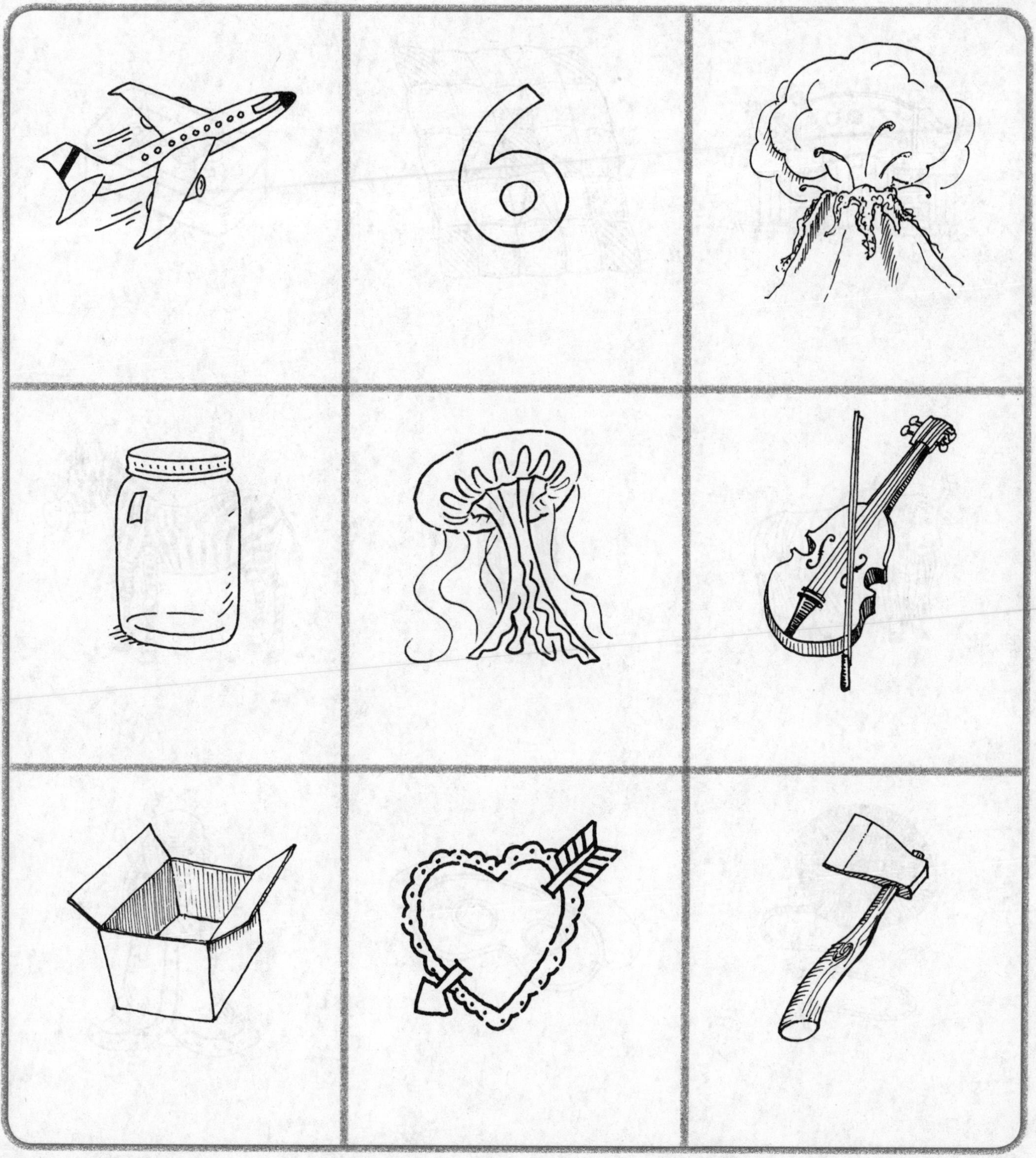

Review Phonics: /ks/x, /v/v, /j/j
Say the name of each picture. Put a marker on each picture if its name ends with the letter *x*. Then put a marker on each picture if it begins with the letter *v* or *j*.

Name ______________________________

ZOO		Soap
	0	

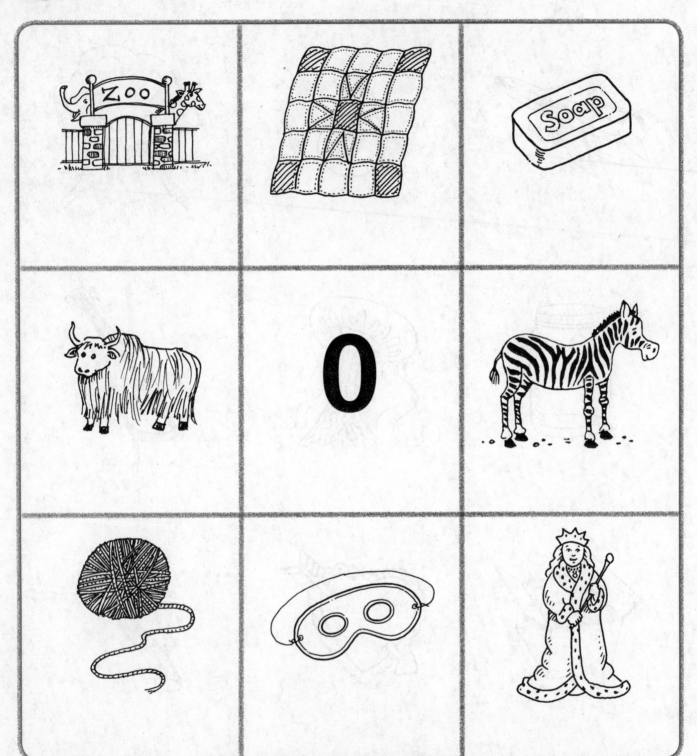

Review Phonics: /kw/*qu*, /y/*y*, /z/*z*
Say the name of each picture. Put a marker on each picture if its name begins with the letters *qu*, *y*, or *z*.

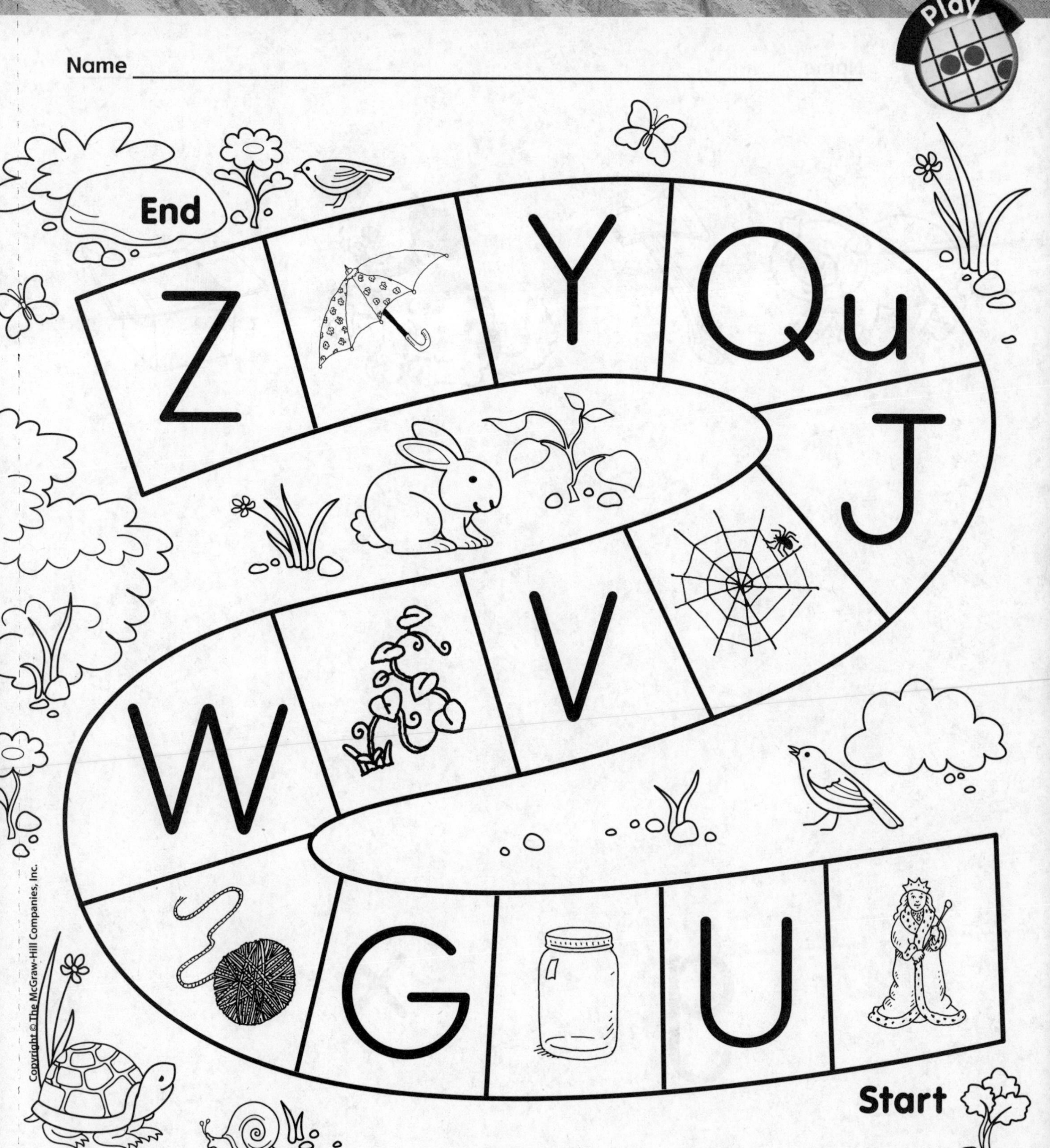

Phonics Review Game: /u/u, /g/g, /w/w, /v/v, /j/j, /kw/qu, /y/y, /z/z
Place a marker on "Start." Move your marker from square to square. When you land on a picture, say the name of the picture and the letter it begins with. If you land on a letter, say a word that begins with that letter. When you reach "End," play again and think of new words.

Name ________________________________

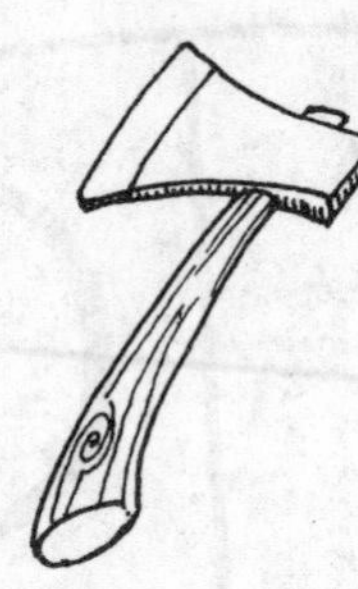

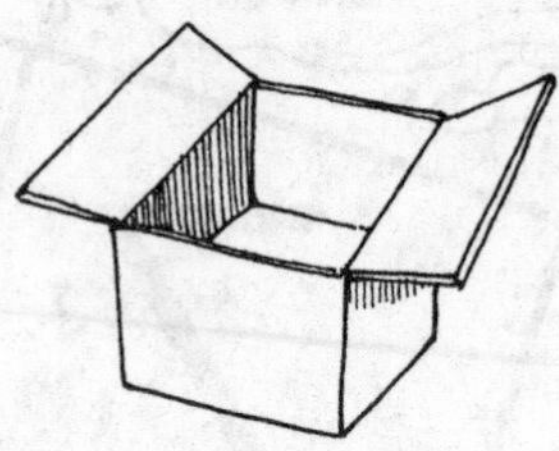

g

Phonics Review Game: /g/g, /ks/x
Say the name of each picture. Draw lines to connect the pictures to the letters they end with.

Name ______________________

"I see me!" said Kit.

They have a lot of fun.

Review High Frequency Words: ***they, have, want, said, this, what, here, for, of, me***
Read the book aloud to a partner. Reread for fluency.

Jim and Kit

"Here it is!" said Jim.

"Do you want to sit?"

"What do you see?"

"I see a hen."

"This is a little cup!"

"It is for you to sip!"

Name ____________________

1.

2.

3.

Category Words: Opposites
Find the two opposites in each row and put markers on them.
Tell about the opposites. Say the opposite words.

Name ____________________

gum jug web

1.

gum

2.

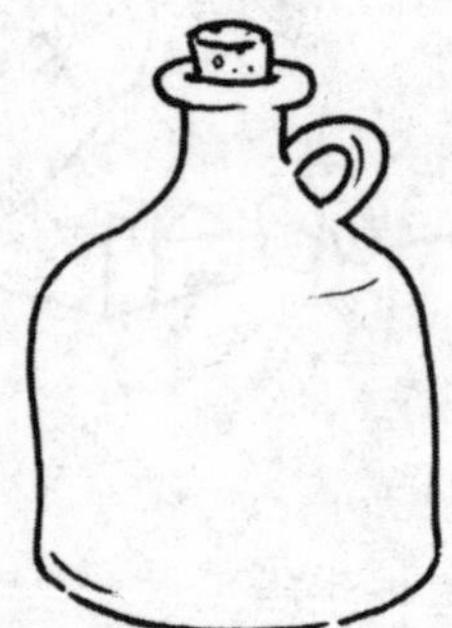

3.

Review Phonics: Blending
Blend the sounds and say the word. Write the word. Repeat the word.

Name ___________________________

yak fox van

I.

van

2.

3.

Review Phonics: Blending
Blend the sounds and say the word. Write the word.
Repeat the word.

Write

Name

1.

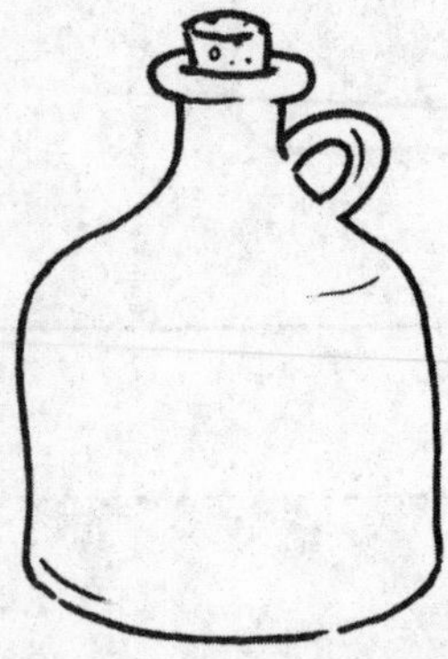

jug

2.

van

3.

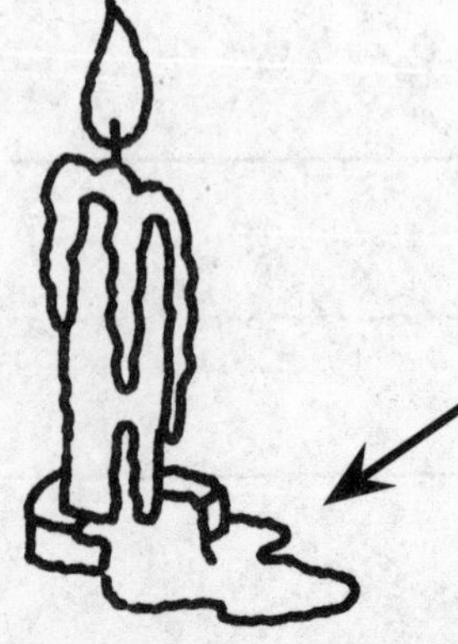

wax

Handwriting Review
Say each picture name. Then say each word as you trace it and write it. Read each word to a partner.

Name ______________________________

Phonemic Awareness: /ā/
Say the name of each picture. Put a marker on each picture if its name has the /ā/ sound.

Name ______________________________

1. 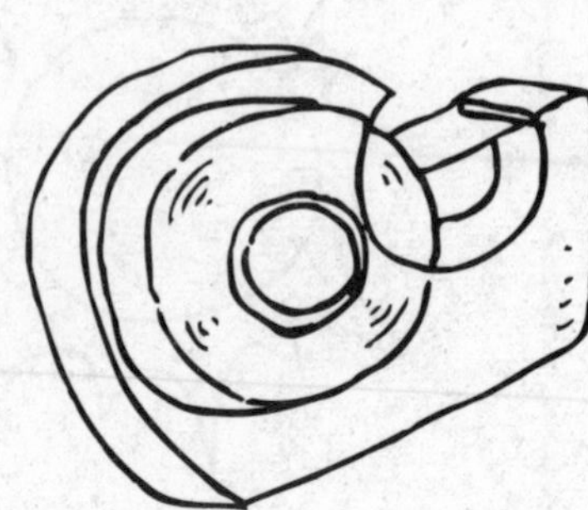

t a p e

2. 

c _ k _

3. 

g _ t _

4. 

v _ s _

Phonics: /ā/*a_e*
Say each picture name. Then write the letters that stand for long *a* in each picture name.

Name ______________________________

I.

2.

3.

Comprehension: Character, Setting, Plot

Look at the pictures about the story *Peter's Chair.*

1. Circle the picture that shows to whom the chair belongs.
2. Circle the picture that shows where the story happens.
3. Circle the picture that shows what Peter does with his chair.

Name

date name bake

1.

date

2.

3.

Phonics: Blending *-ate, -ame, -ake*
Blend the sounds and say the word. Write the word.
Repeat the word.

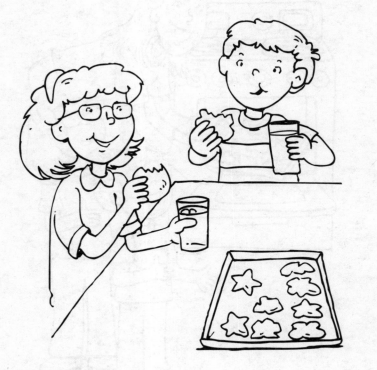

Name ______________________

"I like to help!"

"I like to help, too!"

High Frequency Words: ***help, too***
Read the book aloud to a partner. Reread for fluency.

I Want to Help!

Pam can help mix.

Mack can mix, too.

Pam can help cut.

Mack can cut, too.

Mom can help bake it.

"Can we help?"

Name ____

I.

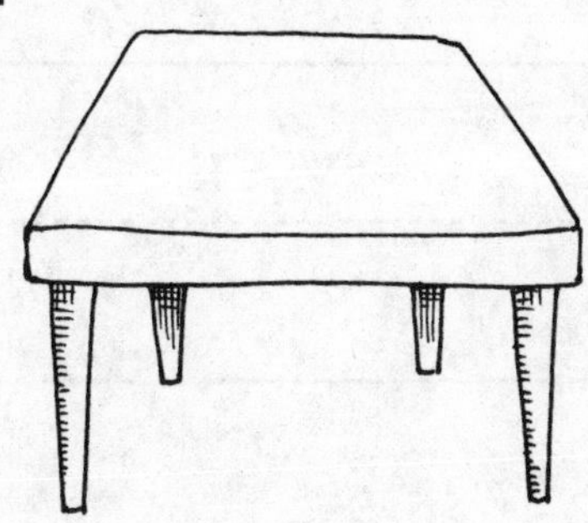

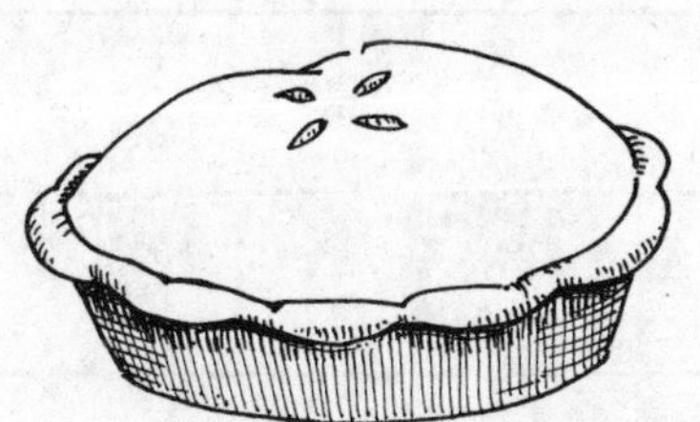

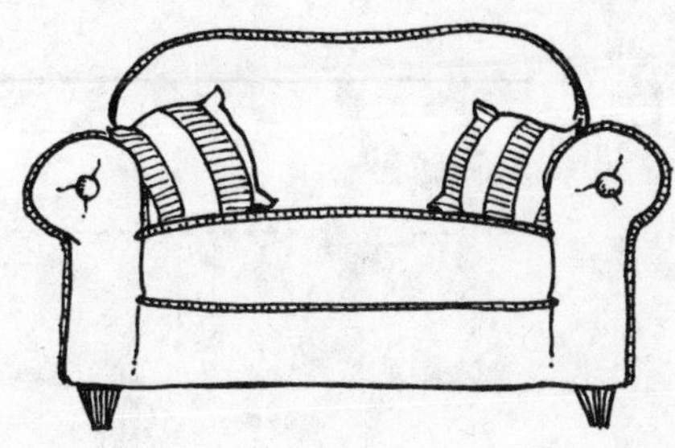

2.

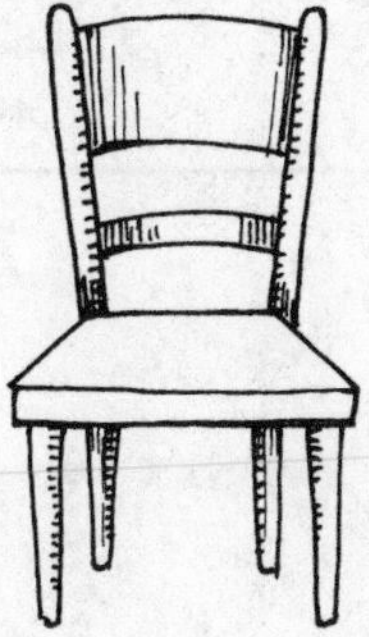

3.

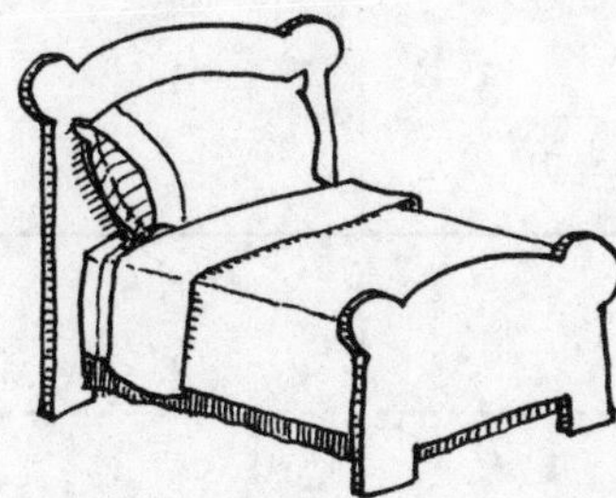

Category Words: Household Furniture
Put a marker on each picture that shows a piece of furniture. Name each piece of furniture. Tell what you can do with each one.

Name ______________________________

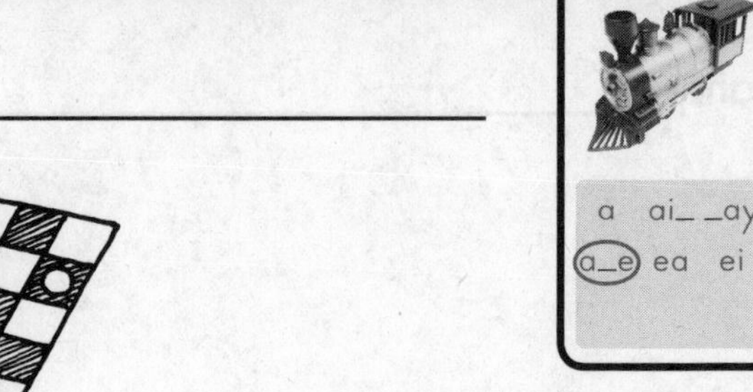

1. It is a game.

2.

3. It is a gate.

4.

Handwriting: Sentences with /ā/a_e
Say each word as you trace it and write it. Then read each sentence to a partner.

Name ____________________

Phonemic Awareness: /ī/
Say the name of each picture. Put a marker on each picture if its name has the /ī/ sound.

Write

Name ______________________________

5

i y i_e
igh ie

I.

v i n e

2.

b ___ t ___

3.

f ___ v ___

4.

b ___ k ___

Phonics: /ī/i_e
Say the name of each picture. Then write the letters that stand for long *i* in each picture name.

Name ______________________________

I.

2.

3.

Comprehension: Character, Setting, Plot
Look at the pictures about the story *Hen Hears Gossip.*

1. Circle the picture that shows the character who loves to gossip.
2. Circle the picture that shows where the story happens.
3. Circle the picture that shows what really happens to one of the animals.

Write

Name ______________________________

hike hive time

1.

time

2.

3.

Phonics: Blending *-ime, -ike, -ive*
Blend the sounds and say the word. Write the word. Repeat the word.

Name ____________________

They can play here!

High Frequency Words: ***play, has***
Read the book aloud to a partner. Reread for fluency.

We Can Play!

We can not play here.

Copyright © The McGraw-Hill Companies, Inc.

We can help.
He has a big sack.

She has a big sack, too.
We put the sack in a bin.

Name ____

Category Words: Farm Animals
Put a marker on each picture that shows a farm animal. Name each farm animal and make the sound it makes.

Name ______________________

i y i_e
igh ie

1.

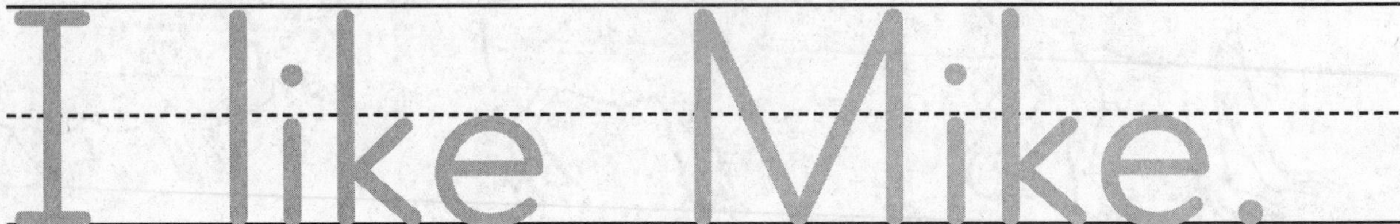

2.

3.

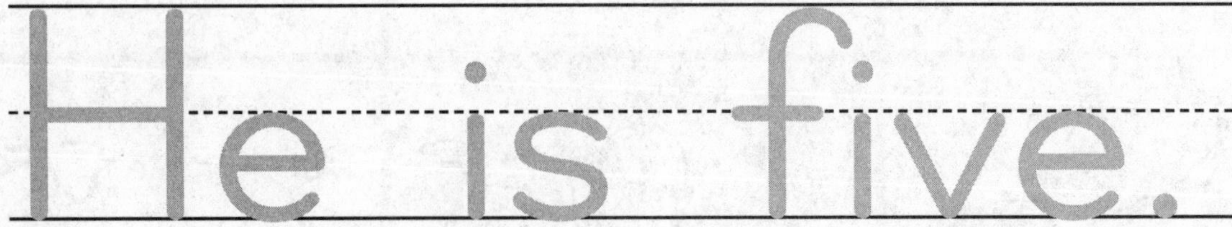

4.

Handwriting: Sentences with */ī/i_e*
Say each word as you trace it and write it. Then read each sentence to a partner.

Name ___________________________________

Phonemic Awareness: /ō/
Say the name of each picture. Put a marker on each picture if its name has the /ō/ sound.

Name ______________________

1. 

p o l e

2. 

c _ n _

3. 

r _ b _

4. 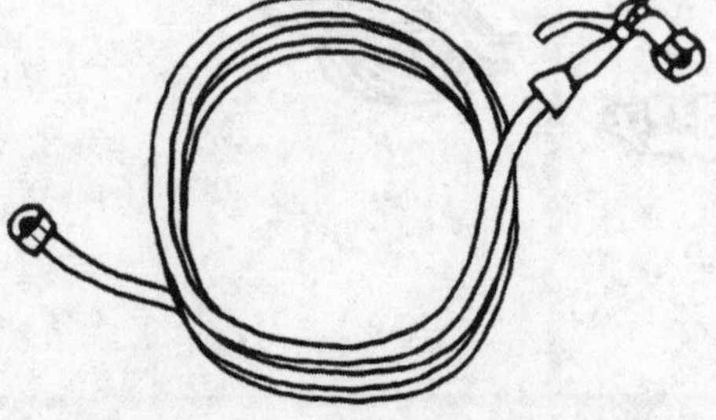

h _ s _

Phonics: /ō/*o_e*
Say the name of each picture. Then write the letters that stand for long *o* in each picture name.

Name

1.

2.

3.

Comprehension: Connections Within Text
The pictures show the steps a baker uses to make bread. Think about the steps in the order they happen. Write *1*, *2*, or *3* next to the picture that matches the order. Talk with a partner about each step.

Name ______________________________

mole nose note

I.

mole

2.

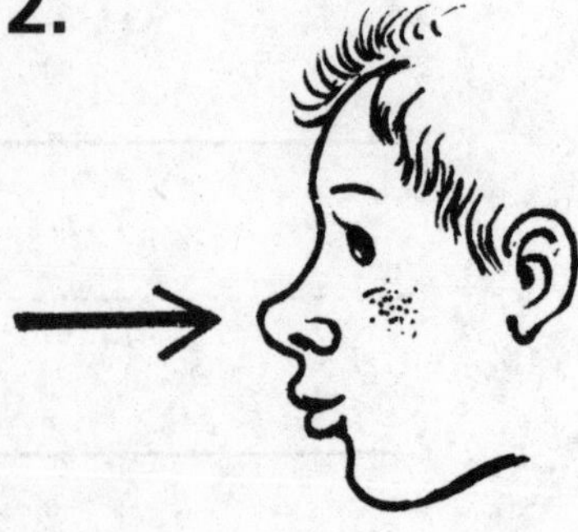

3.

Phonics: Blending *-ole, -ose, -ote*
Blend the sounds and say the word. Write the word. Repeat the word.

Name ______________________

Look, it is big.

Where can it go?

High Frequency Words: ***where, look***
Read the book aloud to a partner. Reread for fluency.

Look at This!

Look, it is little.

What is it?

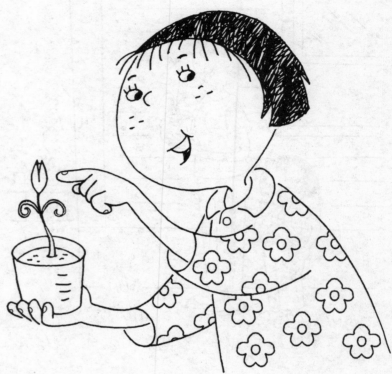

It is in the sun.

It is hot.

Look, it has a bud.

Can you see it?

Name ________________________________

1.

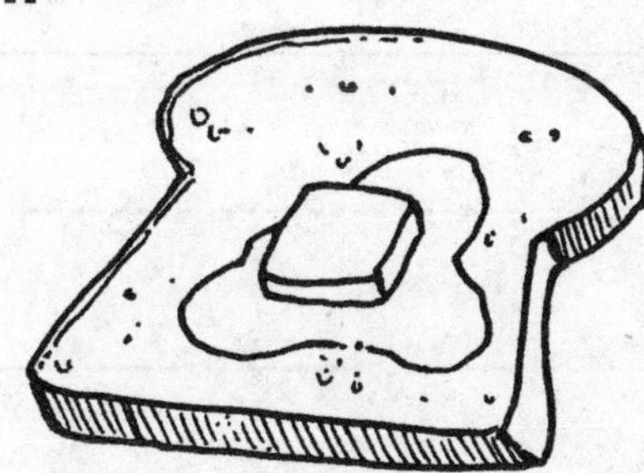

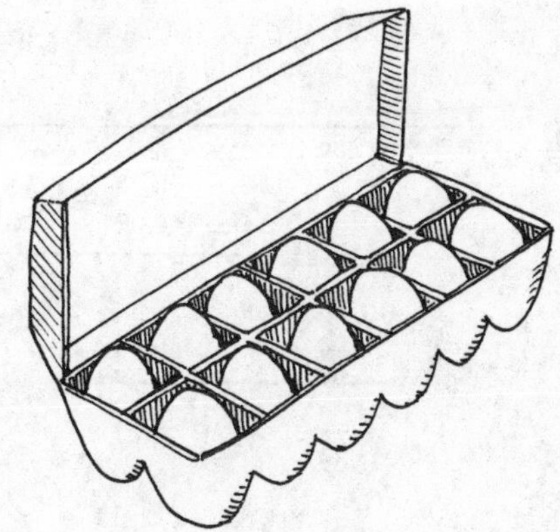

2.

3.

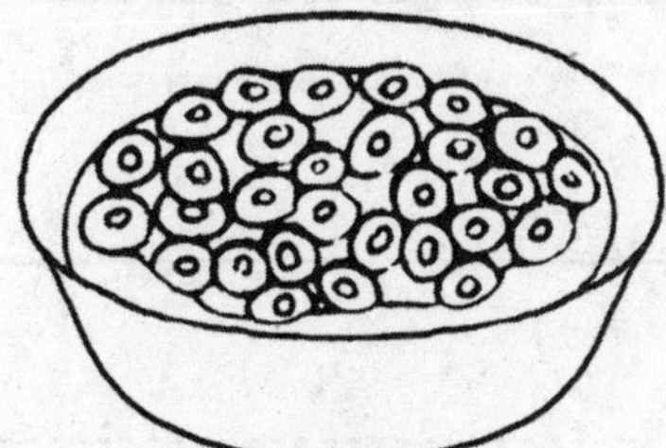

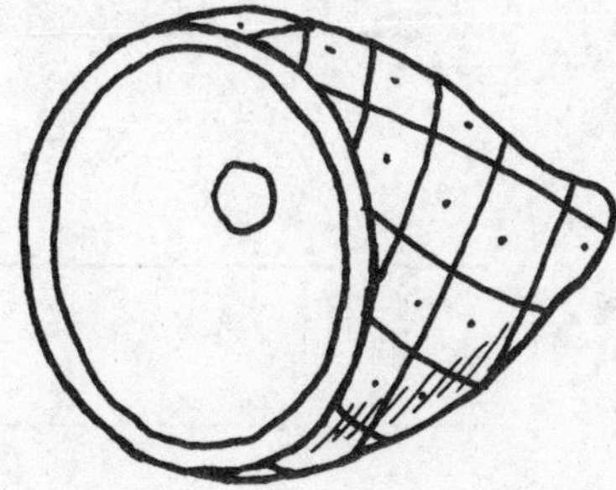

Category Words: Foods Made From Grain
Put a marker on each picture that shows a food made from grain.
Name each food. Tell which foods made from grain you like to eat.

Name ______________________________

1. It is a rose.

2.

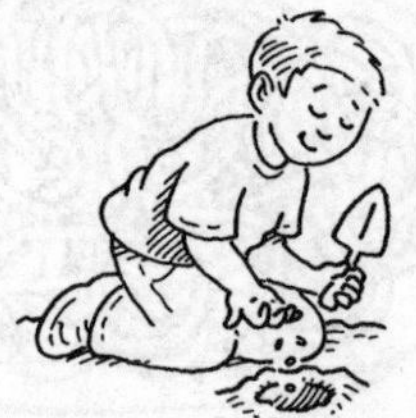

3. I dig a hole.

4.

Handwriting: Sentences with /ō/o_e
Say each word as you trace it and write it. Then read each sentence to a partner.

Name ____________________

Phonemic Awareness: /ū/
Say the name of each picture. Put a marker on each picture if its name has the /ū/ sound.

Name ______________________________

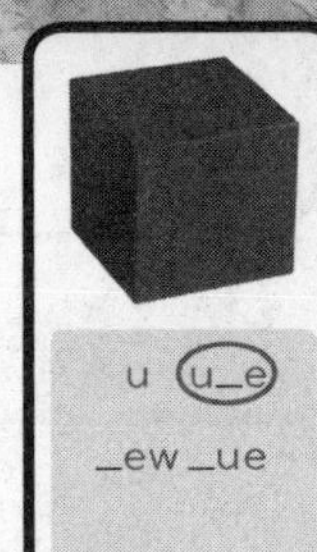

1. 

c u t e

2. 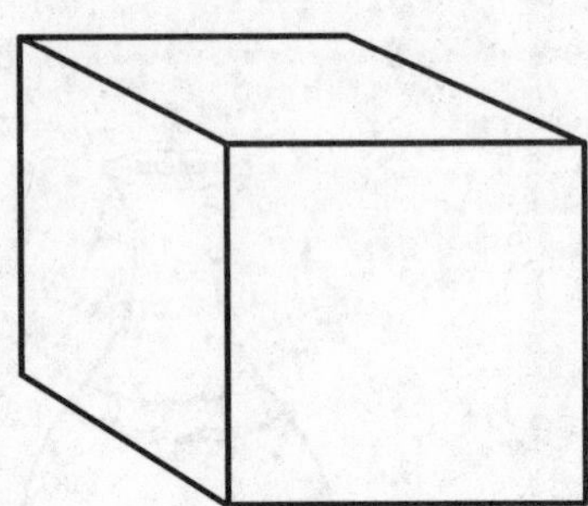

c _ b _

3. 

d _ k _

4. 

t _ n _

Phonics: /ū/*u_e*
Say each picture name. Then write the letters that stand for long *u* in each picture name.

Name ____

I.

2.

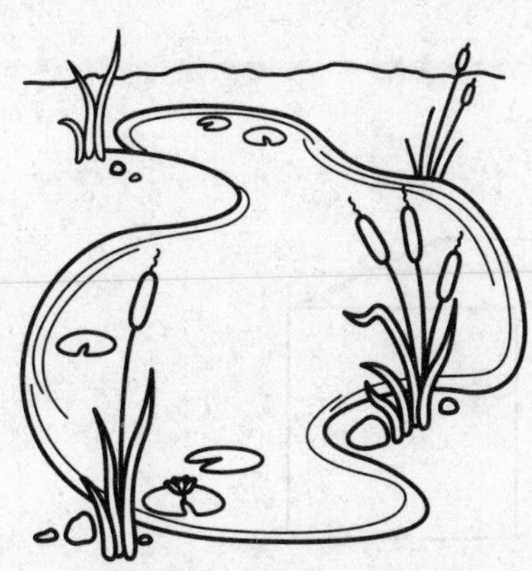

3.

Comprehension: Character, Setting, Plot

Look at the pictures about the story *What's the Big Idea, Molly?*

1. Circle the character who thinks best when fishing.
2. Circle the picture that shows where Frog gets his best ideas.
3. Circle the picture that shows what the animals made for Turtle.

Name ____________________

cube mule June

I.

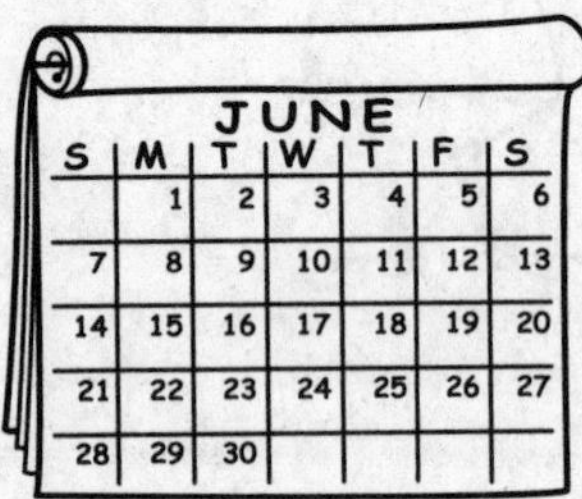

June

2.

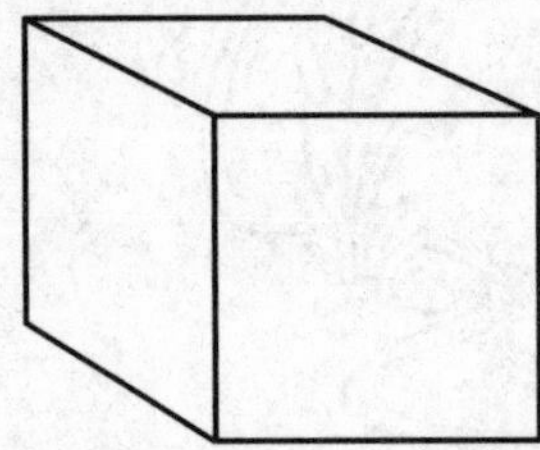

3.

Phonics: Blending *-une, -ube, -ule*
Blend the sounds and say the word. Write the word. Repeat the word.

Name ______________________________

Sam is good at this.

He can help mop.

High Frequency Words: ***who, good***
Read the book aloud to a partner. Reread for fluency.

Who Can Help?

This is not good!

Who can I get to help?

Copyright © The McGraw-Hill Companies, Inc.

Deb can help me fix it.

She is good at this.

This is not good.

Who can help mop?

Copyright © The McGraw-Hill Companies, Inc.

Name ______________________________

1.

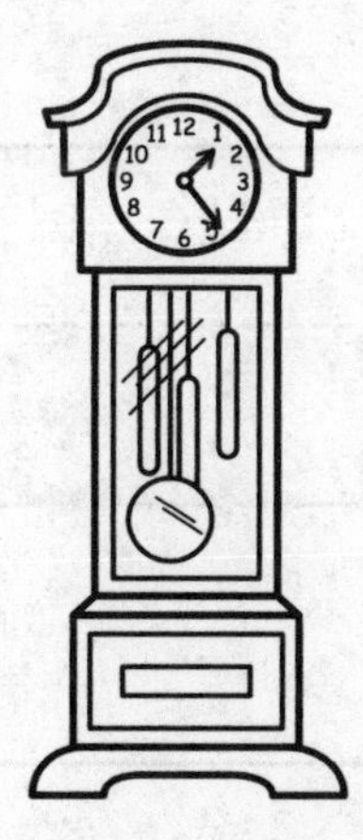

2.

3.

Category Words: Question Words

Look at the pictures and think about questions words.

1. Circle the picture that shows when.
2. Circle the picture that shows where.
3. Circle the picture that shows who.

Name ______________________________

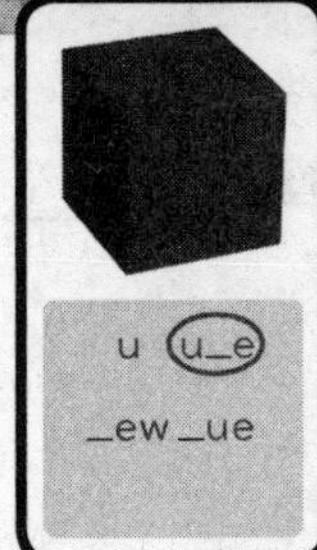

1. It is June.

2. ______________________________

3. Play a tune!

4. ______________________________

Handwriting: Sentences with /ū/*u_e*
Say each word as you trace it and write it. Then read each sentence to a partner.

Name ____

Pete

S M T W T F S
1 2 3
4 5 6 7 8 9 10
11 12 13 14 15 16 17
18 19 20 21 22 23 24
25 26 27 28 29 30 31

Phonemic Awareness: /ē/
Say the name of each picture. Put a marker on each picture if its name has the /ē/ sound.

Name ______________________________

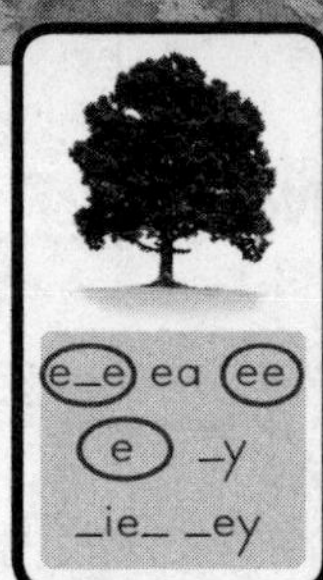

I. 

m e

2. 

w _ _ d

3. 

p _ _ k

4.

P _ t _

Phonics: ***/ē/e_e, ee, e***

Say the name of each picture. Then write the letters that stand for long *e* in each picture name.

Name ______________________________

1.

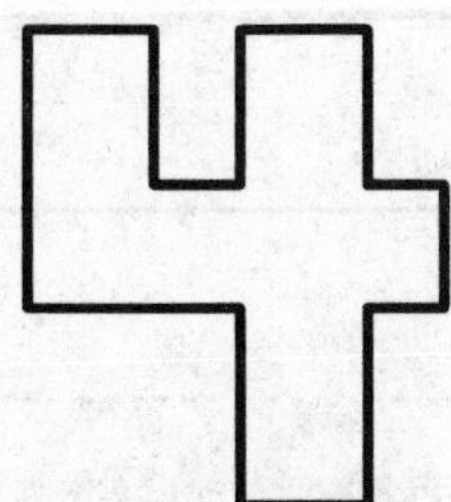

2.

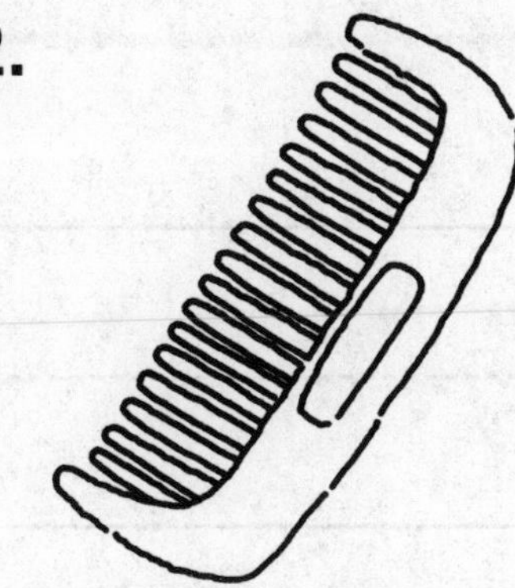

3.

Comprehension: Key Details
Think about the story *All Kinds of Families!* Look at the pictures in each row. Circle the pictures that belong in the same family. Talk to a partner about how the pictures you circled belong in a family.

Name ______________________

beep Pete feed

I.

beep

2.

3.

Phonics: Blending *-eep, -ete, -eed*
Blend the sounds and say the word. Write the word. Repeat the word.

Name ______________________

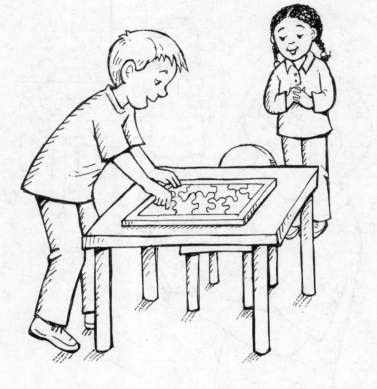

It does fit in here!

Come and see!

High Frequency Words: ***come, does***
Read the book aloud to a partner. Reread for fluency.

Come and See

Can you help me?

Where does it go?

Does it fit here?

No, it does not fit.

Come and see this!

Does it go in here?

Copyright © The McGraw-Hill Companies, Inc.

Name ______________________________

I.

2.

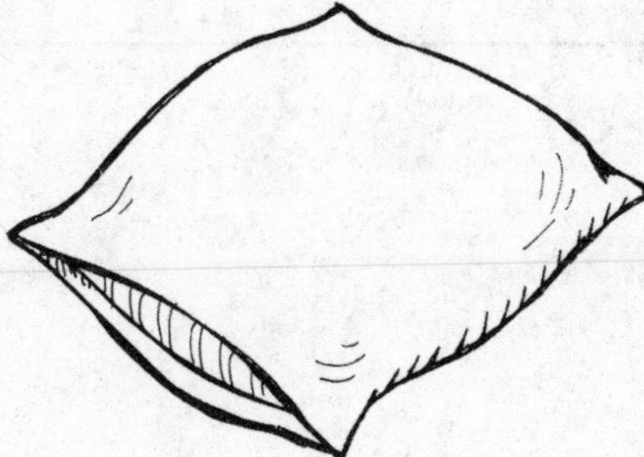

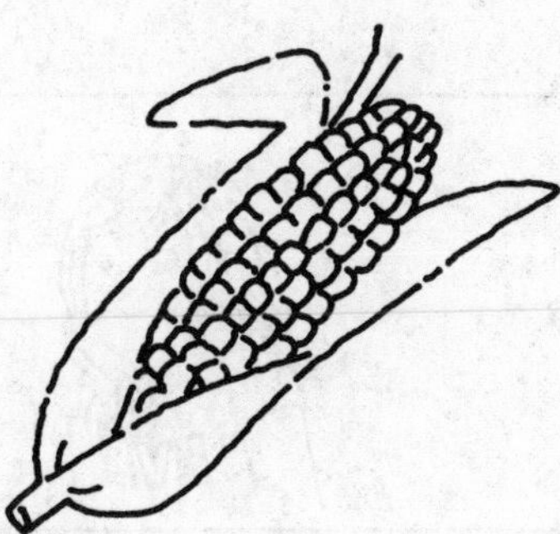

3.

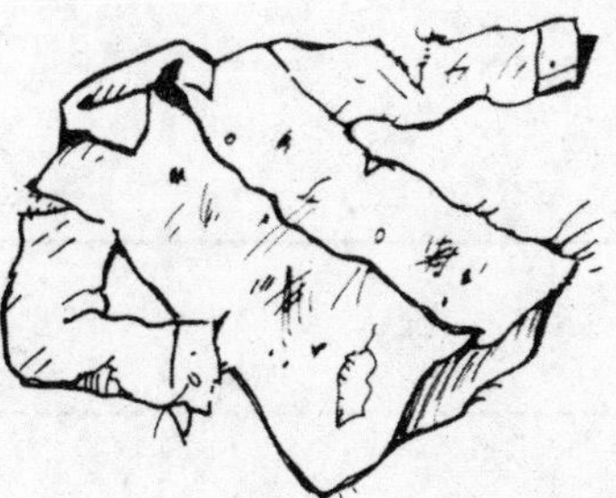

Category Words: Opposites
In each row, put a marker on the two pictures that show opposites.
Say the names of the pictures that show opposites.

Name ________________________________

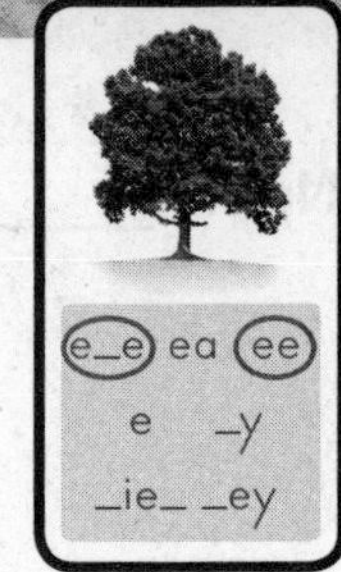

1. I see a bee.

2.

3. I see Eve.

4.

Handwriting: Sentences with */ē/e_e, ee*
Say each word as you trace it and write it. Then read each sentence to a partner.

Name ____________________

Review Phonics: /ā/a_e, /ī/i_e
Say the name of each picture. Put a marker on each picture if its name has the /ā/ or /ī/ sound. Turn to your partner and spell the /ā/ words. Then listen to your partner as they spell the /ī/ words.

Circle

Name ______________________________

1.

2.

Comprehension: Main Topic and Key Details

1. Circle the picture that shows how a mother panda cares for her panda cub.
2. Circle the picture that shows how panda kindergarteners play.

Then talk to a partner about the main topic of *Panda Kindergarten*.

Name ____

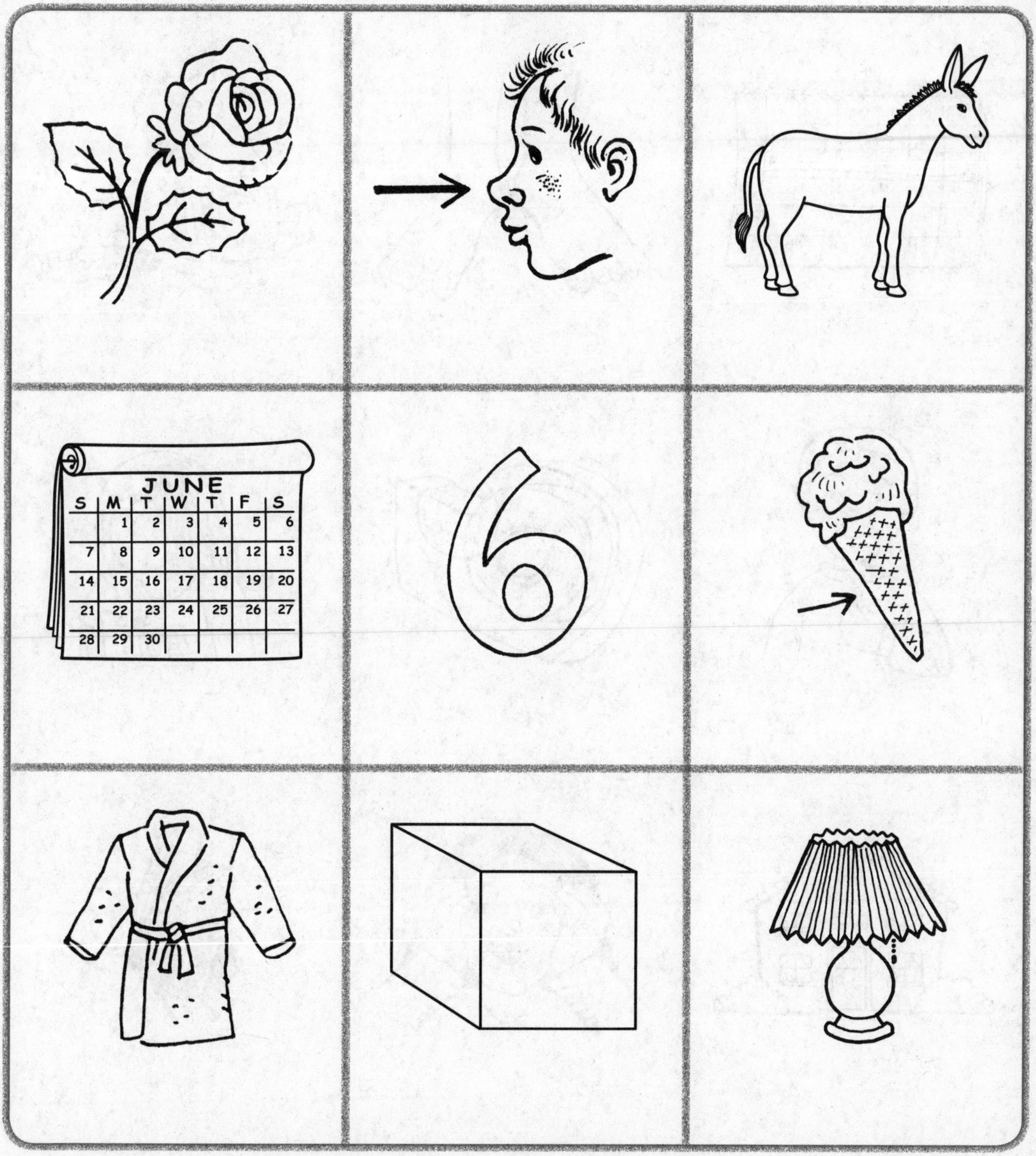

Review Phonics: /ō/*o_e*, /ū/*u_e*

Say the name of each picture. Put a marker on each picture if its name has the /ō/ or /ū/ sound. Turn to your partner and spell the /ō/ words. Then listen to your partner as they spell the /ū/ words.

Play

Name ______________________________

S M T W T F S

EVE

Review Phonics: /ē/e_e, ee, e
Say the name of each picture. Put a marker on each picture if its name has the /ē/ sound. Turn to your partner and spell the /ē/ words.

Name ______________________________

Phonics Review Game: /ā/a_e, /ī/i_e, /ō/o_e, /ū/u_e, /ē/e, ee
Cut on the dotted lines. Fold on the solid lines and tape together to make a cube.

Name ______________________________

Phonics Review Game: /ā/a_e, /ī/i_e, /ō/o_e, /ū/u_e, /ē/e, ee
Toss the cube with a partner. Say the name of the picture that faces up. Say the long vowel sound you hear in the word. Then say another word that has that long vowel sound.

Name ______________________________

It is good to help!

Can you help, too?

Review High Frequency Words: ***help, too, play, has, where, look, who, good, come, does***
Read the book aloud to a partner. Reread for fluency.

We Can Help!

Who can ride a bike?

It does not take gas!

Where can they play?
Come and play here!

Look! She has a seed.
She can pat the seed in.

Name ______________________________

rake hide bike

1.

bike

2.

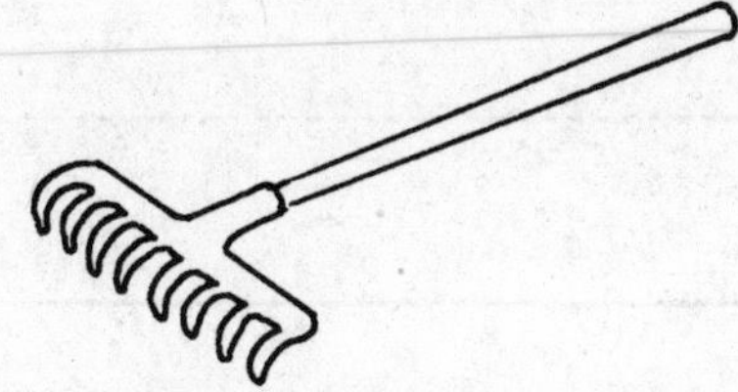

3.

Review Phonics: Blending *-ike, -ake, -ide*
Blend the sounds and say the word. Write the word. Repeat the word.

Write

Name ____________________

bone duke feet

1.

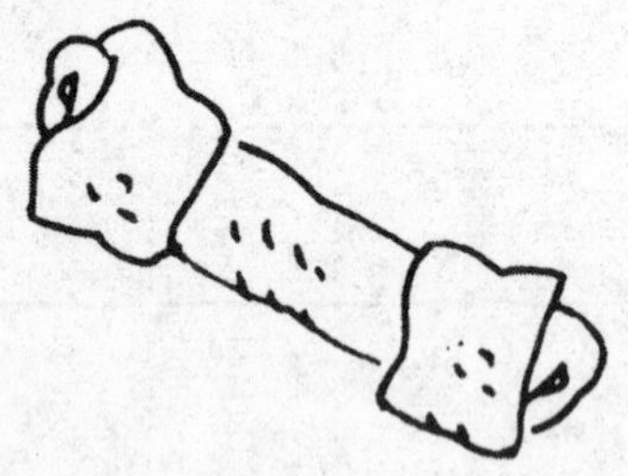

bone

2.

3.

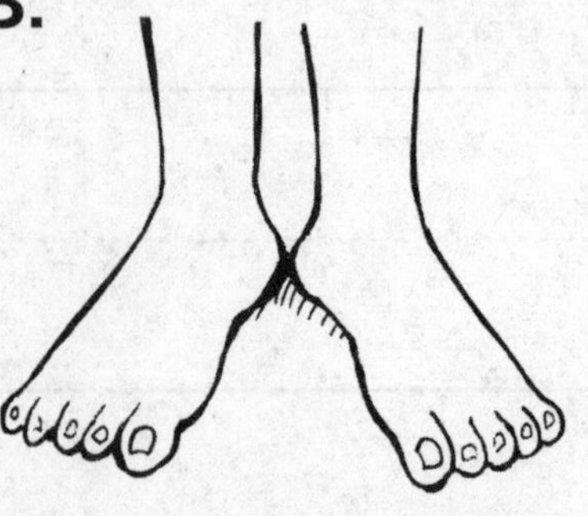

Review Phonics: Blending *-one, -uke, -eet*
Blend the sounds and say the word. Write the word. Repeat the word.

Name ________________________________

I.

2.

3.

Category Words: Names of Baby Animals
Find the baby animals in each row and put markers on them.
Say the name of each baby animal.

Name ___________________________________

The Alphabet

Aa

Bb
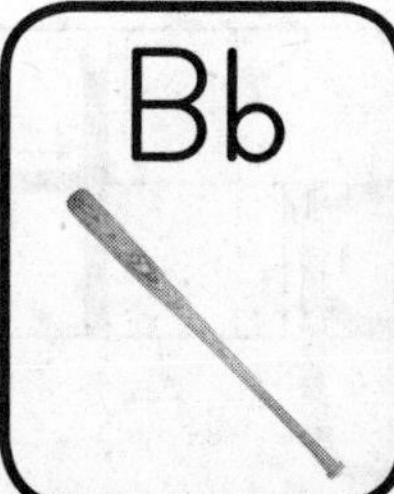

Cc

Dd

Ee
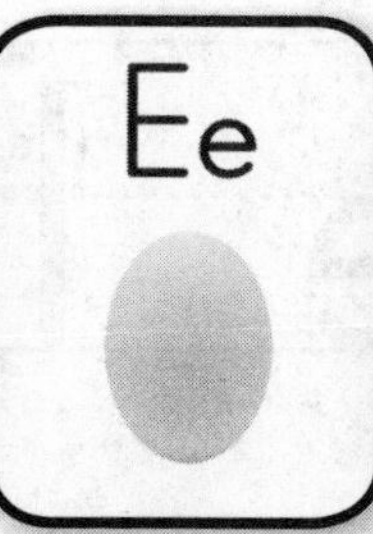

Ff

Gg

Hh

Ii

Jj

Kk

Ll

Mm

Nn

Oo

Pp

Qq

Rr

Ss

Tt

Uu

Vv

Ww

Xx

Yy
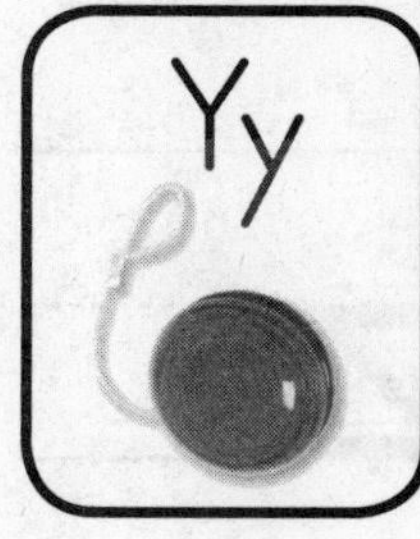

Zz
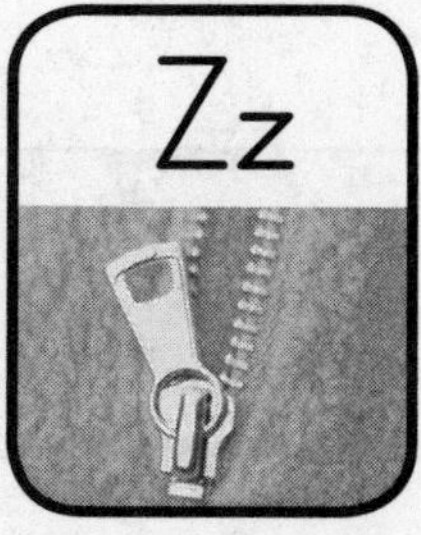

Handwriting Models

Aa Bb Cc Dd

Ee Ff Gg Hh

Ii Jj Kk Ll

Mm Nn Oo Pp

Qq Rr Ss Tt

Uu Vv Ww

Xx Yy Zz

Sound Boxes

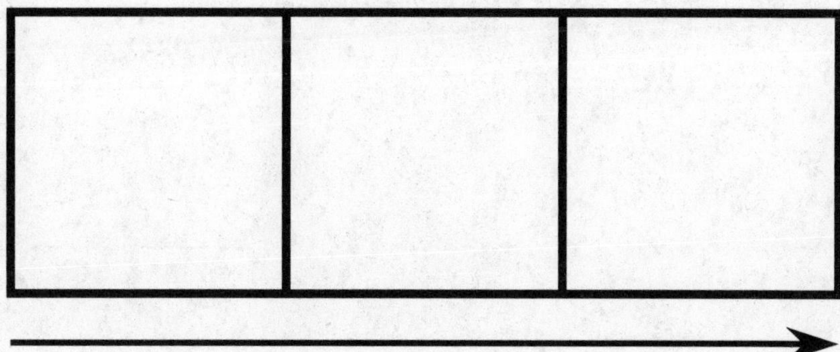

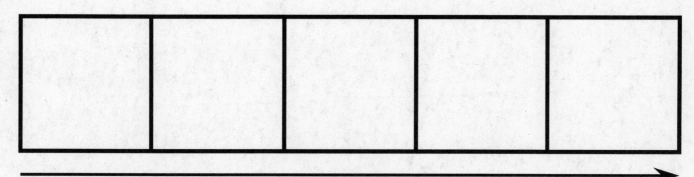

Sound Boxes